HOW TO USE THE MARGIN

At the beginning of each sub-chapter, you see **key terms** in the margin. These are important terms you need to understand the topic. You can find more detailed explanations of the key terms in the glossary (see pp. 206 – 213).

In the margin you also find useful **vocabulary** and **information** to help you working with the materials.

VOCABULARY

INFO

Learning in another language is not always easy. There are some traps and characteristics in every language. The **hot spots** will make you aware of these.

HOT SPOT

INTERNET

You can use the **webcodes and QR codes** to access short film clips, useful internet links, templates to fill in or interactive tasks. Simply enter the webcode in the search field at *www.westermann. de/webcode* or scan the QR code.

WES-116955-321
Links to children's rights at Unicef

HOW TO TRAIN AND CHECK YOURSELF

To be able to open new topics for yourself, you must know how to do it. **Methods** are an important tool for this. On the method pages, you will find important methods explained step by step. Example solutions show you how to get started before you use the method yourself in the tasks.

METHOD

At the end of each chapter, check in the **revision** whether you have learnt the important key terms and contents of the topic.

REVISION

Then broaden your perspective by **looking abroad**. You can discover what the situation is like elsewhere. This helps apply and expand your skills and knowledge from the chapter.

LOOKING ABROAD

HOW TO USE THE APPENDIX

At the end of the book, you will find the appendix. Here you can look up a few things:

As already mentioned, **more help** for the tasks can be found here (see pp. 192 – 201).

MORE HELP

You can also look at some **useful phrases** to improve your language (see pp. 202 – 205).

USEFUL PHRASES

In the **glossary** the key terms for each chapter are explained in more detail (see pp. 206 – 213).

GLOSSARY

And if you want to search for a specific topic, use the **index** (see pp. 214 – 215).

INDEX

Finally, at the very back you find a list of the most frequently used **operators** (verbs used in the tasks) of this textbook.

OPERATORS

westermann

EXPLORING
SOCIETY
ONE

For bilingual classes

Written by:	Andrea Bailer
	Jaqueline Gorman
	Bernd-H. Meichelböck
	Jimmy Miller
	Christina Sorg

Consultant:	Dr. Deanna Nebert

EXPLORING SOCIETY ONE

For bilingual classes

Written by:	Andrea Bailer
	Jaqueline Gorman
	Bernd-H. Meichelböck
	Jimmy Miller
	Christina Sorg
Consultant:	Dr. Deanna Nebert
With contributions by:	Prof. Dr. Joachim Detjen, Florian Grosch, Kevin Pallagi, Dr. Veit Straßner

Druck A² / Jahr 2024
Alle Drucke der Serie A sind im Unterricht parallel verwendbar.
Redaktion: Dr. Shida Kiani
Illustrationen: Yaroslaw Schwarzstein
Umschlaggestaltung: LIO Design, Braunschweig
Layout: Typo Concept GmbH, Hannover
Druck und Bindung: Westermann Druck GmbH, Georg-Westermann-Allee 66, 38104 Braunschweig

ISBN 978-3-14-**116955**-3

Content

4. Democracy in school — 90

5. Local politics — 112

6. Living in global contexts — 132

7. Young consumers — 152

8. Markets and prices — 176

Appendix

Working together – cooperative forms of learning

Think–Pair–Share
Cooperative learning in a three-step system, exchanging ideas and thoughts

1. **Think:** Think about your task individually, solve it and take notes.
2. **Pair:** Present your solution to your partner and find out about his or her solution. Ask your partner questions, exchange ideas, and take notes on a shared result.
3. **Share:** Present your shared solution to the class, look at other solutions and compare them with your own result.

Swap chairs
Comparing and presenting ideas, materials, results with joint evaluation

1. Every student solves the given task and puts his or her sheet of results on his or her chair.
2. Each student picks a different chair and reads the results laid out there. She or he adds feedback to them.
3. Everyone returns to his or her seat and reads the feedback.
4. The class evaluates the results in a group discussion.

Partner presentation
Comparing and presenting ideas, materials, results

1. Read the task. Work individually and prepare a presentation.
2. Agree with your partner who is going to present first.
3. The listener listens carefully and repeats what the speaker has said. The speaker makes sure that the listener reproduces his or her presentation correctly and completely.
4. Swap roles.

Partner quiz
Comparing ideas, materials, results, activating and consolidating learning by formulating and answering questions

1. Get together with a partner.
2. First work on the given task on your own.
3. Based on your solution, find various questions to ask your partner.
4. Ask each other questions in turn. The person asking the question may give hints and tips. After the question has been answered, the person who asked the question reads her or his answer.

Placemat

Using individual thoughts to start a conversation leading to a group product

1. Form groups and divide a sheet of paper into fields equal in size for each participant. In the middle, leave a field free for the results. Everyone writes his or her answers to the task in an outer field without paying attention to the other group members.
2. These results are discussed in the group.
3. After a joint discussion the group notes its results in the middle field.
4. The group presents its results.

Partner jigsaw

Working with a partner and presenting the results to other partners

1. Form groups of four, with two pairs as partners (A + A and B + B).
2. One group (A + A) deals with a different task than the other group (B + B). At first, each group member works alone.
3. A + A and B + B speak about their topic for a set time. This is your chance to discuss open questions.
4. Now A + B and A + B work together. Present the results of your previous partner work to each other. Act once as an expert once and once as a listener.

Jigsaw

Working in groups on different tasks and presenting the group results to each other

1. **The core group:** In the first phase, each member of the group works alone on a different subtopic of the task. When finished, each group member prepares key points for the expert group.
2. **The expert group:** Form new groups, one for each subtopic. These expert groups bring together those who previously worked on the same subtopic. The group talks about the content and deepens its understanding by discussing or asking questions. Members note the results so that they can explain them to others.
3. **Return to your core group:** In the third phase, return to your original core group. Present what you have learned.
4. Evaluate your results in a joint discussion.

Core group

Expert group

Core group

Milling around
Exchanging of information and opinions

1. Walk around the room until your teacher gives you a signal.
2. Then stop and discuss your task with the person closest to you. Move on at the next signal.
3. When the signal sounds again, talk to the next person closest to you.

Bus stop
Learning individually, then adding cooperative learning

1. Each student first works on the task individually.
2. When a student is finished, she or he stands up and waits for the next student to finish.
3. Both students compare their results. They are now an expert team.
4. Repeat this process with additional tasks if necessary.

Tip: You can signify a meeting point in the classroom, for example with a bus stop sign.

Gallery walk
Presenting group results

1. Form groups of the same size, if possible.
2. Each group works on a different topic.
3. The groups now reorganize so that every new group contains one member from every old group.
4. The groups move from station to station. The group's expert presents his or her results to the new team and answers questions.

Graffiti
Individual and cooperative learning, collecting, structuring and visualizing information

1. Form as many groups as there are tasks. Each group receives an assignment and a sheet of paper.
2. Each group begins with its task. Each group member writes down his or her ideas and thoughts about the task without paying attention to what the other group members are writing.
3. After a set time, each person moves to another group table and adds ideas there. Change tables until you get back to your original table.
4. Read all the ideas on the sheet, organize them, summarize the results, and present them to your class.

Good angel – bad angel

Discussing various arguments in small groups in order to reach an opinion

1. Form groups of three and appoint a "good angel", a "bad angel" and an "archangel" in each group.
2. In each group, explain the thesis/statement that you are to discuss.
3. The "good angel" finds arguments in favour of the thesis and the "bad angel" finds arguments against it. Meanwhile, the "archangel" reads all the materials carefully.
4. The "good angel" and the "bad angel" take turns presenting their arguments to the "archangel". There are 30 seconds for each argument.
5. After five minutes, the "archangel" decides in favour of one side and tells the two angels which argument is most convincing.
6. Finally, all the "archangels" present their decision to the class and briefly explain their reasons. Write the most convincing arguments of all the "archangels" on the board and in your folder.

Inside-outside circle

Comparing and presenting ideas, materials, homework, results of individual work

1. Divide into two equally large groups. Then form one inner and one outer circle of chairs. One student from the inner circle and one student from the outer circle are conversation partners.
2. The student from the outer circle asks questions, the other student answers them.
3. After a set time, the conversation partner in the outer circle rotates to face another student. Now the student in the inner circle asks the questions.
4. Repeat the process two or three times.

Fishbowl

Discussing a problem within a small group, while a large group listens and participates

1. A small group sits in a circle of chairs and discusses a problem. One chair remains free for a guest.
2. The remaining students surround the small group in a second, larger circle. They listen while the members of the inner circle present their results.
3. Listeners in the outer circle can take part in the discussion by sitting in the free seat in the inner circle. Those who do so express their opinions and then return to their chairs so that another person can do the same.
4. Members of the inner circle may drop out and join the outer circle. At the end the group discusses the results together.

A new subject

13

12

MASS MEDIA

10

14

TOWN HALL

16

15

17

1   This book aims to introduce you to a new subject. Depending on the *Bundesland* you live in, the subject will have a different name, e.g. *Politik, Politik und Wirtschaft, Politische Bildung, Gemeinschaftskunde* or *Sozialkunde*. The pictures all show different aspects of the subject. Imagine you could use one of these pictures as a cover picture for your folder. Which one would you choose? Give reasons. You may also suggest a completely different picture.

2   **Think-Pair-Share:** List and discuss any expectations and ideas you have about the new subject by answering the following questions:
   a) In what way(s) might the new subject be different from others?
   b) What are you generally looking forward to?
   c) Which topics might be interesting for you?
   d) Is there anything you are worried about?
   e) How would you like to learn (e.g. reading, discussing, group work, …)?

19

18

Planning a class outing

Your task

At the end of the school year, your class is allowed to go on a daytrip – but there is one condition: you must plan this trip yourselves. Use the questions and ideas below to complete this task.

1. How do we want to make decisions?
- Should we make decisions unanimously?
- Should we take a majority vote?
- Would it be best to let a small team plan the trip for us?
- …

2. Where do we want to go?
- A big city?
- A small town?
- A place that is historically interesting?
- A farm?
- A company?
- A parliament?
- An amusement park?
- Into nature?
- …

3. What do we want to do there?
- Sightseeing?
- Visit a museum?
- Learn something about history/politics/the economy?
- Do something creative (e.g. art, a film, …)?
- Do outdoor activities (e.g. hiking, rafting, …)?
- Have a lot of free time?
- …

4. How do we want to get there?
- By bus?
- By train?
- By bike?
- On foot?
- …

5. What do we need money for?
- Travel?
- Entrance fees?
- A course?
- Food?
- …

6. How much money can we spend?
- Are there school rules for class outing budgets?
- How much money should we collect from each student?
- Can we raise more money? If so, how?
- …

Reflecting

When your plan is complete, reflect on the outcome as well as your decision-making process. The following questions should stimulate your discussion, so there is no need to answer all of them.

1. Thinking about the outcome:
- Is your plan realistic?
- Will you be able to raise enough money to pay for everything?
- Does your plan follow school and legal rules (for example, you may not go bungee jumping or stay out for too long)?
- Does your plan take the different interests of your classmates into account?
- Were individual concerns (such as fear of heights) considered?
- Would you be looking forward to this class outing if it were a real plan?
- Might it become a real plan?

2. Thinking about the decision-making process:
- How did you feel during the process?
- Were the discussions moderated effectively?
- How controversial were the discussions? How do you feel about this?
- Did everybody have a chance to come up with ideas?
- Were all the ideas discussed fairly?
- Are you satisfied with your own contributions?
- What would you do differently next time?

Connecting

Connect the task to the new subject.

1. Which aspects played a role in both the pictures on pages 10/11 and in the task you have just completed? Explain.
2. Complete this sentence: "Our new subject is about …"

1

Living together

3

4

?

5

1   **a)** What shapes us? Rank the different influences according to the effect they have had on your personality. Feel free to add more ideas. **MORE HELP**
     b) Compare your result with your partner.

2   Give examples of how the top three factors in your list have influenced you.

3   Which of the influences would you not want to miss? Give reasons.

4   Socialization is the process by which people learn the culture, values, and norms of society. Discuss which factors might be the most important in someone's socialization.

1.1 What is a family? – A difficult question?

M 1 "Modern Family"

M 2 Forms of living together

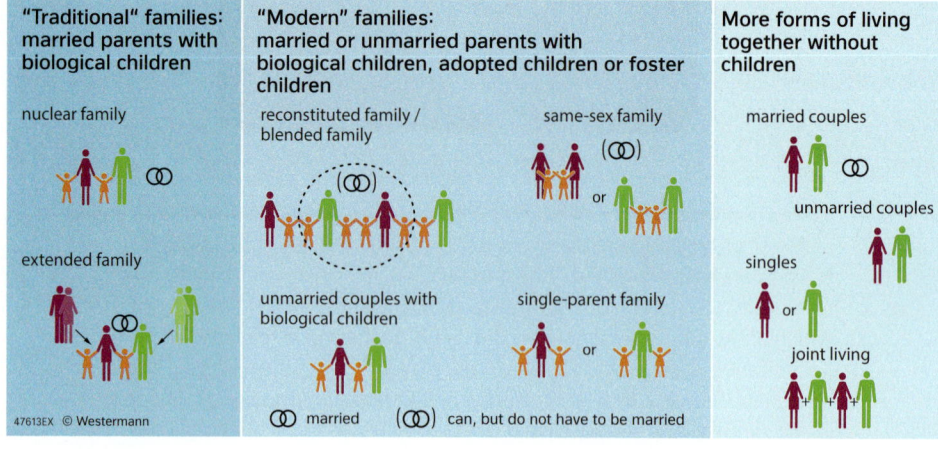

"Traditional" families:
married parents with
biological children

"Modern" families:
married or unmarried parents with
biological children, adopted children or foster
children

More forms of living
together without
children

nuclear family

reconstituted family /
blended family

same-sex family

married couples

extended family

unmarried couples with
biological children

single-parent family

unmarried couples

singles

joint living

47613EX © Westermann

married   can, but do not have to be married

M 3 Family: different definitions

VOCABULARY

committed
verbindlich
scholar
Wissenschaftler/-in
to encompass
umfassen
guardian
hier: Erziehungs-
berechtigte/-r

a) A group of people who are related to each other, such as a mother, a father, and their children.

Family, in: Cambridge Learner's Dictionary, Cambridge: Cambridge University Press & Assessment, https:// dictionary.cambridge.org/dictionary/learner-english/ family [26 Feb 2024]

b) There are narrow definitions of the family, in which the family unit has to consist of a "man and a woman in a committed sexual relationship living together with their children".
Some modern scholars prefer much broader definitions of the family which extend the concept to include anyone an individual thinks of as being "part of the family", such as friends or even pets.

Karl Thompson, What is the Family?, in: ReviseSociology. com, last updated on 12 Jun 2023 (8 Aug 2016), https:// revisesociology.com/2016/08/08/defining-the-family/ [26 Feb 2024] (modified)

c) The term family encompasses all forms of living together that include children and their parents: married as well as unmarried couples, man and woman or same-sex couples, single parents, biological children, stepchildren, foster children, and adopted children. So, a family always consists of two generations: parents/guardians and children living in the same household.

Familien, Wiesbaden: Statistisches Bundesamt (Destatis), https://www.destatis.de/DE/Themen/ Gesellschaft-Umwelt/Bevoelkerung/Haushalte-Familien/Glossar/familien.html [26 Feb 2024] (translated and modified)

d) Family is where people of different generations accept long-term responsibility for one another and in doing so, support and care for each other.

Families, Berlin: Bundesministerium für Familie, Senioren, Frauen und Jugend, https://www.bmfsfj.de/ bmfsfj/meta/en [26 Feb 2024]

e) Family is wherever children are.

Christine Bergmann, Minister for Family, Senior Citizens, Women, and Youth (1998–2002), quoted from: Gute Zitate, o.O. https://gutezitate.com/zitat/188454 [26 Feb 2024] (translated)

1 **Think–Pair–Share:** Define what a family is to you.
2 "Modern Family" is an American sitcom television series. Use the family tree (M1) to explain what is "modern" about this family.
3 Name the different forms of living together (M2) that are represented by the characters in "Modern Family" (M1).
4 Discuss opportunities and challenges of the different forms of living together (M2).
5 a) Compare your definition (task 1) of a family with the definitions in M3.
    b) Which definition of family should the state use when deciding how to support families? Give reasons (M3).

1.2 Changing forms of living together, changing needs?

M1 Forms of living in Germany

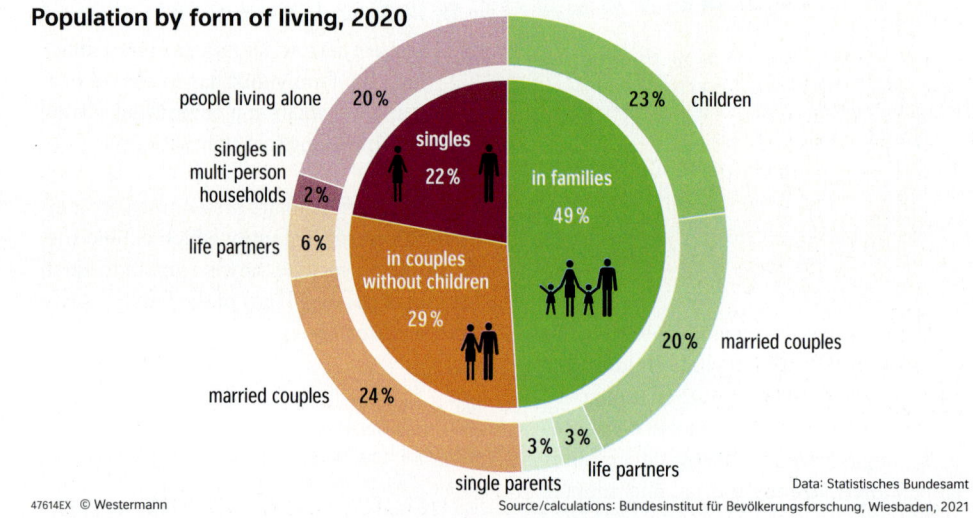

Population by form of living, 2020

people living alone 20%

singles in multi-person households 2%

life partners 6%

married couples 24%

single parents 3%

singles 22%

in couples without children 29%

in families 49%

children 23%

married couples 20%

life partners 3%

47614EX © Westermann

Data: Statistisches Bundesamt

Source/calculations: Bundesinstitut für Bevölkerungsforschung, Wiesbaden, 2021

M2 Number of marriages and divorces

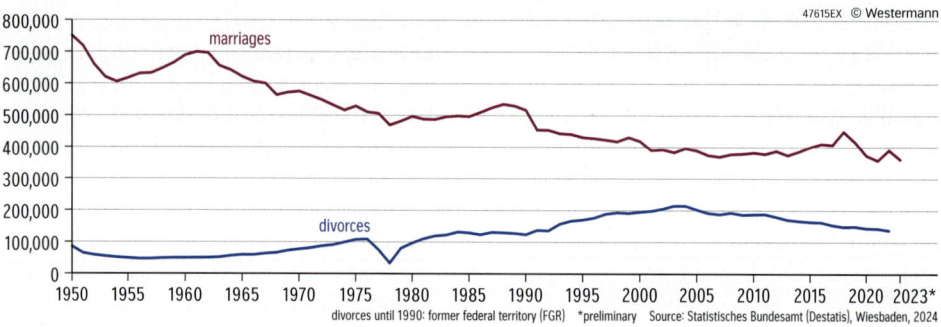

47615EX © Westermann

divorces until 1990: former federal territory (FGR)   *preliminary   Source: Statistisches Bundesamt (Destatis), Wiesbaden, 2024

M3 Development of births

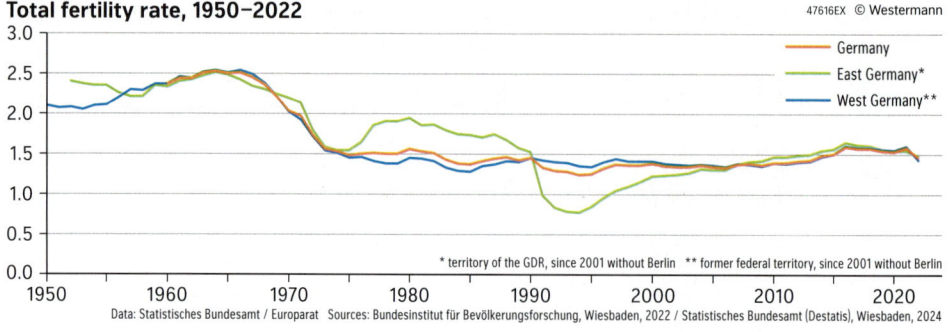

Total fertility rate, 1950–2022

47616EX © Westermann

- Germany
- East Germany*
- West Germany**

* territory of the GDR, since 2001 without Berlin   ** former federal territory, since 2001 without Berlin

Data: Statistisches Bundesamt / Europarat   Sources: Bundesinstitut für Bevölkerungsforschung, Wiesbaden, 2022 / Statistisches Bundesamt (Destatis), Wiesbaden, 2024

M4 Families with children by living arrangement

Families with children under 18 by form of living, 1996–2023

47617EX © Westermann

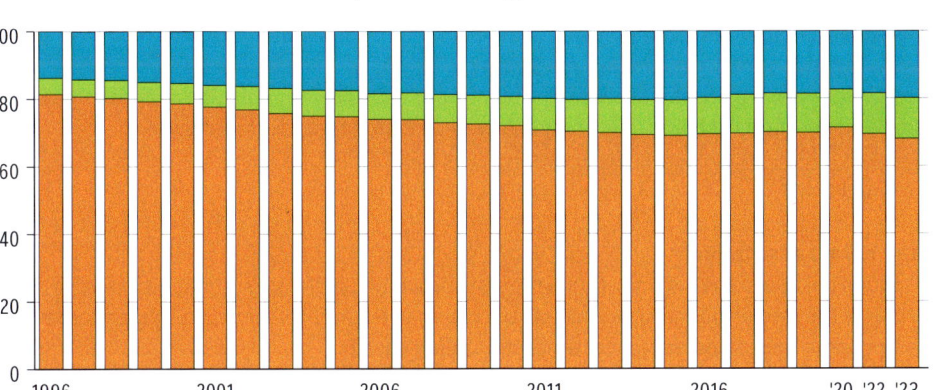

Legend: ■ married couples ■ life partnerships ■ single parents

Data: Statistisches Bundesamt, Mikrozensus
Source/calculations: 1950–2020: Bundesinstitut für Bevölkerungsforschung, Wiesbaden; 2022–23: Statistisches Bundesamt (Destatis), Wiesbaden, 2024

M5 Why family and household structures are changing: some factors

- **Changing gender roles:** More women pursue higher education and join the workforce, so they have more options in addition to (or instead of) motherhood today.
- **Delayed marriage and childbearing:** People marry at an older age. Some women who marry later will also delay having children.
- **Technological advances:** Due to effective birth control methods, women now have greater control over their fertility.
- **Social and cultural changes:** Changing social norms and cultural attitudes towards marriage, cohabitation, and divorce have affected family structures. Acceptance of diverse family arrangements, such as single-parent households, blended families, and same-sex partnerships, has increased.
- **Policy and legal reforms:** Legislative changes, such as the legalization of same-sex marriage, have changed family dynamics and led to the recognition of diverse family forms.
- **Individualism and personal choice:** There is a growing emphasis on individualism and personal fulfilment today, so people tend to set their own goals and desires over traditional family duties.

Statements 1 to 3 adapted from: Changes in Paterns of Fertility, Collins AQA GCSE 9-1 Sociology. Complete Revision and Practice, London: HarperCollinsPublishers, 2022, pp. 36 f. (modified), statements 4 to 6: text by the author

1 Analyse the charts (M1 to M4). ▸ METHOD Statistics, pp. 20 –21
2 Illustrate how the factors described in M5 help explain the developments shown in the charts (M1 to M4). Add more factors if you can.
3 a) Use your findings to discuss the following statements in small groups:
   • "The more children a family has, the more the state should support them."
   • "Single parents should be a top priority for politicians."
   • "Married couples should (not) be treated differently than unmarried couples."
b) Develop a similar statement and discuss it.

How to analyse statistics

Statistics – what are they good for?

Statistics express data in a visual way, which is often more interesting and easier to understand than information in text form. Diagrams compare data or show patterns and trends. No proper scientific study or paper can do without statistics.

However, always turn a critical eye on the quality and reliability of your source. British Prime Minister Winston Churchill once said: "I only believe in statistics that I doctored myself!"

How do I do it?

Step 1: Data description

- Name the title of the diagram. (State the statistical topic, preferably in your own words.)
- Name the kind of diagram (for example bar chart / line graph/pie chart, see margin to the left).
- Quote the source and the year in which it was published.
- Specify the kind of data given. (Is it in per cent or in absolute numbers?)
- Name the year or the time span the data refers to. (Does it refer to a specific point in time or does it show a development?)

Step 2: Analysis

- Describe the general data (developments, patterns, trends).
- Go into detail and compare the most important numbers.
- Name peak and minimum values.
- Keep a lookout for outliers (for example, remarkably high or low values. Ideally, you can explain them in step 3).
- Summarize your findings in a general statement.

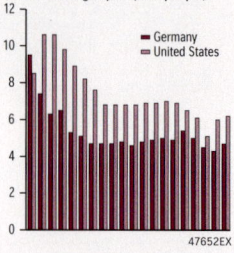

Diagram 1: Marriage rate in Germany and the United States, 1960–2022 (No. of marriages per 1,000 people)

bar chart

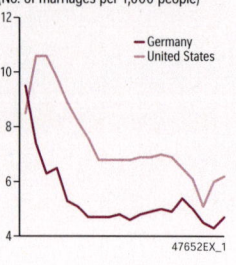

Diagram 2: Marriage rate in Germany and the United States, 1960–2022 (No. of marriages per 1,000 people)

line graph

Vocabulary help

Compare:	double, triple, halve, four times as high as
To go up:	rise, increase, grow, surge, rocket, expand, step up, improve, progress, peak
To go down:	decline, decrease, reduce, drop, plummet, slump, reach a bottom
Finetuning:	slightly, sharply, gradually, gently, steadily
No change:	stabilize, to remain steady/constant/stable/at the same level
Change:	start falling, start rising, level out, fluctuate

Step 3: Draw conclusions

- Now focus on your general statement. Draw a meaningful conclusion on what the data implies. Explain your findings and give reasons for the development or the situation (for example with historical facts or political progression).
- It might be possible to outline effects or consequences (for example on society or nature).
- If you doubt the reliability of your source, it is now time to say so and to give reasons.

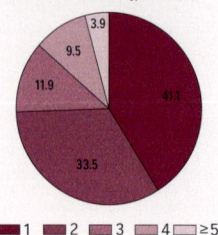

Diagram 3: Amount of people per household in Germany, 2023 (%)

pie chart

Vocabulary help

The data shows that … / The overall development implies that … / The amount of … has dramatically increased / The chart shows that the majority of … /
Therefore, … / Likely, we can expect further … / It can be expected that … / It can be assumed that … because …

Example

Diagram 4: Women born between 1943 and 1998 by number of children, 2018 47619EX © Westermann

Age group	no children	1 child	2 children	3 children	≥ 4 children
1943–48 (70–75)	12.4	26.9	40.8	13.8	6.0
1949–53 (65–69)	15.1	25.8	41.2	12.6	5.4
1954–58 (60–64)	16.7	24.5	40.9	12.8	5.1
1959–63 (55–59)	19.1	23.9	39.5	12.7	4.8
1964–68 (50–54)	20.1	26.5	37.4	11.6	4.4
1969–73 (45–49)	21.3	25.1	37.4	11.6	4.6
1974–78 (40–44)	22.3	24.0	36.6	12.2	4.9
1979–83 (35–39)	27.7	25.6	32.5	10.1	4.1
1984–88 (30–34)	47.3	25.0	20.0	5.7	2.0
1989–93 (25–29)	74.7	15.5	7.4	1.8	0.7
1994–98 (20–24)	91.8	5.9	1.8		0.3

Source: Statistisches Bundesamt (Destatis), Kinderlosigkeit, Geburten und Familien, Ergebnisse des Mikrozensus, Wiesbaden, 2018

Step 1:

The bar chart illustrates the number of children women in Germany have depending on their age group. Four or five years are grouped together, and the figures are given in per cent. The source is the Statistisches Bundesamt and the numbers refer to 2018.

Step 2:

The statistics show that the younger women are, the more likely it is that they are childless. The minimum and the maximum values are both reached by the youngest age group (20-24-year-olds): 91.8 % of this group have no children, whilst only 0.3 % already have four or more children.

The number of children increases quickly in the next three groups. The number of childless women in the second youngest age group drops by almost 19 % compared to the youngest women and then by another 30 % in the third youngest age group (30-34-year-olds). By the time women are 45 and older, we can expect that the number of newborn children will not change significantly any more, so about twice as many women born between 1969–73 (21.3 %) remain childless in comparison to women born between 1943–48 (12.4 %).

Women born between 1943 and 1974 are statistically similar when it comes to having one child (between 23.9 and 26.9 %), as are those having two children (36.6 and 40.8 %), three children (between 11.6 and 13.8 %) and four or more children (between 4.4 and 6.0 %). By the time women in Germany are 30 or older, more than every second woman has at least one child and by the time they are 35 or older, the largest group has two children.

Step 3:

The statistics show that the younger women are in the age group of 75 – 45, the more likely it is that they are childless. There is also a tendency for younger women to have fewer children. Although this cannot be said about women who are 44 or younger, since these women might still decide to have more children, we can expect this trend to continue because higher education results in more ambitious career choices and women's social position has improved along with their paid employment. The resulting smaller population puts more pressure on the social system …

1 Compare how clear and logical diagrams 1 and 2 (p. 20) are. Decide which is more suitable for the data and give reasons for your choice.

2 Contrast the kind of information the pie chart gives with the other two diagrams.

3 Analyse the bar chart (diagram 4).

4 a) Follow the first link under the webcode/QR code and describe diagram 5 to your partner. Ask your partner to draw it without looking at your diagram. When finished, look at the result to see how well you have described the diagram.

b) Swap roles for diagram 6 under the second link of the webcode/QR code.

INTERNET

WES-116955-121
Links to diagrams
5 and 6 for task
4 a) and b)

1.3 Fulfilling the functions of a family – a challenge?

M 1   Home alone?

M 2   The basic functions of a family

1. Socialization and education

One of the functions of a family is to facilitate the process of socialization and education. From early childhood, family members learn
5 values, norms, customs, and behavioral expectations that are important for living in society.

- **Primary Socialization:** This process involves teaching young children basic skills, manners, and language. It's the first
10 step towards understanding the social world.
- **Secondary Socialization:** This stage is about introducing children to larger social institutions, such as schools and religious
15 organizations. It broadens their understanding of societal norms and values.

2. Emotional support

A family serves as the main source of emotional support for its members, providing a
20 safe haven where individuals can express and manage their feelings.

- **Emotional buffer:** Families help members cope with stress and adversity. They offer a cushion against the psychological impact of negative life events.
25
- **Emotional development:** Families also foster emotional development. They teach children how to manage their emotions, nurturing skills like empathy and emotional intelligence.
30

3. Economic security

Families traditionally ensure the economic security of their members. They provide food, shelter, clothing, and other necessities.

- **Resource allocation:** Families manage
35 resources based on the needs of their members. This typically includes distributing income for food, shelter, education, and healthcare.
- **Wealth transmission:** Families also play a
40 role in transferring wealth across generations. This can take on many forms, from inheritance to access to social networks and opportunities.

Functions of a Family, in: Anthroholic.com, o.O., 26 May 2023, https://anthroholic.com/functions-of-a-family [15 Jan 2024] (modified)

M3 The challenges and evolution of family functions

Despite the foundational role of families in society, they face challenges that may alter their functional dynamics. Factors like economic pressures, changing social values, and techno-
5 logical disruptions can influence the way families operate [...].

1. Dual-career families: The rise of dual-career families has shifted traditional familial roles and responsibilities. It has led to more
10 shared household duties and child-rearing responsibilities.

2. Single-parent families: An increase in single-parent families has brought new dynamics to family functions. Single parents often face higher demands in terms of providing 15 emotional support and economic security.

3. Digital influence: Technology has transformed family interactions and socialization. While it brings families closer through virtual communication, it also presents challenges 20 like managing screen time and cyber threats.

Functions of a Family, in: Anthroholic.com, o.O., 26 May 2023, https://anthroholic.com/functions-of-a-family [15 Jan 2024]

VOCABULARY

foundational
grundlegend
to alter sth.
etw. ändern
disruption
Erschütterung,
einschneidende
Veränderung
child-rearing
Kindererziehung
to transform sth.
etw. umformen,
transformieren

M4 "Talk to me!"

Cartoon: Renate Alf, 2016 (translated)

1 Imagine you have to live on your own. What is different? Which problems do you have? (M1) Give examples.
2 Rank the different functions of families according to how important you personally think they are (M2).
3 Describe how families can fulfil the functions described in M2.
4 **Extra:** Sometimes, other people or institutions fulfil the functions of a family. Describe examples.
5 **Placemat:** How can families faced with the challenges in M3 make sure they still fulfil the basic functions of a family? Develop solutions. Also take M4 into account.
▸ METHOD Cartoons, pp. 26 – 27

1.4 Parenting styles – is there a best one?

M1 Values

confidence	commitment	courage	critical thinking
creativity	curiosity	discipline	honesty
fairness	flexibility	independence	kindness
obedience	respect	responsibility	...

M2 Parenting styles

Authoritarian parenting

Parents of this style tend to have a one-way mode of communication where the parent establishes strict rules that the child obeys. There is little to no room for negotiations from the child, and the rules are not usually explained. They expect their children to uphold these standards while making no errors. Mistakes usually lead to punishment. Authoritarian parents are normally less nurturing and have high expectations with limited flexibility. [...]

Authoritative parenting

This type of parent normally develops a close, nurturing relationship with their children. They have clear guidelines for their expecta-tions and explain their reasons associated with disciplinary actions. Disciplinary methods are used as a way of support instead of punishment. Not only can children have input into goals and expectations, but there are also frequent and appropriate levels of communication between the parent and their child. [...]

Permissive parenting

Permissive parents tend to be warm, nurturing and usually have minimal or no expectations. They impose limited rules on their children. Communication remains open, but parents allow their children to figure things out for themselves. These low levels of expectation usually result in rare uses of discipline. They act more like friends than parents. [...]

Uninvolved parenting

Children are given a lot of freedom as this type
35 of parent normally stays out of the way. They
fulfil the child's basic needs while generally
remaining detached from their child's life. An
uninvolved parent does not utilize a particular
disciplining style and has a limited amount of
communication with their child. They tend to 40
offer a low amount of nurturing while having
either few or no expectations of their children.

Terrence Sanvictores/Magda D. Mendez, Types of Parenting Styles and Effects On Children, in: Bethesda, MD: National Library of Medicine, StatPearls Publishing LLC., 18 Sep 2022, https://www.ncbi.nlm.nih.gov/books/NBK568743/ [20 Feb 2024]

VOCABULARY

detached
distanziert, entfernt
particular
besonders, speziell

M3 Parenting styles in pictures

1 Name three things from the table you find most important for children to learn. Feel free to add more ideas (M1).

2 Read the text on parenting styles (M2) and match them with the pictures (M3).

3 Sarah just got her maths test back. It's an F (= fail). Show how different families deal with the situation in role plays. Work in four groups. Each group is assigned a different parenting style. The other groups must guess which parenting style the respective parents use (M2, M3).

4 Which parenting style do you consider the best? Give reasons.
Tip: You can use the method "four corners" for this task. Each corner of the classroom is assigned one of the parenting styles. Each student chooses a corner and gives reasons for her or his choice.

Authoritarian parenting	Authoritative parenting
Permissive parenting	Uninvolved parenting

How to analyse political cartoons

Political cartoon – what is the point?

Political cartoons are drawings that show a critical opinion of a political event or development. They are often funny and exaggerated; however, they do not mainly intend to entertain. They use humour to comment critically on current events. Generally, the audience needs to know about the underlying issue to understand the cartoonist's intent. Therefore, it is vital to stay up to date on what is going on in the world. Political cartoons often deal with controversial topics. They are common in societies with an independent press and freedom of speech.

How do I do it?

Step 1: Description
- Name the title, the cartoonist, and, if stated, the date and the source.
- Describe the image briefly, only including what is necessary for the analysis (no interpretation at this point). If you are allowed to, circle all the important aspects so you do not forget anything.

Step 2: Analysis
The aim of your analysis is to show the artist's perspective on the given issue. In many cases, several of the following tips can help you:
- Identify familiar persons or symbols (see box below). Check if they are portrayed in a positive or negative manner. Read all the labels and captions.
- Cartoons often refer to current political affairs. Make sure to check the publishing date so you do not include more than the historical context allows.
- Look out for exaggeration and caricature. Cartoonists use caricature by exaggerating parts of a person's character or features to make a point. Ask yourself if the artist did this to add meaning.
- Irony is used to highlight the contrast between reality and the ideal.
- Cartoons might play with stereotypes. Point out whether the artist agrees with them or not.

Step 2 ends with a short and precise summary of the artist's overall message.

Common symbols in political cartoons

A lion, John Bull or Britannia for the **UK**

Uncle Sam or an eagle for the **US**, a donkey for the **US Democratic Party**, an elephant for the **US Republican party**

The "German Michel" („deutscher Michel") with his sleeping cap for **Germany**

A bear for **Russia**
A dragon for **China**

Step 3: Evaluation
- Explain whether you agree with the cartoonist's point of view or not. Support your opinion by using details and arguments to prove it.
- You should evaluate how effective the cartoon is. The cartoonist might have left out important facts or relevant arguments. How you justify your opinion is the most important part of your analysis, so do not cut it short!

Example

Step 1:
"Permissive Parenting" is a cartoon drawn by Isabella Bannerman. It was posted on Jim Nolan's Blog on 26 March 2013.
Two children with their bicycles are on a typical suburban street. They look towards the right, where a woman is lying on the street, blocking the way. The adult says "No, no! You don't have to wear helmets! I'll just lie here and be the speed bump!". She does not seem bothered, instead she looks happy. The caption in brackets reads: "Permissive parenting reaches a new low".

VOCABULARY

eagerness
Eifer
to reach a new low
einen neuen Tiefpunkt erreichen

Cartoon 1: Isabella Bannerman, Permissive Parenting, in: Jim Nolan's Blog (jimnolansblog.com), 26 Mar 2013

Step 2:
The children refuse to wear helmets, or the mother does not want to impose the rule on her kids. Either way, she "solves" the safety issue by becoming the speed bump that stops the kids from riding their bikes too fast or too far. She looks content even though she is in danger. She would do anything to please her kids. The children do not look surprised, so it seems that they are used to her behaviour.

The caption names the parenting style as "permissive parenting", which fits the cartoon perfectly. The mother does not set up even a simple rule for the sake of the kids' safety to avoid an argument. Also, other parents would tell children that age to roam the neighbourhood with friends or siblings on their own. She wants to have a close eye on them and even takes part in their spare time activity. Permissive parents do not believe in a hierarchical parenting style. They want to have a friendly relationship with their children and do not like to punish or set limits for them. The artist criticizes this parenting style by exaggerating the woman's eagerness to act as a speed bump. Bannerman thinks this parenting style is not only weak but has become even weaker („reaches a new low") and she likely prefers a different parenting style such as authoritative parenting, which limits children's behaviour more.

Step 3:
I agree / disagree with the artist because …
In my opinion, parents should / should not impose rules / let their kids learn lessons the hard way / be friends with their kids …
I prefer this kind of parenting style to others because … / I prefer [parenting style] to permissive parenting because …

1 Find three more examples for common symbols in political cartoons.
2 Analyse cartoon 2.

I'm so glad we set aside these evenings for "family" time.

Cartoon 2: M Moeller, in: Cartoonstock, 24 Aug 2013

1.5 Should parents be licensed?

VOCABULARY

neglect Vernachlässigung
advice Ratschlag
to second-guess sth. etw. im Nachhinein kritisieren
upbringing Erziehung
primarily vorwiegend, hauptsächlich, in erster Linie
it is incumbent on or upon sb. to do sth. es obliegt jmdm., etw. zu tun
duty Pflicht

INFO

The **Basic Law** (Grundgesetz) is the name of Germany's constitution.

M1 Families in the news

Parents charged with child neglect after boy misses 70 % of school days

Gretchen Hjelmstad, in: Fargo, ND: KVLY, Gray Television, Inc., 4 Jan 2024, https://www.valleynewslive.com/2024/01/04/parents-charged-with-child-neglect-after-son-misses-70-school-days/ [26 Feb 2024]

Exhausted, disconnected and fed up: what is "parental burnout" and what can you do about it?

Alan Ralph, in: The Guardian online, 22 May 2023, https://www.theguardian.com/lifeandstyle/2023/may/22/exhausted-disconnected-and-fed-up-what-is-parental-burnout-and-what-can-you-do-about-it [26 Feb 2024]

Millennial parents say they're bombarded by so much advice it's making them second-guess everything

Charissa Cheong, in: Business Insider, Insider Inc., o.O., 8 Dec 2023, https://www.businessinsider.com/millennial-parents-overwhelmed-advice-doubting-their-instincts-2023-12 [26 Feb 2024]

M2 An extract from the German Basic Law

Article 6
(2) The care and upbringing of children is the natural right of parents and a duty primarily incumbent upon them. The state shall watch over them in the performance of this duty.

Understanding the wording of a law is difficult – in any language. Try to understand the extract from the German Basic Law by finding the statements that paraphrase elements of Article 6 (2).

a) Everybody has the right to have children.
b) Bringing up children is their parents' right. The state usually does not interfere.
c) Children have rights and duties.
d) Parents must look after their children.
e) If parents neglect their children, the state can protect the children (e.g. by deciding children will not live with their parents for a certain time).
f) Parents in Germany must have a certain parenting style.

Text by the author

M3 Should parents be licensed?

VOCABULARY

to accrue
sammeln, erwerben
nutrition
Ernährung
government
mandates
staatliche Vorgaben
to market
vermarkten
mandatory
verpflichtend
feasible
machbar, möglich
to be fined
eine Geldstrafe
erhalten
license for parents
Elternführerschein

The question whether moms and dads should take parenting classes and earn a license is a very controversial one. Here is what some parents in the U.S. say about the issue:

"I do not believe parents should have to study a specific parenting 'style' (unless they choose to) but I do believe they should have to accrue 'parenting credits' in basic child development, psychology, nutrition and communication, before and while raising the future of society."

"Government mandates just don't make sense to me on this topic. I do think that more hospitals, private groups and non-profits could (and should) offer and market classes to parents, however."

"I can only imagine how kids would turn out if everyone was subjected to the same 'ideals' of child-rearing."

"I think that parenting classes would help parents – and ultimately their children – immensely. […] There is so much to know and learn. We require people to have a license to drive a car, to teach, to practice medicine, but we don't require even one class for the most important job in the world – parenting."

"I think parenting classes are the key to breaking the cycle of traditional parenting. Often we all do as our mother for better or worse. Find a good parenting class not just to learn parenting tips, but to learn your own approach to parenting and problem solving."

"The idea might sound good in theory, but in reality it's totally impractical. I don't think something like parenting classes should be government-regulated or mandatory. I wouldn't want the government advising me how to parent, plus it doesn't even seem feasible to enforce. If a pregnant mother refused to take a 'mandatory' parenting class, what would happen? Would she be fined? Arrested? Reported?"

"I certainly don't want the government telling me how to raise my children."

"It's hard to say whether it should be a requirement for parenting classes in order to raise children because I feel that the government is already far too involved in the average American's private life. However, I do feel that parenting – or the lack thereof – is one of the root causes of many of the problems affecting our society today, such as crime rates, unemployment, teen pregnancy and more. At the very least, they should be offered or marketed more toward expectant couples by hospitals and physicians."

Michelle Maffei, Should parenting require a license?, in: SheKnows, SheMedia, LLC., o.O., 2 Sep 2013, https://www. sheknows.com/parenting/articles/1009213/should-parenting-require-a-license/ [20 Feb 2024] (modified)

1 Explain what the newspaper headlines have in common (M1). **MORE HELP**

2 **Bus stop:** Complete the task in M2 and connect Art. 6 (2) GG to the headlines in M1. **MORE HELP**

3 Some politicians have suggested introducing a mandatory license for parents. In M3 you can find arguments for and against this idea. Sort them into pros and cons. **MORE HELP**

4 **Good angel – bad angel:** Discuss whether parents should be licensed, starting from the arguments in M3. ▸ Useful phrases (A), pp. 202 – 203

1.6 Division of labour in families – fair play?

childcare
Kinderbetreuung
parental leave
Elternzeit

M 1   Families with children by living arrangement

Ideal division of professional and family work 2007 and 2019
in per cent

47620EX © Westermann

Question: This list describes different family forms. Apart from your current life situation: which would you prefer to live in?

■ Parents with children under the age of 18: 2007   ■ Parents with children under the age of 18: 2019

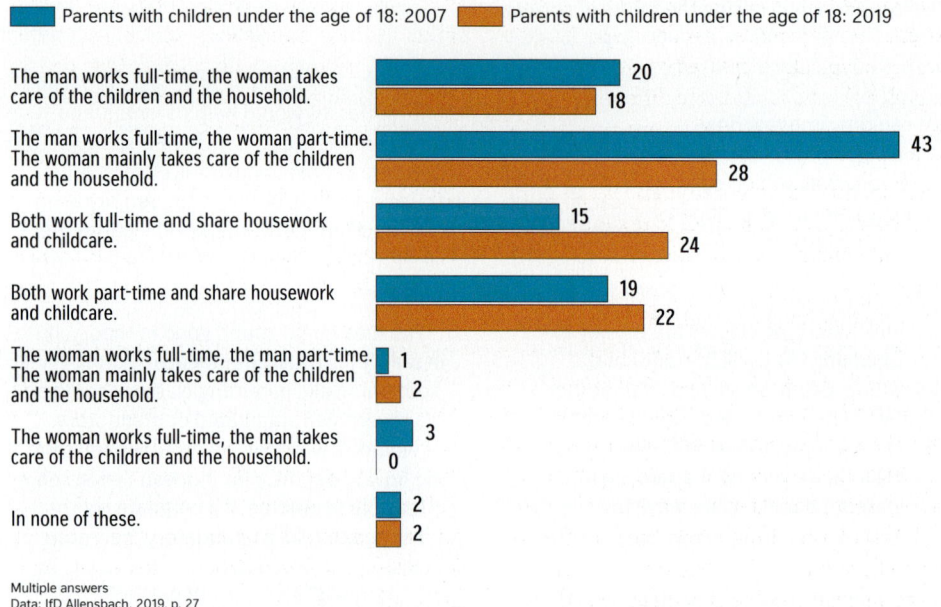

The man works full-time, the woman takes care of the children and the household. — 20 / 18

The man works full-time, the woman part-time. The woman mainly takes care of the children and the household. — 43 / 28

Both work full-time and share housework and childcare. — 15 / 24

Both work part-time and share housework and childcare. — 19 / 22

The woman works full-time, the man part-time. The woman mainly takes care of the children and the household. — 1 / 2

The woman works full-time, the man takes care of the children and the household. — 3 / 0

In none of these. — 2 / 2

Multiple answers
Data: IfD Allensbach, 2019, p. 27
Source: Familie heute. Daten. Fakten. Trends. Familienreport 2020, Berlin: Bundesministerium für Familie, Senioren, Frauen und Jugend, p. 130

M 2   Real division of labour in families

Employment constellations of working couples with children under 18 in the household in per cent

47621EX © Westermann

■ Father full-time/mother part-time   ■ Mother full-time/father part-time
■ Both full-time   ■ Both part-time

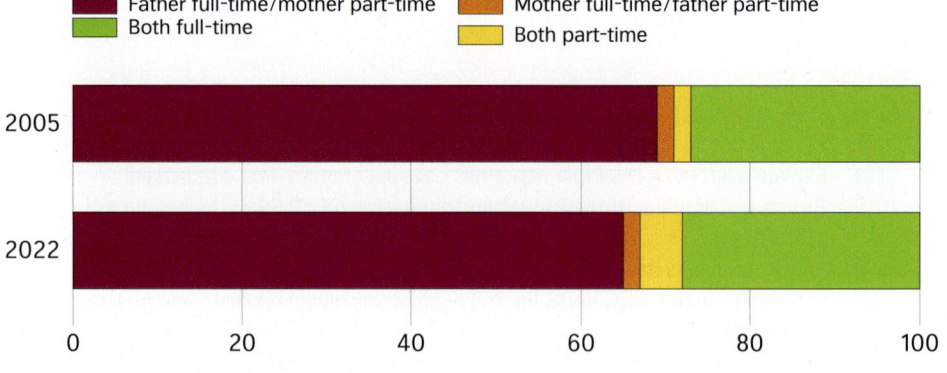

Source: Statistisches Bundesamt (Destatis), Wiesbaden, 2024

M3 What explains the gender division of labour and how can it be redressed?

Centuries of economic growth and **campaigning** have enabled equal rights for men and women in **the developed world**. But there remain **gaps** in the economic standing of women
5 and men across all high-income countries.

Women still make systematically different education choices from men, and in contrast to men, they often earn less when becoming a parent. What's more, gender gaps in paid
10 work are typically increased by gender gaps in unpaid work, which leads to differences in access to leisure and economic prestige that favour men.

These **inequalities** naturally raise issues of re-
15 **distributive** justice, related to unequal access to employment opportunities and life satisfaction. [...]

One key **constraint** for women is their primary role in raising and caring for children. Evi-
20 dence from several countries shows that while childbirth is fairly neutral for men's careers, it causes a large and **persistent** drop in women's earnings. On becoming a parent, women are more likely than men to leave employment
25 and, if they remain in work, they tend to favour family-friendly working conditions. These include flexible schedules and shorter hours, which are less helpful for career development and **progression**.

30 The resulting motherhood **penalty** is not significantly reduced by the availability and generosity of childcare support policies, nor by the introduction of parental leave rights that are exclusively reserved for fathers. As a re-
35 sult, it's natural to think about the deeper roots of these inequalities, which are related to social norms about **appropriate** gender roles in the household and the workplace.

One can think of norms as social rules about what is appropriate and inappropriate for
40 men and women to do in society. For example, the male **breadwinner** model has a clear concept for gender roles in the family, with consequences for women's investment in their careers.

45 In some cases, norms stem from **intrinsic** beliefs about gender roles. In others, they are mostly shaped by peer pressure and the negative effects breaking a certain norm can have on your image. It isn't easy for policy to
50 reshape personal beliefs, and it's debatable to what extent **third parties** should be allowed to **interfere** with decisions taken within families.

Barbara Petrongolo, What explains the gender division of labour and how can it be redressed?, Bristol: Economics Observatory, 11 Sep 2023, https://www.economicsobservatory.com/what-explains-the-gender-division-of-labour-and-how-can-it-be-redressed [4 Mar 2024] (modified)

VOCABULARY

to campaign for sth.
sich für etw. engagieren
the developed world
die Industrieländer
gap
Lücke, Abstand
inequality
Ungleichheit
redistributive
umverteilend
constraint
hier: Hindernis, Einschränkung
persistent
anhaltend
progression
Entwicklung
penalty
Strafe
appropriate
angemessen
breadwinner
Hauptverdiener/-in, Ernährer/-in
intrinsic
intrinsisch, innerlich
third party
Dritte
to interfere
eingreifen

INFO

Parental leave
can be taken by both mothers and fathers. However, mothers take parental leave more often and for longer. In 2022, 45.2 % of working women and 3.0 % of working men in Germany with a youngest child under the age of 3 were on parental leave. The average length of leave requested was 14.6 months for mothers and 3.6 months for fathers.

1 a) Which of the options in M1 do you consider the best arrangement for families with children? Make a class survey.
   b) Compare the results of your survey to the data in M1.
2 **Extra:** Compare M1 and M2. Try to find reasons for the differences.
3 Use M3 to explain M2.
4 Develop ideas what the state, employers, and families themselves could do to close the gap between the ideals and realities of the division of labour in families in Germany. Choose your top three. **MORE HELP**
5 "Gender equality starts at home." Comment on this statement.

1.7 Gender leisure gap – a political problem?

M 1 Equality?

M 2 Time for paid and unpaid work

Paid and unpaid work

47622EX © Westermann

Persons aged 18 and over, in hours per week

■ Paid work ■ Unpaid work

2022

	Paid work	Unpaid work	Total
Women	16 h 00 min	29 h 52 min	45 h 53 min
Men	23 h 48 min	20 h 42 min	44 h 30 min
Total	19 h 49 min	25 h 23 min	45 h 12 min

2012 / 2013

	Paid work	Unpaid work	Total
Women	16 h 09 min	29 h 29 min	45 h 38 min
Men	25 h 13 min	19 h 21 min	44 h 34 min
Total	20 h 35 min	24 h 32 min	45 h 06 min

Deviations due to rounding
Source: Statistisches Bundesamt (Destatis), Zeitverwendungserhebung, Wiesbaden, 2022

M3 Women are earning more money. But they're still picking up a heavier load at home

MICHEL MARTIN, HOST: A new report tells us women are **making bank** at work and carrying a big load at home, too. What a shock to hear this. The Pew Research Center combed several national surveys to come to this finding. NPR's Andrea Hsu gives us more details.

ANDREA HSU, BYLINE: Here's the gist. In marriages between men and women, a growing share of women are earning as much or more than their husbands. And yet, even in those marriages, women are still spending more time on housework and caregiving than the men. Kim Parker is director of social trends research at the Pew Research Center.

KIM PARKER: In many ways, I think public attitudes are kind of **lagging** behind the economic realities that husbands and wives are facing these days.

HSU: Pew found that in 45 % of U.S. marriages now, women make roughly as much or more than their husbands. That's triple what it was half a century ago when far fewer women were in the workforce.

PARKER: They're very much almost on equal footing with men in the workplace. Yet there's still these attitudes about what's really valued in terms of the contributions that they make.

HSU: Pew surveyed more than 5,000 people about those attitudes. They asked them, what does society value more in men and women – their contributions at work or at home?

PARKER: What we found was that a majority of Americans say that society values men's contributions at work more than what they do at home.

HSU: But for women, it was totally different. Only 1 in 5 respondents says society puts greater value on what women do at work. Close to a third said society favors what women do at home. And here's the curious thing – young people, those under 30, were the most likely to take that view.

PARKER: They're almost more cynical about it, which is interesting.

HSU: On the other hand, Parker says, older people tend to think society puts equal weight on what women do at work and at home. She says maybe that's because older people have witnessed a lot of change over their lifetimes.

PARKER: Whereas for young people, they might just see the imbalance now, but they haven't lived through the arc of the advancements women have made in the workplace.

HSU: Daisy Chin-Lor has lived that arc. She worked in corporate leadership roles for years while raising a family. She's now interim head of the Institute for Women's Policy Research.

DAISY CHIN-LOR: I think that in the past there was an assumption that there are certain roles that you play, and that's what women do. Men think we like to do it. I think we have to do it. There is some innate nature to it, but I think there's a lot more discussion about it.

HSU: And that she sees as progress.

Andrea Hsu, NPR News.

Andrea Hsu, Women are earning more money. But they're still picking up a heavier load at home (transcript), Washington, D.C.: National Public Radio (NPR), 13 Apr 2023, https://www.npr.org/transcripts/1168961388 [20 Feb 2024]

INTERNET

WES-116955-171
Listen to this radio feature (M3) on NPR.

VOCABULARY

making bank
umgangsprachl.: Kasse machen
gist
Hauptpunkt, Kern
to lag behind sth.
hinter etw. zurückbleiben

INFO

In this context, **"byline"** refers to the name of the journalist who reported or wrote the news story.

Article 24, Universal Declaration of Human Rights
Everyone has the right to rest and leisure, including reasonable limitation of working hours and periodic holidays with pay.

---

1 Think of a sentence to put into the thought bubble (M1).

2 Analyse the bar chart (M2). ▸ METHOD Statistics, pp. 20 – 21

3 a) Name possible reasons for the gender leisure gap.
   b) Compare your ideas to the reasons described in M3.

4 Discuss whether the gender leisure gap is a private or a political problem.

5 **Gallery walk:** Develop a set of measures that can help the woman in M1.
   Take different levels into account:
   • What can women themselves and their families do?
   • What can employers do?
   • What political solutions can you think of?

1.8 How can Germany fight child poverty?

M1 Poverty: your associations

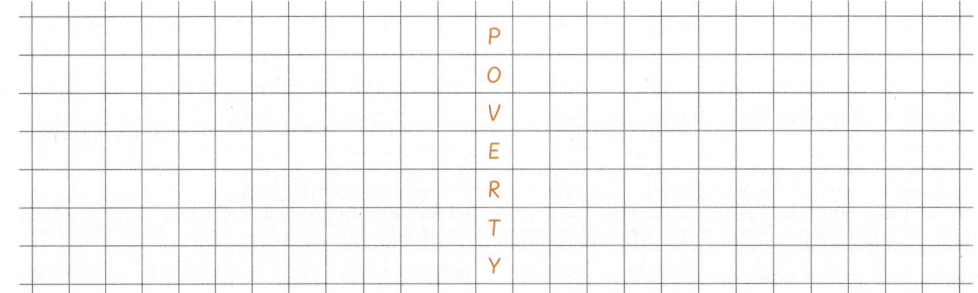

M2 Moments when people realized they were poor

a) "I was always overwhelmed by not knowing what to say after Christmas break when teachers would go around the room and ask what presents everyone got. There were times when Christmas wasn't celebrated or even mentioned in my family. So when the teacher got to me, I wouldn't know what to say. I would just shrug my shoulders and hope the questions didn't get any more specific."

b) "[…] Everyone on my soccer team wore [brand-name] cleats, while I wore off-brand ones. A girl on the team called me out and asked when my parents were going to buy me 'real' cleats. I'm pretty sure I told her to [shut up], but it embarrassed me and affected me mentally. I thought, I don't belong here."

c) "I remember getting yelled at by my Spanish teacher for not typing up an assignment, but we didn't have a computer at home."

d) "Realizing the reason my mom 'wasn't that hungry' when she took us to [a fast food restaurant] was that she couldn't afford food for herself. I used to get mad when she would ask for a bite. I'd say, 'I thought you weren't hungry. Maybe you should get your own.' When I realized the real reason, I'd tell her I was full before finishing half my sandwich and drink and most of my fries so she could have them. She cried when she realized I had found out her secret. I still give most of my fries to other people now."

a) to d) from: Molly Capobianco, People Are Sharing Their Childhood Memories Of Realizing They Were Poor, And Wow, People Need To Be Nicer To Kids, New York, NY: BuzzFeed, 24 Nov 2022, https://www.buzzfeed.com/mollycapobianco/people-share-moment-they-realized-they-were-poor [27 Feb 2024]

M3 Definitions of poverty

Absolute poverty means lacking the basic necessities of life. Health and even life itself are threatened.
The World Bank define poverty as income of less than US $2.15 per day.

Steve Harris, Longman Study Guides: A-Level and AS-Level. Sociology, Harlow: Longman, 1996, p. 165 (modified/figures added)

Relative poverty exists when people earn so much less than the average pay that they are unable to participate in what have come to be regarded as ordinary living patterns. For European countries, usually a relative poverty line of 60 per cent of the national median income is used. In Germany, the at-risk-of-poverty threshold for a single person was a monthly income of €1,310 in 2023.

M4 At-risk-of-poverty rate among families and children

At-risk-of-poverty rates among families / children, Germany, 2005 – 2021*

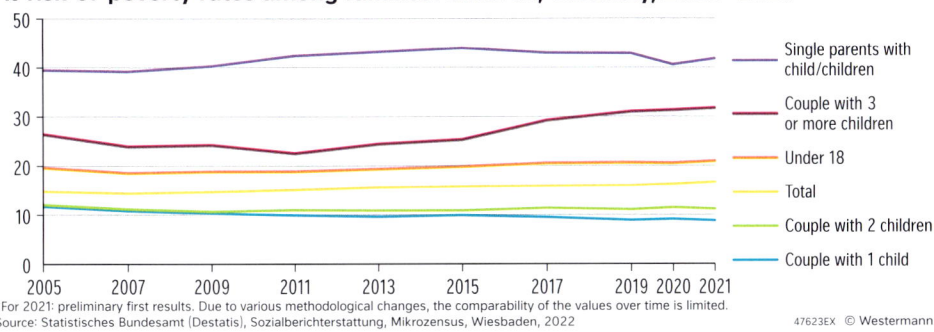

*For 2021: preliminary first results. Due to various methodological changes, the comparability of the values over time is limited.
Source: Statistisches Bundesamt (Destatis), Sozialberichterstattung, Mikrozensus, Wiesbaden, 2022   47623EX © Westermann

M5 What are the reasons for child poverty in Germany?

One of the main reasons for this is that the parents' financial situation has a direct impact on the children. This means that if parents work in the low-wage sector or are dependent on social benefits, there is, simply put, little left for the children. Due to their income situation, they often suffer from an unhealthy diet, poorer educational opportunities, and less social participation [...]. According to a survey of children and young people (aged 10–17) conducted by the Deutsches Kinderhilfswerk in 2023, another main reason for the persistence of child poverty is the lack of support and encouragement in education.

How much poverty is there in Germany?, in: vostel Blog, Berlin: vostel volunteering UG, 19 Dec 2023/last updated: 10 Jan 2024, https://vostel.de/blog/en/poverty-germany/ [4 Mar 2024]

M6 Possible measures against child poverty

- more financial support for low-income families
- more financial support for single parents
- free childcare (nursery and kindergarten)
- a stronger focus on equal opportunities in education policies
- free school meals
- more affordable housing
- financial literacy programs
- a higher minimum wage
- more flexible working options for parents
- more research on poverty
- ...

Text by the author

1. What do you think of when you hear the word poverty? Find words that contain the letters of the word poverty (M1).
2. Read M2 and add more aspects to your list from task 1.
3. a) Explain which kind of poverty (M3) the people in M2 have experienced.
   b) Give reasons why it is important to make a difference between absolute and relative poverty (M3).
4. Illustrate reasons for child poverty in your own words (M4, M5).
5. a) Rank the suggested measures according to how effective they are (M6). Feel free to add more measures.
   b) Discuss the pros and cons of the measure you find most effective (with your partner).

1.9 Meeting different expectations – a dilemma?

M1 Pleasing everyone: impossible?

M2 Role conflicts

a) Role conflict happens when there are contradictions between different roles that a person takes on or plays in their everyday life. [...] To truly understand role conflict, though, one [5] must first have a solid grasp of how sociologists understand roles, generally speaking. Sociologists use the term "role" [...] to describe a set of expected behaviors and obligations a person has based on his or her position in life and relative to others. All of us have multiple [10] roles and responsibilities in our lives[:] [...] son or daughter, sister or brother, mother or father, spouse or partner, friend, [...] or professional [...].

Because we all play multiple roles in our lives, [15] all of us have or will experience one or more types of role conflict at least once.

Ashley Crossman, What Is Role Conflict in Sociology?, in: ThoughtCo, New York, NY: Dotdash Meredith, 30 May 2019, https://www.thoughtco.com/role-conflict-3026528 [15 Apr 2024]

b) The most obvious example of role conflict is work/family conflict, or the conflict one feels when pulled between familial and professional obligations. Take, for example, a mother who is [5] also a doctor. She likely has to work long hours at the hospital and may even be on call several nights a week, taking her away from her children. Many individuals who find themselves in this position describe feeling conflicted and [10] distressed about their situation.

In role strain, the demands of a single role become overwhelming. A boss may have many responsibilities to juggle, including management, innovation, and organizing events. Both role conflict and role strain can potentially [15] lead to role exit, where an individual stops identifying with a particular role. For example, a boss may become so frustrated with all her responsibilities that she quits her job.

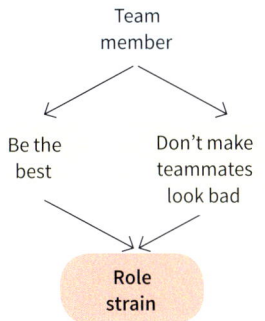

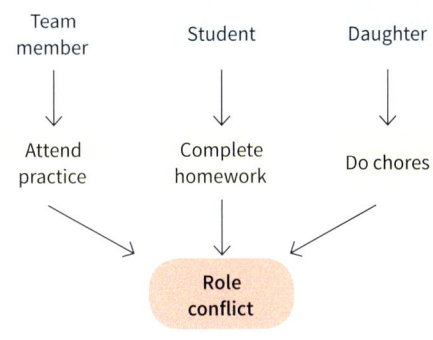

VOCABULARY

chore
Haushaltsarbeit
to loom
sich abzeichnen

M3   The weekend dilemma

Tom is a 14-year-old secondary school student. It is Friday afternoon; school has just finished, and he is excited about the weekend. He is looking forward to spending time with his
5 friends, but he is also aware of the growing pile of homework waiting for him at home.
Tom's parents have been stressing how important it is for him to keep up with his schoolwork, especially as there are several important
10 exams this month – including maths and history. They have reminded him several times this week that his grades need to improve, and they expect him to spend more time studying. But Tom's friends have been planning a week-
15 end trip to the mountains for weeks. They have been talking about it non-stop and he does not want to miss out on the fun. His friends are expecting him to join them, and he knows it will be a great opportunity to relax and unwind after a hectic week of classes. 20
As he stands outside the school gates, torn between wanting to spend time with his friends and the **looming** responsibilities of his academic workload, he realizes he has a decision to make. Will he put his studies first and go 25 straight home to do his homework, risking disappointment from his friends? Or will he decide to enjoy some quality time with his friends, knowing that this could affect his grades and upset his parents? 30

Text by the author

1   **a)** Starting from M1, make a list things other people expect from you.
     Use different colours to highlight expectations that …
       • … conflict with each other.
       • … contradict your personal wishes.
   b) Compare your results with your partner.
   c) Discuss which expectations others have that are worth living up to.
2   Illustrate the difference between role strain and role conflict by more examples (M2).
3   **a)** Explain whether Tom's situation can be described as role strain or role conflict (M3).
   b) Discuss Tom's choices and decide what he should do.
4   **Extra:**
   a) Act out the consequences of this decision by doing a role play in front of the class:
     • If you decide that Tom should go straight home, act out the phone call in which he explains his choice to his best friend.
     • If you decide he should go on the weekend trip with his friends, act out the scene when Tom comes home on Sunday evening and has to face his parents again.
   b) Give each other feedback on your role plays. **MORE HELP**

1.10 Peer pressure – overwhelming?

M 1 Who would you ask for advice in these situations – your parents or your friends?

- You feel a teacher has treated you unfairly.
- You do not know what to wear to Kim's birthday party.
- You have had a bitter argument with your best friend. 5
- You are afraid you will have to repeat this school year if your marks do not improve.

- You are in love with a boy or girl from your class and do not know how to deal with it.
- You worry that you are not attractive enough. 10
- You feel lonely.
- Your parents want you to work harder for school.

Text by the author

M 2 Peer groups

A peer group is a social group whose members have common interests, social status, and age. This is where children can escape supervision and learn to form relationships on their own. 5 The influence of the peer group is usually strongest during adolescence. However, peer groups tend to have only short-term influence, unlike the family, which has a long-term influence.

10 Unlike family and school, peer groups let children escape the direct supervision of adults. Among peers, children learn to form relationships on their own. Peer groups also offer the chance to discuss interests that adults may not 15 share with their children (such as clothing and popular music) or allow (such as drugs and sex). Peer groups have a significant impact on the psychological and social adjustment of individuals in the group. They provide a perspective 20 outside of the individual's point of view. Peer group members also learn to develop relationships with others in the social system. Peers, especially group members, become important social "guides", teaching members about cus- 25 toms, social norms, and different ideologies.

Peer groups can also teach members about gender roles. During socialization, group members learn about gender differences, social and cultural expectations. While boys and girls are very different, there is not a one-to-one link 30 between sex and gender role with males always being masculine and females always being feminine. Both genders can contain different levels of masculinity and femininity.

Adolescent peer groups provide support for 35 children and teens as they assimilate into adult society. As a result, they become less dependent on their parents, feel more independent, and connect with a much larger social network. Peer group cohesion is defined by 40 factors such as group communication, group consensus, and group conformity concerning attitude and behavior. As members of peer groups interconnect, and agree, a normative code emerges. 45

This normative code can become very rigid, dictating group behavior and dress. Peer group individuality is increased by normative codes, and intergroup conflict. If a group member does not conform to these codes, he or she may 50 be rejected by the group. The term "peer pressure" is often used to describe instances where an individual feels indirectly pressured to match their behaviour to that of their peers. Taking up smoking and underage drinking are 55 two of the best-known examples. Despite the often-negative connotations of the term, peer pressure can be used in a positive way.

Peers groups, in: LibreTexts. Social Sciences, o.O., https://socialsci.libretexts.org/Courses/Collin_College/Introduction_to_Sociology/04%3A_Socialization/4.02%3A_The_Role_of_Socialization/4.2.05%3A__Agents_of_Socialization/4.2.5E%3A_Peer_Groups [15 Apr 2024] (modified)

M3 A tough decision

I think they're pretty, but before I decide, let me get some social validation.

Cartoon: Mark Dubowski, 1 June 2015

VOCABULARY

to navigate
sich einen Weg bahnen, etw. durchstehen
to be vulnerable to sth.
anfällig für etw. sein
boundary
Grenze
substance
hier: Drogen oder Alkohol
susceptible
empfänglich

M4 Navigating negative peer pressure

Negative peer pressure can be challenging to navigate, particularly for young people who may be more **vulnerable** to social influence. However, there are several strategies that in-
5 dividuals can use to resist negative peer pressure. These strategies include:

- **Setting boundaries:** It is important to set boundaries and communicate them clearly to peers. For example, an individual may
10 decide not to engage in **substance** use and communicate this boundary to their friends.
- **Seeking out positive peer groups:** Seeking out positive peer groups can
15 provide an alternative source of social support and reduce the influence of negative peer pressure.
- **Developing self-confidence:** Developing self-confidence can make individuals less **susceptible** to negative peer pressure. 20 Self-confidence can be developed by setting and achieving personal goals, engaging in activities that one enjoys, and surrounding oneself with positive influences. 25
- **Seeking adult support:** Seeking support from trusted adults, such as parents, teachers, or counselors, can help individuals navigate negative peer pressure and make informed decisions. 30

Understanding Peer Groups: The Importance and Influence of Social Connections, Delhi: Marg Erp Limited, 2 May 2023, https://margcompusoft.com/m/peer-group/ [15 Apr 2024]

1 Decide who you would ask for advice in the situations in M1. Give reasons.
2 Visualize the most important information on peer groups in a systematic way. Make sure you include both positive and negative aspects of peer groups. **MORE HELP**
3 Analyse the cartoon (M3). ▶ METHOD Cartoons, pp. 26–27
4 Imagine the following situation: All of Kim's close friends vape regularly. For some time, they have been trying to convince her that she must join them if she really wants to belong to their clique. Kim, however, does not want to. Discuss which of the tips in M4 might help Kim best in this situation.

Grouping terms: analysing families and society

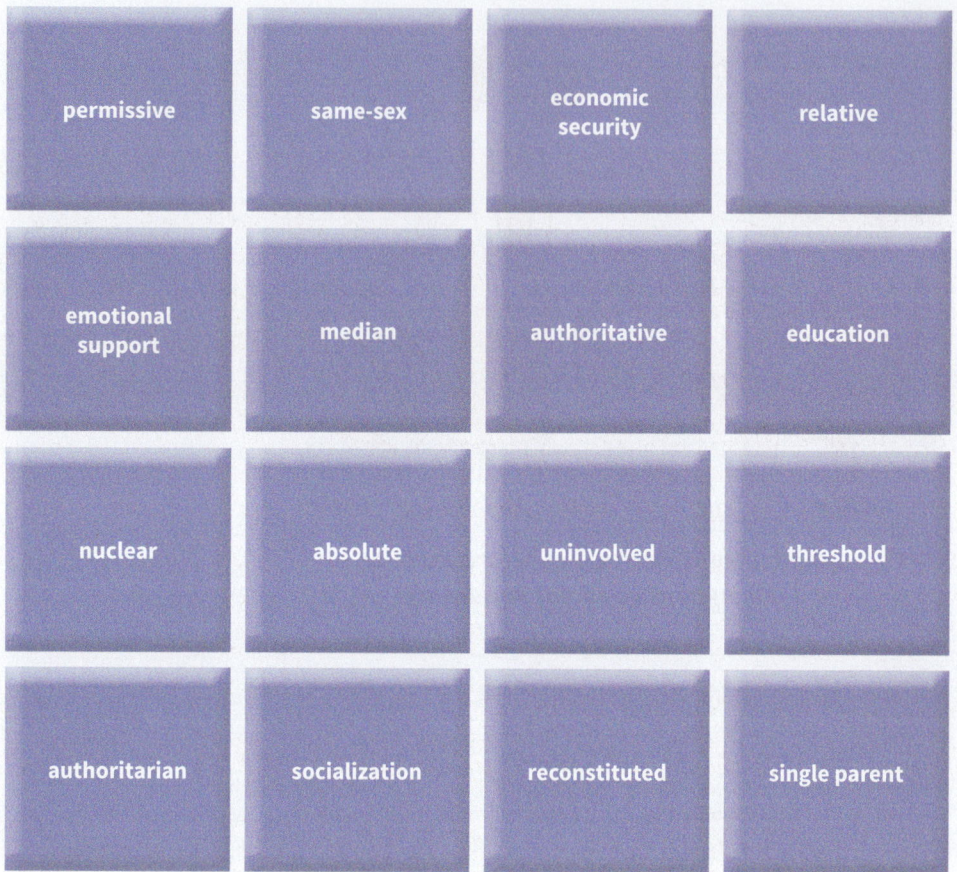

permissive	same-sex	economic security	relative
emotional support	median	authoritative	education
nuclear	absolute	uninvolved	threshold
authoritarian	socialization	reconstituted	single parent

Elevenie: reflecting on families and peer groups

An elevenie is an eleven-word poem of five lines, with each line performing a specific task in the poem:

Row	Words	Content	Example
1	1	The topic of the poem, e.g. an object, a problem, a thought, …	*Homework*
2	2	A more detailed description of the word / What does it do?	*Piles high*
3	3	Where is the word from row 1, or how is it?	*On my desk*
4	4	What are your thoughts about it?	*Waiting to be done*
5	1	Conclusion: What is the result? (often a commentary or a summary word)	*Never-ending*

1   Group words that belong into the same category. Find a heading for each category.
2   Try to find more terms that belong in the same category.
3   Write an elevenie on either families or peer groups.

What is cohousing?

Cohousing communities are intentional communities, created and run by their residents. Each household has a self-contained, private home as well as shared community space.
5 Residents come together to manage their community, share activities, and regularly eat together.
Cohousing communities can be intergenerational, welcoming anyone of any age and any
10 family structure, or specifically to cater for people who are older or are communities of common interest, for example for women or LGBT groups.
Typical communities range from 10 to 40 house-
15 holds. All adult residents are encouraged to take part in decision making; some communities also require residents to undertake a set number of hours work for the community.

47644EX © Westermann

Common house with various shared rooms such as kitchen, playroom and guest rooms

Flats and houses

Heating supply

Playground

Community garden with gathering places

Small gardens

Parking

Design of a typical cohousing neighbourhood

About cohousing, UK Cohousing Network, o.O., https://cohousing.org.uk/about-cohousing-2/ [27 Mar 2024] (modified)

VOCABULARY

cohousing
gemeinschaftliche Wohnformen
LGBT
Abkürzung für Lesbian, Gay, Bisexual and Transgender

What are the pros and cons of cohousing?

Cohousing can help to overcome the loneliness that many people experience in big cities.

Not everybody can afford to buy a home in a cohousing project. So cohousing is not an opportunity for poorer people.

Living with people with different lifestyles, habits, and preferences can lead to conflicts.

Because many things are shared, cohousing can help residents to save money.

As people share space and resources, cohousing is a greener way of living.

As many facilities are shared, you cannot customize them as you wish.

You can have a direct impact on the community you live in because decisions are made democratically.

Both the work you have to do for the community and democratic decision-making can be time-consuming and tiring.

1 What is a home? Describe this concept in your own words.
2 Compare living in a cohousing community to living in a family.
3 Do research on cohousing projects in different countries (for example, Germany, Denmark, the UK, the U.S., or Canada) and present them to each other.
You can take the following aspects into account:
• How many people live in this community?
• Who lives there (singles, families, elderly people, …)?
• What are the facilities like (private homes, shared spaces, design, …)?
• How are the communities organized? How do they make decisions?
• What does community life look like?
• Does the project have a specific vision or values?
• Can you find any reports of people's experiences with this project? What are its strengths and weaknesses?
4 a) Your parents have suggested moving into a cohousing community. Would you welcome this plan? Give reasons.
b) Discuss whether cohousing might be the future of living together.

INTERNET

WES-116955-191
Some useful links for your research

2

Podcast Virality Television Books Radio Influencers Apps Story Streaming Print Blog Digitalization Livestreaming Gaming Media Report Journalism Magazines Article Memes Photography Emoticons Infotainment News Film Music Advertising Influence Video Hashtags Newspapers

Media and its role in our lives

Across

2. This media records and shares thoughts or experiences in written or multimedia form.
4. This media mainly prints news and information.
5. Showing or listening to content on an electronic device without downloading it.
7. Sending out audio or video content in real time over the internet.
9. A popular platform for sharing short videos in a global community.

Down

1. Making and sending audio content, often on diverse topics.
3. This widely used electronic device receives signals and shows moving images and sound.
6. Communicating through images and text, often used for humour or commentary.
8. Sending audio content to a wide audience, often through channels like FM or AM.

1 What comes to mind when you think about media? Compare and discuss your thoughts with a partner. Use the word cloud and the images on the left. **MORE HELP**

2 Solve the crossword. Use the webcode/QR code or write the missing words in your folder. **MORE HELP**

3 a) Media Diary: List the diverse media types you typically interact with, estimate how much time you spend daily or weekly on each, and identify the main media platforms you use. **MORE HELP**

b) Discuss your findings in a group: Why are certain types of media so popular among your peers?

4 Create a collage illustrating how media impacts your life. Use pictures from magazines, printouts, or your own drawings to illustrate both the positive and negative influences of your experience with media.

2.1 Can the media shape society?

| M 1 | Media in our lives

| M 2 | How do we find out what is going on in the world?

How and where we find information and facts about the world is really important:

- It helps us make decisions and understand the world around us.
5 - We like to know what is happening in other countries, what our government is doing, and even what famous people are getting up to!

We find most of this information through the
10 media.

Key fact
"The media" is a name for all the different ways of communicating with lots of people at once.

There are three main types of media where 15 you can get news:

- print media, such as newspapers and magazines
- broadcast media, such as television and radio 20
- online media, such as websites and social media

Key fact
We still get news from traditional media sources (newspapers, television, and radio) 25 but we find out lots from newer sources like the world wide web and social media.

What is the media?, in: Bitesize, London a.o.: BBC, https://www.bbc.co.uk/bitesize/guides/zhbstrd/revision/1 [1 Dec 2023]

1 State the functions of media portrayed in M1.
Give examples of additional roles that media fulfil in our society.
2 Explain how various media sources help keep us informed about current events (M2).
3 Identify the changes in media usage since the 19th century and explain their significance and role in the development of our society (M3).
4 **Gallery walk:** Create a poster illustrating how media influences us and how we influence the media. Use graphics, diagrams, or symbols alongside explanatory text to depict these relationships.

M 3 Evolution of mass communication – some milestones

about 40,000 BCE	In the Stone Age, people communicated via cave paintings. The oldest painting to date was discovered in Indonesia and is at least 45,500 years old.
about 3,000 BCE	The Summerians invented cuneiform writing, one of the first writing systems. They used clay tablets as writing material. The Egyptians also had a writing system, the hieroglyphics. They used papyrus scrolls for writing.
about 1440	Johannes Gutenberg invented the printing press in Mainz. This made it possible to mass-produce texts.
1650	The first daily newspaper was published in Leipzig.
1820s	The first lasting photograph was created with a "camera obscura".
1830s	With the help of the electric telegraph, it was possible to send messages over long distances.
1860/70s	The telephone was invented. People in distant places could talk to each other in real time.
1920s	The first entertainment radio broadcast aired in 1923, but only a small audience could afford to pay for radios and licensing fees.
1930s	Public television stations aired the first full-length programs to inform and entertain a broad audience from 1935 onward. In Nazi Germany, radio and television were used for propaganda.
1940s	On 21 May 1949, freedom of the press was enshrined in Article 5 of the German Basic Law: "Every person has the right to freely express and disseminate opinions in speech, writing, and pictures, and to access information without hindrance from generally accessible sources."
1950s	Radio reached nearly every household in Germany. Television became a mass medium, with some programs reaching 90 percent of the population.
1960s	The Second German Television channel (ZDF) was founded in April 1963, and regional programs followed from 1964 to 1969, increasing the competition for audience attention.
	In 1969, the US military connected several computers and created the first internet: the ARPANET. But for a long time, only a few experts could use it.
1980s	Private cable and satellite programs started on radio and television. Radio stations increased from 40 to over 230 within a few years. People spent an average of six hours daily on radio, television, and newspapers.
1990s	The Word Wide Web was born and made it possible for people all over the world to network with each other.
2000s	Social media platforms, including Facebook and Twitter, along with numerous blogs, started. The iPhone, the first internet-capable smartphone, was released in 2007. Television and radio stayed popular, while (print) newspaper reading declined.
2010s	Almost all German households had internet access. Online videos became popular. Various apps and social media platforms made it easier to make and share content such as videos, articles, and podcasts.

Text by the author, from 1920s adapted from: Geschichte der Medienwelt, Düsseldorf: Landeszentrale für politische Bildung Nordrhein-Westfalen, https://www.politische-bildung.nrw.de/digitale-medien/digitale-demokratie kompetenz/newsroom-40/geschichte [1 Dec 2023] (translated and modified)

VOCABULARY

BCE
(Before Common Era)
v. u. Z. (vor unserer Zeit)
cuneiform writing
Keilschrift
clay tablets
Tontafeln
to air
ausstrahlen, senden
enshrined
verankert, festgeschrieben
internet-capable
internetfähig

INFO

ARPANET
Advanced Research Projects Agency Network

2.2 Does social media bring people together or drive them apart?

M1 The social media have more …

positive
aspects

negative
aspects

M2 Benefits and challenges of social media

M3 Is social media good for you?

Elena: "Hello, my name is Elena. I'm 14 years old and I'm from Ruse in Bulgaria. My question is, what are the benefits of social media? This question is important to me because a lot
5 of people consider social media unhealthy."
Joe: "We see it all the time. There's loads of stories around about how bad social media is for us and how large parts of our lives are in the hands of a few massive companies.
10 I'm Cybersecurity Reporter at the BBC, which means that a big part of my job is holding these big companies to account. I spend a lot of time looking at the negative sides of social media and I pretty much take the positives for
15 granted. So getting this question is actually really good for me because it can remind me of all the good things that have come about since social media was invented.

I grew up in a time before social media. Not quite that long ago! We still had mobile 20 phones and the internet, but it wasn't quite like it is now. Everything was much slower and much more difficult. People still mainly communicated by phone call, which means that if you made plans, you had to stick to 25 them. Or you could leave your mate waiting in the rain.

And now we're more connected than ever. Most of us are spending time every day with our friends online and sharing our lives with 30 people across the world. If you're feeling isolated or lonely or if you feel like there's something you need help with, you can find a community through social media who can share their experiences and help you out. All this 35 communication can lead to a greater under-

standing of each other and also bring some real change. It's hard to imagine something like the climate strike movement spreading as
40 far or as fast as it has, without social media. It helped **amplify** the voice of a 15-year-old activist in Sweden, so she's been heard around the world. And there are some pretty direct benefits too.
45 Tools have been made that encourage people to make the world around them better, whether that's by giving money, telling your friends and family you're safe or by donating blood. In fact, this alone has led to more than 50 million people becoming blood donors around the
50 world, literally life savers.

So, there really are some great benefits to social media but it's still really new. These apps are **emerging technologies** and when things affect the way that we live and work and do
55 things as much as social media has, it takes a long time to work out what the **knock-on effects** could be. It's probably up to the next generation to work through some of these problems and hopefully, if they do a good job,
60 we'll be talking a lot more about the positive sides of social media in the future."

Is social media good for you? (video transcript), BBC My World, cit. in: LearnEnglish Teens, London: British Council, https://learnenglishteens.britishcouncil.org/study-break/video-zone/is-social-media-good-for-you [12 Nov 2023]

VOCABULARY

to amplify
verstärken
emerging technologies
entstehende Technologien
knock-on effect
Dominoeffekt
bullying
Mobbing
to prey upon sb.
jmdn. ausnutzen, auf jmdn. Jagd machen
to harass sb.
jmdn. belästigen
to demean sb.
jmdn. herabwürdigen
to hurt sb.
jmdn. verletzen
to upset sb.
jmdn. aufregen
lineup
hier: Positionslinie

M4 The face of cyberbullying

Sadly, **bullying** behavior has been around since the beginning of civilization. Bullying has consistently taken form as stronger people **preying upon** the weak, and now, with the
5 rise of technology, it has also become widespread online.

Cyberbullying has become a growing problem in countries around the world. Essentially, cyberbullying doesn't differ much from the type
10 of bullying that many children have unfortunately grown accustomed to in school. The only difference is that it takes place online. […]

Cyberbullying is any type of **harassing**, threat-
15 ening, **demeaning** language. It can also involve embarrassing another person online. Typically, this is done through mean comments, online rumors, and even sexual remarks. […] Essentially, anything that is posted online that's intended **to hurt** or **upset** some-
20 one else, regardless of what the topic is, is considered to be cyberbullying.

There isn't a single platform where all of the cyberbullying takes place, and no online space is completely free of cyberbullying. Since
25 most children and young adults access the internet via their mobile devices, this is the most common medium through which they experience this type of harassment.

Cyberbullying statistics show that Instagram
30 is the most common platform for cyberbullying, closely followed by Facebook and Snapchat. Many people experience cyberbullying while playing online multiplayer games as well. While YouTube is among the online plat-
35 forms with the highest number of users, only a tenth of users have so far reported experiencing cyberbullying there.

Ogi Djuraskovic, Cyberbullying Statistics, Facts, and Trends (2023) with Charts, in: FirstSiteGuide blog, FirstSideGuide, o. O., 4 Oct 2023, https://firstsiteguide.com/cyberbullying-stats/ [12 Nov 2023]

1 In your eyes, are the positive or negative aspects more prominent in social media? Create a **lineup** on this question (M1). Provide examples to support your argument.
2 Evaluate the positive and negative impacts of social media and relate them to your personal experience. **MORE HELP**
3 Compare the views in M3 and M4 regarding the role of social media.
4 Is cyberbullying worse than conventional bullying? Use M4 and discuss your findings in a group.
5 **Placemat:** Develop a list of practical tips on how to counter cyberbullying.

How to convince someone in a debate

Debate – what is it good for?

In a democratic society, it is normal that people have different opinions on how to deal with an issue. Is it a good idea to block airports to protest climate policies? Should 16-year-olds be allowed to vote in a general election? A discussion is a way to express your opinion and to listen to other arguments. A different point of view may even change the way you see a problem. Sometimes, it is possible to find a compromise. In any case, it is important that you learn how to argue your point. How about practicing your skills by defending the position you do not believe in?

How do I do it?

Step 1: General preparation

- Do the necessary research on the subject. It is vital that you know your facts. Make sure that they are facts, not assumptions. If you cannot find solid evidence for your opinion, then you might simply be wrong. ▸ METHOD Sources, pp. 52–53
- It is helpful to brainstorm ideas and to write them down. This way, you can make a list of smart arguments. Consider which ones are stronger or weaker and put them in order. A convincing string of arguments connects the points well. This makes it easier for your listeners to follow.
- A good argument looks at the issue not only from your own point of view, but from many different perspectives. Put yourself in someone else's shoes! The more viewpoints you can offer, the better.
- Anticipate how the other side will argue and prepare counter-arguments.
- Be polite and make it easy for people to change their minds. You have a better chance of changing their view if you welcome them instead of making them feel stupid for believing in a certain way. Otherwise, their pride might not allow them to change their minds even if your arguments are convincing.

Step 2: Work on each argument

- Go through each point on your list. A good argument starts with a clearly stated main point. Keep it simple.
- You then add supporting statements or explanations.
- Last, give an example and, if possible, evidence. ▸ Useful phrases (A), pp. 202–203

An exemplary argument structure

Main point:	Cyclists should always wear a helmet,
Support:	because it reduces the risk of severe injuries. A helmet softens the blow to the head after a fall.
Example:	My brother had a bike accident last year. He fractured his arm and the broken helmet strongly suggested that he would have faced a harder time without it. A study commissioned by the Baden-Württemberg Ministry of Transport concluded that a helmet reduces the risk of severe head injuries by 80 % (HFC study from 2017).

Example

Debate topic: Should parents have more control over their children's use of social media?

Possible aspects of the debate:

Safety
- Online predators
- Cyberbullying
- Inappropriate content
- …

Trust and respect
- Kids might lose trust in parents.
- They feel that parents do not respect them.
- …

Overwhelming impressions
- Kids need help to cope with the number and content of inter-actions.
- …

Invasion of privacy
- Conversations with friends should stay private.
- Making one's own decision is a normal part of growing up.
- …

Unhealthy amount of time
- It is too tempting for most kids to spend their entire time online, and it is not healthy for their social development.
- It is unhealthy to stare into a screen for such a long time.
- …

Example of an argument:
Parents should monitor and limit their child's use of social media because too much time on social media is not good for children's mental and physical development. Excessive screen time has been linked with higher depression rates, poor sleep, obesity risks, and behavioural problems. A Gallup survey from 2023 showed that just over half of US teenagers spend at least four hours a day on social media apps.

1 Debate the above topic. Prepare by using the method suggestions.

2.3 Unmasking fake news and image manipulation – easy to spot?

KEY TERMS

disinformation
Verbreitung von
gefälschten
Informationen,
Desinformation
fake news
gefälschte
Nachrichten
image manipulation
Bildmanipulation
propaganda
Propaganda
(= Manipulation der
öffentlichen
Meinung)

VOCABULARY

digitally altered
digital verändert

M 1   Examples of image manipulation

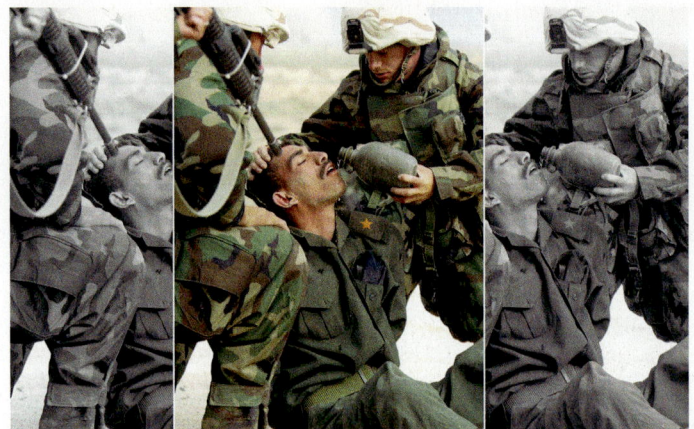

a) The photo in the centre was taken during the Iraq war in 2003. It shows an Iraqi soldier surrounded by American soldiers. The German artist Ursula Dahmen made this collage of it to show how image sections and colours can manipulate the viewer.

b) The photos show a 2008 missile test in Iran. The original is on the right, while the manipulated photo is on the left side. The Iranian government copied a missile into the altered version to hide an ignition which failed.

M 2   Seeing is believing

Most of us are familiar with the saying: "Seeing is believing." However, what if what we see tricks us?

In quality media produced by journalists, content and images are generally fact-checked for accuracy. Naturally, the selection of images by the media, as well as the perspective from which they are taken, always influences us. However, the rise of social media, where anyone can share content, together with the growth of artificial intelligence, has fundamentally changed the landscape. Numerous images we come across on the internet today and which we accept as fact, are either photomontages or manipulated. Most of us understand that visual content is digitally altered in today's world, particularly since we know about image editing programs. However, even with this awareness, why do we often believe what we see and fall for manipulated images? Image manipulation did not start with the invention of image editing programs. Even in the 20th century, pictures were altered to influence the observer.

Text by the author

M3 Fake news

HOW TO SPOT Fake news

Look out for strange or unfamiliar URLs, such as those that end in .com.co

Check the site's "About" section—if it has one. Often, you'll find clues to whether the site is legitimate and whether it follows acceptable editorial standards.

Be wary of articles labeled "sponsored content"

Such content typically means a company, organization, or perhaps even a government entity paid for it.

Be wary of Bloggers

Some bloggers lack expertise on a subject. Check blog posts against coverage of the same topic in the mainstream media.

Click the links

Much like citations in a research paper, links are supposed to provide clear evidence that supports the claims a journalist wants to make. When you see a link, click it to see if it really supports what the writer had to say. Also, see if it links to an outside source or if it's linking to another post or piece by that same author.

Consider the source

Is it legitimate and trustworthy? What do searches on the authors' names tell you about their qualifications? Legacy media, like the Washington Post and New York Times, as well as major network news (ABC, CBS, NBC) tend to have more credibility.

Search the topic

Do an Internet search for any other stories on the topic, using keywords. The more stories you find on a topic, the more likely it is that the story in question has some merit.

Check the root sources

Good stories will have multiple root sources, with various publications, websites and television broadcasts all using their own reporting with multiple, varied sources to confirm information. If you rely on stories with many quality sources, it will help you separate the weaker pieces from the stronger ones.

Watch for bias

Are the writers fair and impartial, or are they promoting their own views or those of a political party, pressure group, or other entity?

When in doubt, don't cite

Don't use information in an assignment, broadcast it on social media, or tweet it in a way that implies it's true if you suspect that it is not. Nothing kills fake news faster than healthy skepticism and a commitment to quality research.

*Sources:
Dynamics of **NEWS REPORTING & WRITING**
Vincent F. Filak
and the editors of
CQ RESEARCHER

SAGE Publishing

1. Look at the photomontage M1 a) and explain how your response changes when the image is only visible in fragments.
2. Compare the images in M1 b) and analyse them, considering the image caption.
3. Have you encountered fake news before? Search online for examples, and then use the information in M3 to verify.
4. a) Starting with M1 and M2, identify possible reasons for spreading manipulated images and fake news.
   b) Comment on why people use media to manipulate others and the reliability of the media platforms involved in this behaviour. **MORE HELP**
5. **Milling around:** Develop creative approaches to assess how reliable media information is.

How to deal with online sources

VOCABULARY

reliable
verlässlich,
zuverlässig

Why do I have to be careful with my sources?

Getting information has never been easier. Simply type a keyword into a search engine and it does not take a second to find more text than you could ever read. The sheer amount can be overwhelming, and everything you read will not have the same quality.

Professional journalists produce quality media. These journalists worry about losing their reputations. Fellow journalists counter-check their stories and the public watches them closely.

Other sources offer anyone, no matter how qualified, the opportunity to share their ideas online. There is no quality check. Worse, the content we read might be written by someone who actively tries to influence us with his or her own ideas about what is going on in the world. Artificial Intelligence and deep fake programmes make matters worse.

This confuses a lot of people and gives them the impression that they cannot trust anything they read any more. However, we must accept this challenge and find ways to deal with the "data jungle". Here are some tips to find reliable and accurate information online.

How do I do it?

INTERNET

WES-116955-232
Links to tips for
internet searches and
correct citation

Step 1: Search strategy

- Most search engines have tools to help you find information. Use the webcode/QR code on the left for more information.
- Narrow down the number of results by thinking about the most relevant keywords for your search.

Step 2: Can I trust the source? Use the ADAM approach

Age

- How old is the information you found? Is it still relevant? Depending on the topic, you can relax. If you are looking into a current political issue, even information that is one week old might be out-of-date. If you are doing research on a historical topic, your sources may be older but still relevant.
- If the website has many links which do not function, it is a sign that the homepage is out of date.
- Be aware that not all official websites, such as those of the federal government or other institutions, provide all information with a publication date. Therefore, it is also important to know how trustworthy the publisher is (see "Author").

Depth

- How detailed is your source? Does your source offer explanations, good evidence, and sources for its claims?
- Counter-check individual points. Do other (or at least the majority of) sources agree? There are different websites that help to check on information (for example Mimikama, ARD-Faktenfinder, dpa-Faktencheck, Correctiv). The fastest way to check is to use a search engine, then type in a factfinder of your choice and add the keywords relating to your search. Example: "ARD-Faktenfinder: Brandgefahr e-Autos". ▸ webcode/QR code, p. 51
- How professional does the source appear? Are there grammatical errors or typing mistakes?
- Look at the language. Is it highly emotional and populistic or rather factual, academic, and objective?
- Are there advertisements? If yes, are they obvious or rather hidden?

Author

- Who is the author of the information and who owns the site on which it was published? At best, you will find both. However, many official websites do not always give an author's name because the institution itself is responsible for the publication. Then you need to know the owner of the site. Is it a private person, an organization (frequent website ending: .org), a public authority (for government authorities in the USA: .gov, German institutions generally use: .de), a company (frequently, especially for international companies: .com). It is never a good sign if you cannot find out who wrote or published the information. You can try to find out who owns a website by doing a "whois search" (see webcode/QR code to the right).
- If you find the author, check out his or her reputation by searching for the person online. What are the author's qualifications? What do other sources say about the author? Looking at sources that quote your author can give you hints. The operator "link:URL" finds websites that refer to the homepage in question. The more reputable the institutions, the better.
- Are there signs that the author has a conflict of interest (for example because a specific company pays for him or her)?
- Be aware that publishing information ("Impressum") is not as common in English-speaking countries as it is in Germany. If you do not find it on a German website, it is a cause for concern.

INTERNET

WES-116955-233
Some links on how to check out who owns a website

Money

- Does a person or company benefit from a study or text financially? For example, if a study on the benefits of owning a hedgehog is paid for by the National Hedgehog Foundation, you should not be too surprised that the outcome is clearly "yes".

Step 3: Proper citation

- Always name your source. If you use someone else's ideas, diagrams, or texts without mentioning your source, you commit an academic offence called plagiarism. Do not underestimate this problem. You might think that no one will notice because there is so much information out there. However, there are many tools which quickly identify plagiarism – and after all, it is only fair to give credit to the person who made the content.
- There are rules on how to list your sources at the end of your work. For example, name the author, the title and where and when it was published exactly. Ask your teacher about your school's standard protocol for citation ("Methodencurriculum"). If there is no such thing at your school, use the webcode/QR code on p. 52 for help.

Example:

Aliev, Alim: Zwischen Angst und Widerstand. Leben auf der Krim seit 2014, in: Aus Politik und Zeitgeschichte, 74. Jg., 6–8/2024, hrsg. v. d. Bundeszentrale für politische Bildung, Bonn, 03.02.2024, https://www.bpb.de/shop/zeitschriften/apuz/543975/aus-politik-und-zeitgeschichte-2024/ (Abruf: 21.02.2024)

1 You are asked to give a presentation. Use the ADAM approach. Choose one of the following topics for your online research:
a) (Attempted) Manipulation of public opinion during the last US election.
b) Hommingberger Gepardenforellen.

2.4 AI – blessing or curse?

M 1   AI and its role in journalism

Cartoon: Chappatte 3 March 2023

M 2   AI at school

"Can I go home since
AI does all my schoolwork for me now?"

Cartoon: Nate Fakes, 10 July 2023

M3 Pope in a puffer? Identifying an AI-generated deepfake

Several services are available online [...], which are open to the public and let anybody generate a fake image by entering what they'd like to see. [...] These tips help you look for
5 signs indicating an image may be artificially generated, but they can't confirm for sure whether it is or not. There are plenty of factors to take into account, and AI solutions are becoming more advanced, making it harder to
10 spot if they're fake. [...]
One of the first things you should pay attention to is how humans are represented in the picture. [...] Look at the hands, feet, ears, and noses. Then assess whether they look unnatural or
15 not. For instance, there may be **inconsistencies**, such as an unusual number of fingers, abnormal shape, or peculiar positioning. Similarly, look at facial details that might look strange, especially around the eyes and on the ears, as
20 these are often harder to generate for AI. [...]
[I]t's also important to look at all the elements in the picture, such as clothes and accessories. Check if these make sense or whether the **shading** and details are accurately represented. [...]
25 [C]heck the lighting and the shadows, as AI often struggles with accurately representing these elements. [...] Also, make sure the overall scene is realistic and use common sense. For example, it's unlikely a lion would be hav-
30 ing dinner with a family of penguins while wearing a pearl necklace and holding silverware with its paws. Finally, if something feels **awkward**, fact-check unusual events online using a search engine, reliable sources, and news outlets. If you don't find anything online
35 or only data from unknown sources, the image may be AI-generated.

AI-generated image of Pope Francis wearing a puffer jacket

Hagop Kavafian, How to identify AI-generated images, in: Android Police, Saint-Laurent, QC (Canada): Valnet Inc., 22 June 2023, https://www.androidpolice.com/identify-ai-generated-images-how-to/ [24 May 2024]

VOCABULARY

inconsistency
mangelnde Übereinstimmung/Harmonie
shading
Schattierung
awkward
merkwürdig, seltsam

1 Choose a task:
   a) Analyse cartoon M1. Explore both the advantages and disadvantages that result from using AI in journalism.
   b) Analyse cartoon M2. Refer to your personal experience with AI at school.
      ▸ METHOD Cartoons, pp. 26 – 27

2 How can you tell if an image is genuine or created by AI? Summarize the clues in the text (M3) using your own words and apply them to the example of Pope Francis.
   MORE HELP

3 Write an article for a school newspaper, blog, or podcast discussing the pros and cons of artificial intelligence. Use examples to help illustrate your points.

4 **Extra:** Can you tell the difference between a real video or picture, or one that has been generated by artificial intelligence (AI)? Take the quiz using the webcode/QR code.

INTERNET

WES-116955-241
Link to the BBC Quiz:
AI or real?

2.5 How much personal information are we willing to reveal?

M 1   Sharing your private life on the internet

M 2   Digital footprint

A digital footprint includes all traces of your online activity, including your comments on news articles, posts on social media, and records of your online purchases. This can also
5 include the websites you frequent, any messages sent, and data you've added online. Whenever you post something online, share content, or even when a website collects your information by installing cookies on your de-
10 vice, you create a digital trail or footprint. This includes your IP address, login details, and other personal information. Information that others post about you also gets added to your data trail. It could show up when some-
15 one searches for your name online. Your online identity can influence different aspects of your life. [...]

The digital footprint you leave behind is important because:

- It's basically permanent once the data is   20
available to the general public, especially
with social media posts.
- It can determine your reputation online,
which is almost as important as your
offline reputation.   25
- Employers can investigate potential new
hires before making a final decision.
- Colleges and universities can investigate
prospective students' social media before
sending out acceptance letters.   30
- Your words, images, and videos can be
misinterpreted or even altered for
malicious purposes.

Bad actors may share your private messages with a larger group of people and potentially damage friendships, relationships, and reputations.

35

Cybercriminals can steal and use your personal information for phishing purposes or create fake accounts using your data.

40

Clare Stouffer, What is a digital footprint and how can you protect it, Tempe, AZ: NortonLifeLock Inc., 25 Jul 2023, https://us.norton.com/blog/privacy/digital-footprint. [27 Feb 2024]

M3 GDPR personal data

European Union's General Data Protection Regulation (GDPR)

47558EX © Westermann

The GDPR asserts that everyone has a right to the protection of their personal data. With that, GDPR restricts how companies collect, store and use the personal data of customers. The rules give consumers the power to deny the collection of their personal data, to fact check data that is collected and even to have their data erased from a company's databases.

The GDPR defines personal data as any information related to a person that can be used to directly or indirectly identify them, including:

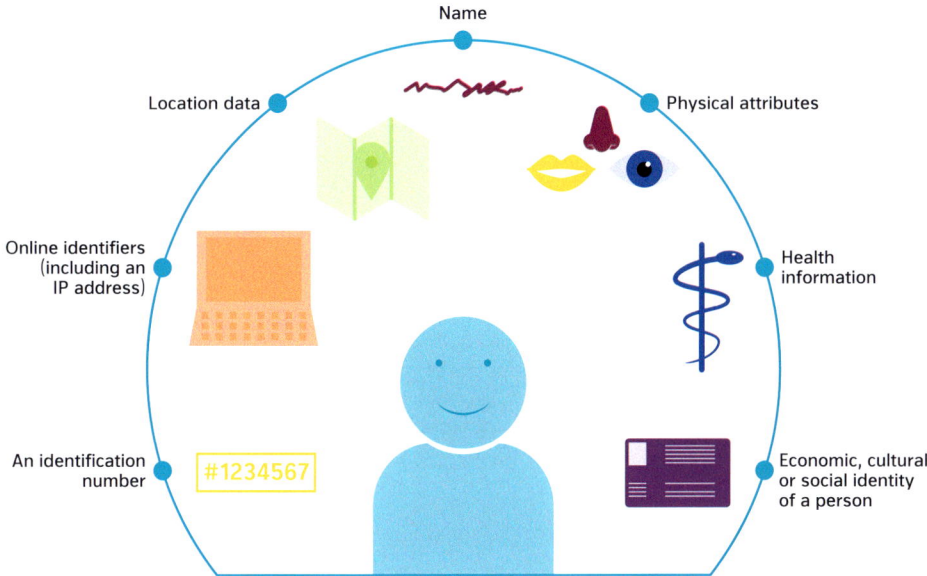

Quelle: Bridget Botelho, What does the GDPR definition of personal data include?, Newton, MA: TechTarget, 14 Mar 2018, www.techtarget.com (modified)

1   List the types of personal information people share online and give reasons why people are willing to share this type of information.

2   Jigsaw:
   a) Consider the situations illustrated in M1: Who might have published each image and why? What risks are there in publishing such images, and for whom?
   b) Evaluate each situation from the perspective of third parties, such as parents, friends, classmates, teachers, and potential employers.

3   Illustrate the concept of a "digital footprint" and the resulting risks (M2).

4   Visualize your own digital footprint. Think of areas such as shopping, finances, fitness, health, news consumption, reading habits, social media activity …

5   Discuss whether the GDPR helps to reduce the risks you found in task 3. **MORE HELP**

6   **Extra:** Do some research on what users can do to improve their own digital footprints.

Word search puzzle: world of (modern) media

G	I	F	A	K	E	N	E	W	S	A	D	O	R
L	G	P	R	I	P	A	D	D	R	E	S	S	E
C	O	N	T	E	N	T	T	A	N	I	S	N	A
O	N	L	E	I	E	M	N	I	O	H	A	A	C
N	I	A	R	G	S	I	L	M	G	N	N	B	H
L	R	B	R	O	A	D	C	A	S	T	F	A	N
I	P	R	I	N	T	M	E	D	I	A	E	R	I
N	O	I	T	A	M	R	O	F	N	I	S	I	M
E	C	Y	B	E	R	B	U	L	L	Y	I	N	G
N	O	I	T	C	E	T	O	R	P	A	T	A	D
A	G	W	H	I	N	T	E	R	N	E	T	O	M
J	O	U	R	N	A	L	I	S	M	M	S	I	T
O	P	R	O	P	A	G	A	N	D	A	R	A	A
C	O	N	R	P	L	P	H	I	S	H	I	N	G

accurate
genau
impartial
unparteiisch
counterfeit
gefälscht
subtle
raffiniert, unter-
schwellig, fein, subtil
deceitful
betrügerisch,
täuschend

Matching exercise: types of news presentation

a) accurate   **b)** biased   **c)** credible   **d)** misleading   **e)** reliable
f) sensationalist   **g)** unbiased   **h)** authentic   **i)** manipulative   **j)** objective

1) Presenting information precisely and truthfully
2) Based on facts and correctness
3) Providing information in a fair and impartial manner
4) Able to be trusted or believed
5) Free from prejudice or favoritism
6) Genuine and not counterfeit or copied
7) Attention-grabbing, often at the expense of precision
8) Intended to influence opinions by creating false impressions
9) Showing a preference or prejudice for or against something
10) Exercising control or influence over others in a subtle or deceitful manner

1 Find all 14 words related to "the media" hidden in the word search puzzle. **MORE HELP**
2 Create a mind map that visualizes the key terms addressed in chapter 2.
▸ METHOD Visualization, pp. 136 – 137
3 **a)** Assign the adjectives a) to j) in the word bank to their correct meaning 1) to 10).
b) Find their German translation and their opposites in English and German.

US teenagers' cyberbullying experiences

VOCABULARY

name-calling
Beschimpfung
rumour
Gerücht

Per cent of US teens who say they have experienced cyberbullying online or on their cellphone

Any type of cyberbullying listed below	59
Offensive name-calling	42
Spreading false rumours	32
Receiving explicit images they didn't ask for	25
Constantly asking where they are, what they're doing, who they're with, by someone other than parent	21
Physical threats	16
Sharing explicit images of them without their consent	7

Note: Respondents were allowed to select multiple options. Those who did not give an answer or gave other responses are not shown.
Survey conducted 7 Mar – 10 Apr 2018
Source: Pew Research Center, 2022

47561EX © Westermann

1 Describe the bar chart. ▸ METHOD Statistics, pp. 20 – 21
2 Compare the situation of teenagers in the USA regarding their experience with cyberbullying with your own situation.
3 **Think–Pair–Share:** Present an influencer from either the UK or the USA. Then, analyse the similarities and differences in how social media personalities influence fashion trends, consumer behaviour, and lifestyle choices in these countries and in Germany.
▸ Why are influencers effective?, p. 157, M3
4 **Choose a task:**
   a) Write an article for English-speaking students on your school's website, exploring the influence of social media on our lives in Germany.
   b) Create a blog for an English-speaking audience about (fake) news in Germany.

1

2

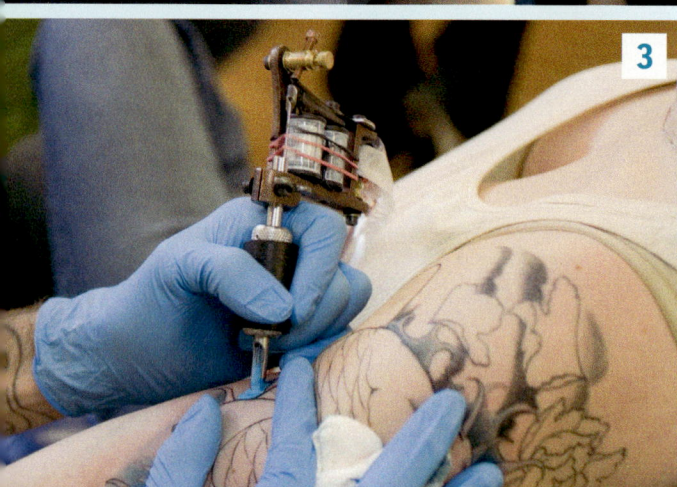

3

4

5

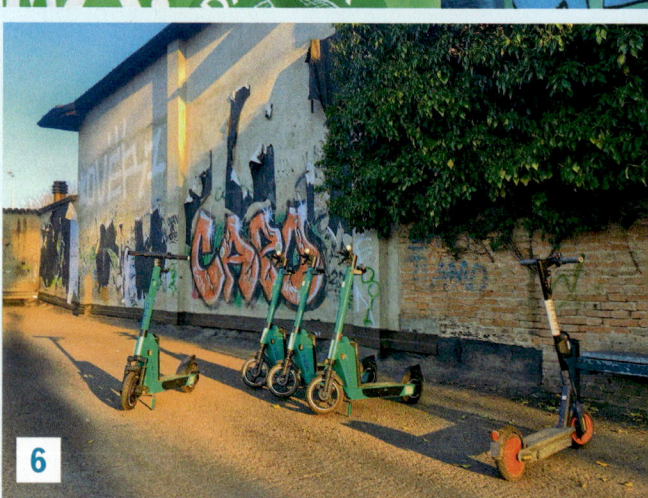

6

7

8

Young people and the law

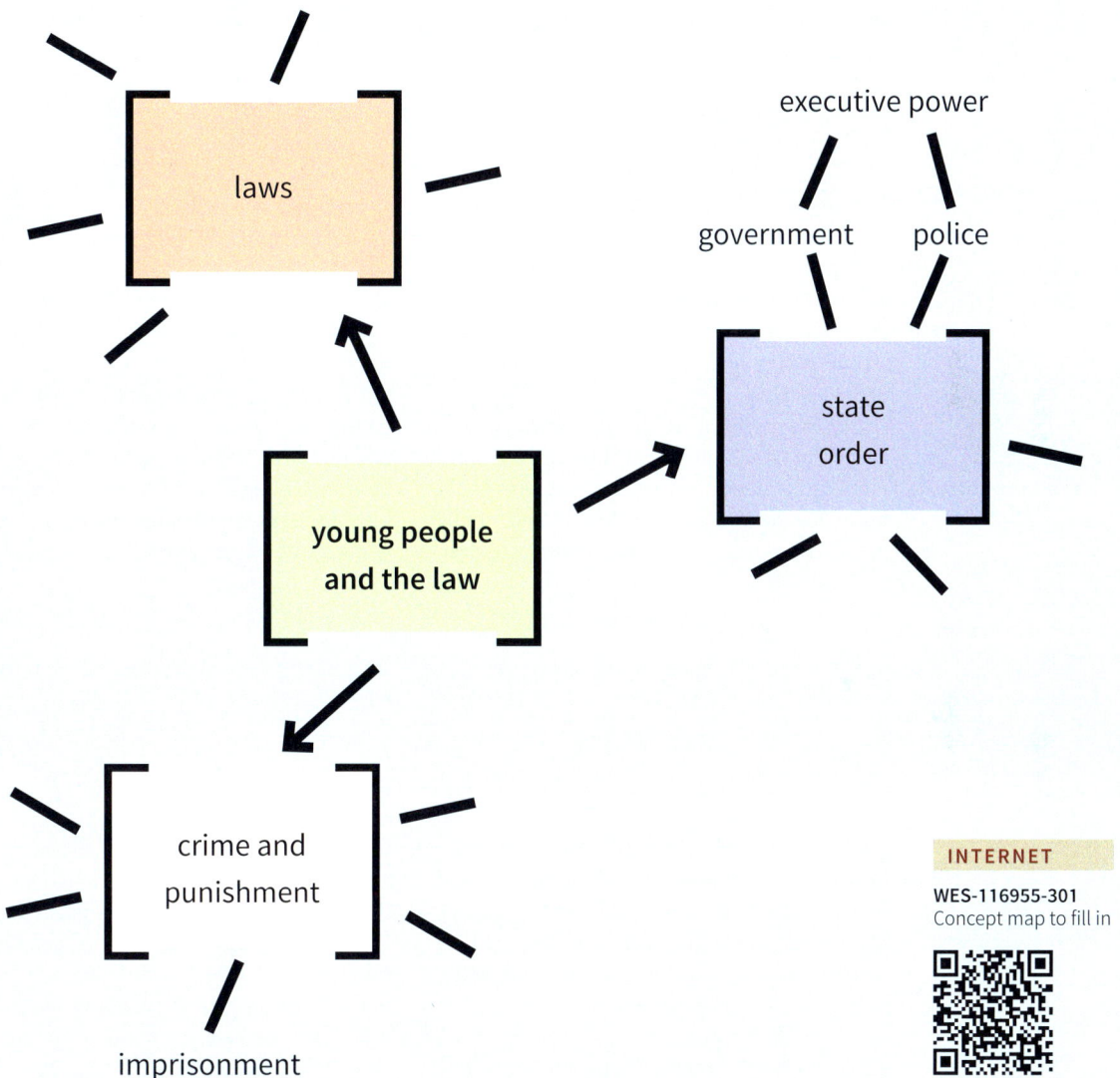

laws

young people
and the law

executive power

government   police

state
order

crime and
punishment

imprisonment

INTERNET

WES-116955-301
Concept map to fill in

1 Describe the photos and explain what they have to do with German laws.
Collect key terms of law and order in class. ▶ Useful phrases (B), pp. 203 – 204

2 Copy the concept map and complete it with terms that you already know about
"the law", "crime and punishment", as well as "state order". Throughout this unit,
you should add more aspects to show your progress in knowledge and vocabulary.
▶ METHOD Visualization, pp. 136 – 137

3.1 Laws – what are they good for?

KEY TERMS

law
Gesetz
legal order
Rechtsordnung
**separation
of powers**
Gewaltenteilung

VOCABULARY

the essence
das Wesentliche
to trigger a tantrum
einen Wutanfall
auslösen
offside
Abseits
convention
Sitte, Konvention
arbitrary
willkürlich
to take precedence
Priorität haben
to dismantle sth.
etw. zerlegen

INFO

Anarchy
is a society without
rulers. In some
definitions, anarchy
describes a society
without rules
and laws.

HOT SPOT

The term **law** (plural:
laws) generally refers
to a specific legal
regulation (Gesetz),
the term **"the law"**
refers to the legal sys-
tem (Rechtssystem,
"das Recht").

M 1   How practical would a world without rules be?

Consider, [...] how rules are the essence of sport, games and puzzles – even when their entire purpose is supposedly fun. The rules of chess, say, can trigger a tantrum if I want to
5 "castle" to get out of check, but find that they say I can't; or if I find your pawn getting to my side of the board and turning into a queen, rook, knight or bishop. Similarly, find me a football fan who hasn't at least once raged
10 against the offside rule. But chess or football without rules wouldn't be chess or football – they would be entirely formless and meaning-less activities. Indeed, a game with no rules is no game at all.
15 Lots of the norms of everyday life perform pre-cisely the same function as the rules of games – telling us what "moves" we can, and can't, make. The conventions of "pleases" and "thank yous" that seem so annoying to young children
20 are indeed arbitrary – but the fact that we have some such conventions, and [...] that we agree

what they are, is part of what makes our social interactions run smoothly. [...] Of course, there has long been an appetite among some people for a less formalised society, a society without 25 government, a world where individual freedom takes precedence: an anarchy. The trouble with anarchy, though, is that it is naturally unsta-ble – humans continually, and spontaneously, generate new rules governing behaviour, com- 30 munication, and economic exchange, and they do so as rapidly as old rules are dismantled.

Nick Chater, Could we live in a world without rules?, London: BBC, 21 Feb 2020, https://www.bbc.com/future/article/20200220-could-we-live-in-a-world-without-rules [17 Aug 2023] (modified)

M 2   Difference between rules and laws

Rules and laws are different types of instruc-tions that are designed to help us understand how to participate safely and fairly in groups and society. Though rules and laws can be
5 similar, the consequences of not following laws are much more serious.
Rules are instructions for a place or situation, such as school, home or sports teams. They can be made by people who have authority,
10 such as teachers, parents and coaches. Some-times they are made with the input of the whole group. Different groups have rules. Group rules only apply to people who are part of that group. Other people don't need to fol-
15 low those rules. There can be consequences

for group members who break the rules. These consequences may not affect the person who broke the rules anywhere except in the group. Laws are rules that apply to all people at all times and have legal consequences if they are 20 not followed. They are made by parliaments and [form the basis for jurisdiction by courts]. Laws help us all to behave safely, fairly and re-spectfully. Examples of laws that students need to follow are wearing a seatbelt [like 25 everyone else] [...] and going to school. There are major consequences for people who break laws such as having to pay a fine or going to jail. The police and the courts are both respon-sible for making sure the laws are followed. 30

Introducing ... rules and laws, Canberra: Commonwealth of Australia/Parliamentary Education Office, 3 May 2022, https://peo.gov.au/understand-our-parliament/how-parliament-works/bills-and-laws/introducing-rules-and-laws [7 Jan 2024] (modified)

M3 Functions of the law

Explanation	Function	Example

I) The function is to rule, control and predict social behaviour. Behavioural standards uphold this. If these standards are broken, people can bring cases before court.

II) The state and its citizens must accept the law for it to function properly. In return, the law offers freedom, equality, and protection against arbitrary state action.

III) The function is to create a legal order everyone respects and follows. Only state organs can do this – not private people, as this power must stay in the hands of the state.

IV) The function is to make laws accessible and available to the public. The laws must be clear and precise. New laws must not have retroactive effects.

V) The function is to reach the agreement of opposing interests. Thus, it calms conflicts and ideally prevents new conflicts.

1) peace

2) obligation

3) order

4) legal security

a) rule of law and Basic Law, separation of powers

b) Representatives in parliament make laws; everybody accepts the way the laws are made; Basic Law and rule of law, separation of powers.

c) Everyone can read the laws (they are also online), commentary helps to clarify them, forums help out, laws cannot be made to punish someone after the fact.

d) traffic regulations, compulsory school attendance, legal age for drinking alcohol and smoking, etc.

e) Everyone can file a (justified) complaint, sentences (as in prison sentences) deter crimes.

Based on: Mathias Hütwohl, Einführung in das Recht. Grundzüge des Rechtssystems und der Rechtsmethodik, München: C.H. Beck, 2022, pp. 4 ff. (translated and modified)

VOCABULARY

to rule
herrschen, regieren
to predict
voraussagen
to bring a case
before court
einen Fall vor Gericht bringen
obligation
hier: Verbindlichkeit
accessible
zugänglich
available
verfügbar
precise
präzise, genau
retroactive
rückwirkend
to calm
beruhigen
to file a complaint
eine Klage einreichen
sentence
hier: Strafe
to deter
abschrecken

HOT SPOT

Difference between "safe" and "secure"
Being "safe" means that someone is not in danger or cannot be harmed.
If something is "secure", it is protected so that nobody can get into it, steal it or commit a crime involving it.

1 **Think–Pair–Share:** Create a scenario in which your community does not know any rules. Try to answer the following questions:
a) What would everyday life look like?
b) What would happen if some people were much stronger than others?
c) How would the community react to certain crimes like theft or murder?
d) What would people do to feel safe and secure?

2 Based on the author's main points (M1), explain the necessity of rules in your own words.

3 **a)** Explain the difference between rules and laws (M2). Create a table.
b) **Extra:** Assess whether it makes sense to separate rules from laws, especially if there are differences in every country.

4 **a)** Assign the explanations to the functions of law, as well as the examples (M3).
MORE HELP
b) Add the functions to your concept map from the beginning of the unit.

5 Discuss: Are laws just a tool to protect people? **MORE HELP** ▸ Useful phrases (A), pp. 202–203

3.2 Children's rights in Germany – good enough protection for future generations?

M 1   Children in different situations

M 2   Children's rights and why they matter

Children are individuals. [They] are neither the possessions of parents nor of the state [...]; they are equal members of the human family. Children start life as totally dependent beings. [They] must rely on adults for the nurture and guidance they need to grow towards independence. Such nurture is ideally found from adults in children's families, but when they cannot meet children's needs, it is up to the state as the primary duty bearer to find an alternative in the best interests of the child. [...] The healthy development of children is [important] to the future well-being of any society. Because they are still developing, children are especially vulnerable – more so than adults – to poor living conditions such as poverty, inadequate health care, nutrition, safe water, housing and environmental pollution. The effects of disease, malnutrition and poverty threaten the future of children and therefore the future of the societies in which they live.

The costs to society of failing its children are huge. Social research findings show that children's earliest experiences significantly influence their future development. The course of their development determines their contribution, or cost, to society throughout their lives.

Child rights and why they matter, New York, NY: UNICEF, https://www.unicef.org/child-rights-convention/child-rights-why-they-matter [16 Sep 2023]

M3 Children's rights to be enshrined in the German Basic Law

Children's rights are to be specifically en-shrined in Germany's Basic Law, the Cabinet has decided. This is to underline the special importance of children and their rights. The
5 rights of parents are not to be restricted in any way.

In Germany children have all the same basic rights as adults but also need special protec-tion. Until now, this has not explicitly been
10 stated in the Basic Law, Germany's constitu-tion. To make clear how important children and their rights are in our society, their rights are to be explicitly enshrined in the Basic Law, making them more visible. [...] There are four
15 elements involved in the constitutional amendment:

- The bill clearly states that children are holders of basic rights, which have to be respected and protected. These include, in
20 particular, the right of children to develop as responsible individuals.

- The best interests of the child have to be **appropriately** taken into account, **thus** enshrining the principles of the best interests of the child in the constitution. At the same time, the use of the term "appropriate" ensures that the interests of other holders of basic rights are also considered, insofar as these potentially contradictory interests have to be **reconciled** properly.
- Children's **entitlement** to a fair hearing before the law is also **reasserted**. The best interests of the child can only be appropri-ately taken into account if the actual interests of the child in question have previously been **ascertained**.
- This bill does not change the primary responsibility of parents or the role of the state to watch over them in the performance of this duty and guard against **jeopardizing** best interests of the child, both of which are already laid out in the German Basic Law.

Children's rights to be enshrined in the German Basic Law, Berlin: Presse- und Informationsamt der Bundesregierung, 20 Jan 2021, https://www.bundesregierung.de/breg-en/service/archive/rights-of-child-in-basic-law-1841338 [17 Sep 2023] (modified)

M4 Article 6 (2) Basic Law

(2) The care and upbringing of children is the natural right of parents and a duty primarily incumbent upon them. The state shall watch over them in the performance of this duty.

1 **Placemat:** Look at the pictures (M1) and list a few rules that parents, in your opinion, should obey for their children to become healthy and happy adults. You may add more ideas.

2 Explain in your own words why children need special care and what might happen if they do not get it (M2).

3 Analyse the state's main obligations to protect and fulfil children's rights (M3).
  Focus on:
  a) the main goal of the amendment,
  b) what exactly is protected,
  c) exceptions.

4 **a)** Compare the current article (M4) and the planned amendments (M3). **MORE HELP**
  b) Assess how they benefit children and whether they improve their protection.
  c) Extra: Do research on the current status of the enshrinement of children's rights in the Basic Law.

INFO

The Cabinet
Members of a cabinet are usually called cabinet ministers or secretaries.

25 **Constitution**
contains the basic principles of a nation that determine the powers and duties of the government and guarantee certain
30 rights to the people in it. In Germany, the constitution is called the "Basic Law".

VOCABULARY

35 **to enshrine sth. in**
etw. bewahren/ verankern in
Basic Law
Grundgesetz
constitutional amendment
40 Verfassungsänderung
bill
Gesetzesentwurf
appropriately
angemessen
thus
daher, folglich
to reconcile
hier: in Einklang bringen
entitlement
Berechtigung, Anspruch
to reassert sth.
etw. erneut zum Ausdruck bringen, hervorheben
to ascertain sth.
etw. feststellen
to jeopardize sth.
etw. gefährden, aufs Spiel setzen
to be incumbent
erforderlich sein

3.3 Rights and duties of adolescents – appropriate for youth?

KEY TERMS

capacity for tortious liability
Deliktsfähigkeit
criminal capacity
Strafmündigkeit
legal capacity
Rechtsfähigkeit
minor
Minderjährige/-r
parental permission
elterliche Zustimmung

VOCABULARY

privacy
Privatsphäre
independence
Eigenständigkeit
belly piercing
Bauchnabelpiercing
age limit
Altersgrenze
bodily harm
Körperverletzung
punishable by law
strafbar
to claim damages
Anspruch auf Schadensersatz erheben
occupational disadvantages
berufliche Nachteile
invalid
ungültig

HOT SPOT

Difference between "must" and "have to":
The modal verb "must" expresses personal *obligation*. The semi-modal verb "have to" expresses that the subject is bound to act in a specified manner, *because of some external pressure* (e.g. by law or because of other's expectations).

M1   Situations in a teenager's life

1   2   3

M2   Body jewellery – a question of age?

Once a teenager reaches the age of 12 or 13, parents often confront discussions about the teenager's privacy and wishes for growing independence. Whether they discuss the first
5 tattoo or a belly piercing, parents and teenagers will often disagree.
However, at what age is the teenager allowed to get a tattoo or a piercing? The answer is not so easy, as it may differ from country to coun-
10 try, sometimes even from state to state. In Germany, there is no age limit. However, if the teenagers return home with a surprise under the skin made of ink or of steel or acrylic, they might risk trouble with their parents. But the
15 tattoo artist or the piercing studio will face much bigger consequences.
Technically, getting tattooed or pierced is bodily harm. It does not matter if it is an earring, a tongue, or a belly piercing. Bodily harm
20 is punishable by law unless the person has given permission. And that is the point: it is relevant whether the person has reached mental maturity – not his or her age. The tattoo artists have to answer all your questions and explain what risks might occur before 25 they are allowed to start. If they don't do that, you might claim damages. The same goes for the piercer: Do young customers fully understand what they are about to do? Are they aware of the risks and the follow-up care? Are 30 they informed about occupational disadvantages that might arise? And even then, without written parental permission, the studios risk a lot, especially if something goes wrong. If your parents were against it and you were 35 not legally able to decide, your signature is invalid and thus, your permission – and without permission, one might return to the criminal offence: bodily harm.

Ab wann darf man sich tätowieren lassen?, in: Recht Relaxed, Berlin: Bundesministerium der Justiz, https://www. recht-relaxed.de/WebS/RechtRelaxed/DE/KoerperSex/TattoosPiercings/tattoosPiercings_node.html [16 Sep 2023] (translated and modified)

M 3 Extracts from the German Criminal Code and the German Civil Code

From the Criminal Code (Strafgesetzbuch)	From the Civil Code (Bürgerliches Gesetzbuch)
§ 223: bodily harm (1) Whoever physically assaults or damages the health of another person **incurs a penalty** of imprisonment for a term not **exceeding** five years or a **fine**. (2) The attempt is punishable.	**§ 1626: parental custody, principles** (1) The parents have the duty and the right to care for the minor child (parental custody). [...] (2) In the care for and **child-rearing** of the child, the parents take account of the growing ability and the growing need of the child for independent responsible action. They discuss questions of parental custody with the child to the extent that, in accordance with the stage of development of the child, it is advisable, and they seek agreement.
§ 228: consent Whoever **inflicts** bodily harm with the victim's consent is only deemed to act unlawfully if, despite that consent, the act offends common **decency**.	**§ 823: liability in damages** (1) A person who, intentionally or **negligently**, unlawfully injures the life, **limb**, health, freedom, **property** or some other right of another person is **liable** to provide compensation to the other **party** for the damage arising therefrom.

VOCABULARY

to incur a penalty
sich strafbar machen
to exceed
überschreiten
fine
Geldstrafe
to consent
zustimmen
to inflict
zufügen
decency
Anstand
custody
Obhut, Sorgerecht
child-rearing
Kindererziehung
negligently
fahrlässig
limb
Leib (= Körper)
property
Besitz
liable
haftbar
party
Partei

M 4 On the way to full legal age in Germany

At the age of **18** you are of **legal age**. You can make **legal contracts** and conduct **lawsuits**. You are also **responsible for any damage you may cause**. You can **marry** and **vote in federal elections**. If you are charged **in criminal court, the judge can treat you as an adult** according to the laws.

At the age of **16** you must carry an **identity card or passport** with you. You can go to **restaurants and public dance events until midnight**. You can get an **AM or A1 (motorcycle) driver's licence**. You can be **sworn in at court**. You can make your **last will** before a notary public.

At the age of **15** you can **work legally** (from the age of 13 only light work with many restrictions is permitted). You can also get a **moped driver's licence**.

At the age of **14** you can decide your **religious identity**. This is the same age when you have **limited criminal capacity** (= you can be charged as a criminal under juvenile criminal law).

At the age of **12** your parents cannot change your **religious confession** against your will.

At the age of **7** you have **limited contractual capacity** and **limited capacity for tortious liability** (= you maybe held responsible for damage you cause).

At the age of **6** you reach the first legal age limit and must attend **school**.

At **birth** you have **legal capacity**. You have rights and duties during your lifetime.

4756zEX © Westermann

INFO

Criminal Code
regulates the legal relationships between citizens and the state. It anticipates violations of the law and is intended to prevent criminal offences.

Civil Code
regulates the legal relationships between citizens (e.g. contracts, compensation for damages).

---

1 Describe the situations in the pictures (M1) and decide which require parents to give their permission and why.

2 Apply the laws (M3) to the examples given in M2. ▸ METHOD Law, pp. 68 – 69

3 Explain
  a) why a tattoo or a piercing might be considered a criminal offence but might still not be punished. **MORE HELP**
  b) what conditions have to be met so that a tattoo or piercing is not considered a criminal offence. **MORE HELP**

4 Describe the chart (M4).

5 Fishbowl: Discuss whether some aspects such as getting a piercing or a tattoo should be included in the regulations and whether the age limits are appropriate (M4).

How to deal with laws

The law – what is it good for?

In Germany, the most important laws are written down in our constitution, the Basic Law („Grundgesetz"), where its separate parts are called "articles", as well as in the Criminal Code ("Strafgesetzbuch", StGB) and the Civil Code ("Bürgerliches Gesetzbuch", BGB). In the latter, the parts are called "sections". The sign for sections is § (in German you would say "Paragraf"). If you ever read a few sections of the "BGB", you might have thought that you would rather sit at dinner next to your smelly aunt for three hours. However, learning to understand the laws is worth the effort.

The law may seem unpleasant because it is written in general terms. It must apply to as many cases and situations as possible. It must also be precise so that no one misunderstands it. This makes legal language seem distant and unworldly. However, if you follow the steps below, you may discover the beauty in a text that many people have put a lot of thought into to help make our society better. Ideally, the law means justice and predictability. Without laws, we would fall back into the times of "the stronger your muscle, the more right you are". If you know your rights, no one can take advantage of you easily. So look at it this way: Since you work in school mainly with your head, understanding the law saves you many hours in the gym to get what you want. Just follow the steps below to learn how effective German laws are.

How do I do it?

Step 1: Prepare the content

- If you are looking for a specific article or section, check out the table of contents (on the first few pages) or the subject index (on the last few pages).
- Make sure that the book of laws in front of you is the latest edition. Laws change frequently.

Step 2: First reading

- Read the article or section slowly and thoroughly. Write down or highlight words you do not know. Look them up online or in a dictionary. Write them next to the text (if allowed).
- Break down very long sections into several smaller units of meaning.

Step 3: Second reading: Go into detail

- Now reread your task and focus only on the aspects that help to answer the question. Highlight the keywords in a different colour. Remember that the law might be written in difficult language, but often the content can be quite simple. Do not be discouraged!
- In many cases, you must separate the elements of the offence ("Tatbestand") from the legal consequences ("Rechtsfolge"). Think of it as an "if … then …" structure. The elements of the offence are the "if" part. The legal consequences only apply if all the elements of the offence are given. Note keywords to make a visual summary.

Step 3: Answer the question

Give a precise, short answer to the question. Later you can justify and explain it (if necessary). Try to say or write what the law means in your own words.

INTERNET

WES-116955-331
Here you can find more information on how to quote laws.

How to talk about (German) laws – examples

	in German: § = Paragraf	in English: § = section
BGB/Civil Code	§ 108 (Paragraf 108) ↳ Absatz 1 ↳ Satz 1	§ 108 (section 108) ↳ paragraph 1 ↳ sentence 1
GG/Basic Law	Artikel 1 Absatz 1	Article 1 paragraph 1

Example

Poppy is desperate for some money. Her friendly neighbour drives past her house in his dirty convertible and offers her 20 Euros to clean his car. Poppy agrees and runs back into the house to get some cleaning supplies. Her mother has overheard the conversation and shakes her index finger. "That's not going to happen, sweetheart … There is some homework waiting for you upstairs." Poppy is furious and, as every educated14-year-old would do, digs out her Bürgerliches Gesetzbuch to check whether her mother has a right to deny her this juicy deal.

> ein/-e 7–18 Jährige/-r

> wenn man Verträge selbst abschließen darf

§ 106 Beschränkte Geschäftsfähigkeit Minderjähriger
Ein Minderjähriger, der das siebente Lebensjahr vollendet hat, ist […] in der Geschäftsfähigkeit beschränkt.

§ 107 Einwilligung des gesetzlichen Vertreters
Der Minderjährige bedarf zu einer Willenserklärung, durch die er nicht lediglich einen rechtlichen Vorteil erlangt, der Einwilligung seines gesetzlichen Vertreters.

> eine Äußerung, die eine Rechtsfolge herbeiführt (z. B. Vertragsangebot oder Kündigung)

> wenn auch eine Gegenleistung erwartet wird

A few weeks later, Poppy goes shopping for a new smart watch. Her parents are generally open to such things, but they do not know about this particular shopping spree. The watch is expensive and the shop assistant is worried he will get into trouble if he sells it to an underage girl. What does the BGB say about the situation?

> der Sorgeberechtigten, meist die Eltern

> meist der Verkäufer

§ 108 Vertragsschluss ohne Einwilligung
(1) Schließt der Minderjährige einen Vertrag ohne die erforderliche Einwilligung des gesetzlichen Vertreters, so hängt die Wirksamkeit des Vertrags von der Genehmigung des Vertreters ab.
(2) Fordert der andere Teil den Vertreter zur Erklärung über die Genehmigung auf, so kann die Erklärung nur ihm gegenüber erfolgen; eine vor der Aufforderung dem Minderjährigen gegenüber erklärte Genehmigung oder Verweigerung der Genehmigung wird unwirksam. Die Genehmigung kann nur bis zum Ablauf von zwei Wochen nach dem Empfang der Aufforderung erklärt werden; wird sie nicht erklärt, so gilt sie als verweigert.

> Direkt: Die Aussage des Minderjährigen reicht nicht.

> Die Eltern können es sich auch nochmals anders überlegen.

> Keine Antwort der Eltern bedeutet „nicht genehmigt".

Elements of the situation	Legal consequences
Prerequisite ("if …")	Consequence ("then …")
If a teenager buys something without his/her parents' knowledge,	then the contract is not legal without their explicit consent.

1 Your 7-year-old brother looks over your shoulder and wants to know what you are up to. Explain §106–108 to him in simple words. **MORE HELP**

3.4 Contractual capacity in Germany – an exaggerated restriction?

M 1 A failed shopping spree

Ben, a 13-year-old exchange student from the United States, is your guest. One day, he decides to buy a new games console for about € 450. He returns angrily from a store. He tells you that he was not allowed to buy the games console because it was too expensive. He does not understand the problem because he had shown the money and was ready to pay. 5

> "That's exaggerated! Why did the lady not let me buy it? She even asked me how much pocket money I get, and I told her that I usually get $ 35 a month. I also told her that I have more money with me because I'm an exchange student. Do I look like a criminal?."

Text by the author

M 2 § 110 German Civil Code: performance effected with means of the minor's own

A contract concluded by the minor without the approval of the legal representative is deemed effective from the outset if the minor effects performance under the contract with means that were made available to the minor for this purpose or for the minor's free disposition by the legal representative or by a third party with the representative's approval. 5

M 3 § 110 teaches responsibility!

Auch für Verkäufer ist der Taschengeldparagraf wichtig. Verkäufer müssen nicht befürchten, dass die Eltern kleinere Einkäufe der Kinder rückgängig machen, zum Beispiel wenn das Kind sich ein Buch oder einen Film kauft. Bei Unsicherheit und größeren oder hochpreisigen Einkäufen verlangen einige Händler eine Zustimmung der Erziehungsberechtigten. Zwar gibt es keine genaue Geldgrenze, doch kleinere Einkäufe stellen in der Regel kein Problem für Kinder und Jugendliche dar. Verkäufer müssen jedoch bedenken, dass bestimmte Käufe und Zahlungen nicht dem Taschengeldparagrafen 5 10 unterliegen. Dazu zählen: Handyverträge, Abonnement, Ratenzahlung, Mitgliedschaften mit Monatsraten. 15
Ein 14-jähriger Teenager darf also beispielsweise keine Mitgliedschaft im Fitnessstudio oder Zeitschriften-Abonnements abschließen, ohne ausdrückliche Zustimmung der Eltern. Des Weiteren ist es Minderjährigen zum Beispiel 20 nicht erlaubt, ein Pferd zu kaufen, da das Tier genügend Pflege benötigt, aber auch weil mit dem Kauf weitere Kosten anfallen, zum Beispiel die Stallmiete, Tierarztkosten und Versicherungskosten. 25

Taschengeldparagraph: Wie Eltern und Kinder davon profitieren, München: Generali Deutschland AG, 3 Jan 2019, https://www.generali.de/journal/taschengeldparagraph-wie-eltern-und-kinder-davon-profitieren- [7 Apr 2024]

M4 Recommendations for pocket money by the German Youth Welfare Office (2023)

Age	Pocket money per month in €
6 – 7	ca. 4 – 8
8 – 9	ca. 8 – 12
10 – 11	ca. 16 – 21
12 – 13	ca. 21 – 26
14 – 15	ca. 26 – 38
16 – 17	ca. 38 – 60

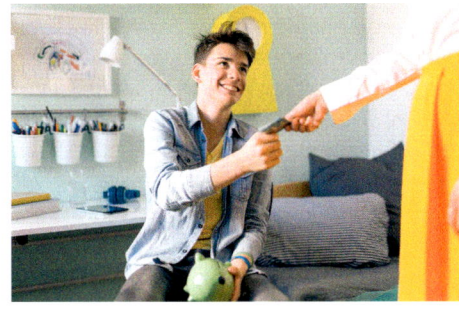

Data: Wie wichtig ist Taschengeld für Kinder?, in: Jugendämter.com, Ingelheim, GOW Media GmbH, https://www.jugendaemter.com/wie-wichtig-ist-taschengeld-fuer-kinder (translated and modified) [26 June 2023]

M5 Contractual capacity in the USA

In most states of the USA, students **are short of the capacity** to make contracts. Thus, minors who **authorize** contracts can either **stick** to the deal they had made, or they can **void** the contract. There are **exceptions**: in many states, a minor cannot void a contract for basic needs, such as accommodation, food, and clothing.

Moreover, a minor is only allowed to void a contract if under the age of majority. In most cases, majority begins at the age of 18. If a minor has not voided the contract before then, the contract can no longer be voided.

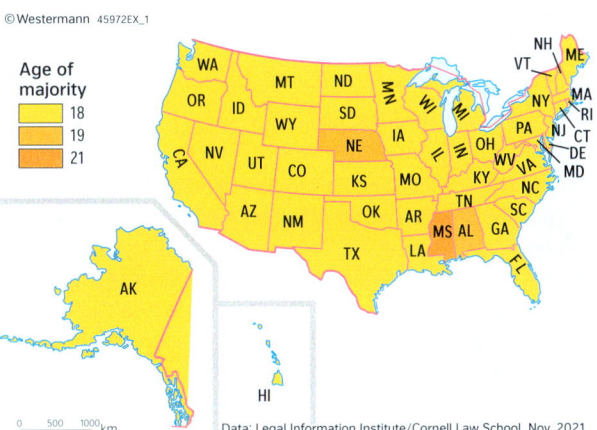

Text by the author

1 Talk with a partner about the case (M1): what could have been the reasons why Ben was not allowed to buy the games console?

2 Summarize in your own words under what conditions a minor is allowed to buy something without the parents' approval (M2). **MORE HELP** ▸ METHOD Law, pp. 68 – 69

3 Outline the main aspects of § 110 in English (M3). ▸ METHOD Mediation, pp. 72 – 73

4 a) Analyse M4 and explain to what extent this information **complements** M3.
b) Use your findings to write a dialogue between Ben and you which explains the situation legally and how he could still get his games console.

5 **Extra:** Read about the American concept of contractual capacity (M5) and compare it to the German law. Find similarities and differences.

6 **Milling around:** Discuss whether contractual capacity is an exaggerated restriction for young people. ▸ Useful phrases (A), pp. 202 – 203

How to mediate content

Mediation – what is it good for?

Mediation is a summarizing technique that helps people to communicate even if they do not share the same mother tongue. Instead of translating a whole written or spoken text, move only the important information from one language into another.

You should note that the person you mediate for might not have the same cultural background as you do. You cannot simply translate some terms, for example, "Taschengeldparagraf", because there is no such thing in the US or in the UK.

How do I do it?

Step 1: Prepare the content

- Read your task and choose only the details your addressee needs. Leave out all unnecessary information. Your task is to not only translate language, but also explain the context by giving only the important information.
- Watch out for keywords.
- Take your addressee's perspective and background into account. You might have to give additional information, depending on how much your partner knows about political or geographical aspects. For example, the US president is the head of government as well as the head of state. The German president is only the head of state. Depending on the context, you might have to point out this difference so that you do not confuse your partner.
- Feel free to change the structure of the text.
- Leave out your opinion.
- Name the original source.

Step 2: Adjust your language

- Do not translate word for word. Use your own words, but do not change the meaning.
- Do not panic if you cannot think of the exact English word you need. Describe your way around unknown English words. Use synonyms or paraphrase. You can even use a word that means the opposite and negate it.
- Use the proper register. This means that you use a different style if you talk to a friend than if you write to your headteacher. In general, your word choice should match the intention of the text.
- Match your style to your task's objective: you might have to this in a blog, a letter, an e-mail, or a direct conversation.

Informal	Formal
Hi George,	Dear Mr Jones,
Hope you're well! I just wanted to let you know …	I am writing to inform you …
Sorry for…	Please accept my apologies for …
As soon as possible …	At you earliest convenience …
Love/Take care/See you soon	Sincerely/Regards
Jenny	Jennifer Matthews

INFO

Concepts that might have to be explained:
- Basic Law
- Geschäftsfähigkeit
- Youth Protection Act
- Taschengeld-paragraf

Example

VOCABULARY

state election
Landtagswahl

M 1   Verschiedene Altersgrenzen bei Wahlen verwirren junge Menschen

Der Superwahltag in Berlin im September 2021 wurde offenbar nicht nur wegen zahlreicher Pannen bei der Durchführung zum Debakel. Wie eine Studie der Otto-Brenner-Stiftung zeigt, gab es auch Verwirrung um das Mindestalter für Wahlberechtigte. 16- und 17-Jährige durften an der Wahl zur Bezirksverordnetenversammlung teilnehmen, nicht aber an den Abstimmungen für Abgeordnetenhaus und Bundestag. Zehn Prozent der für die Studie befragten 16- und 17-Jährigen gaben nun an, nicht von ihrer Wahlberechtigung zur Bezirksverordnetenversammlung gewusst zu haben. Ein, wie es in der Studie heißt, „nicht unerheblicher Teil" der Befragten ging außerdem fälschlicherweise davon aus, auch bei der Bundestagswahl abstimmen zu dürfen. Der Politikwissenschaftler Thorsten Faas von der FU Berlin sprach von Fehlwahrnehmungen, die er auf einen „Flickenteppich aus Altersgrenzen" zurückführte.

Verschiedene Mindestalter zur Wahlberechtigung gibt es nicht nur in Berlin. In elf Bundesländern dürfen 16- und 17-Jährige inzwischen an Kommunalwahlen teilnehmen, in sechs Ländern zudem an Landtagswahlen. Bei der Europawahl [2024] wird die Altersgrenze ebenfalls bei 16 Jahren liegen. Für Bundestagswahlen gilt weiterhin das Mindestalter von 18 Jahren.

ZEIT ONLINE/dpa, Verschiedene Altersgrenzen bei Wahlen verwirren junge Menschen, in: Die Zeit online, 22 Jan 2023, https://www.zeit.de/politik/deutschland/2023-01/deutschland-wahlrecht-studie [1 Feb 2024]

Task: Your parents' friend Joshua is a respected American high school teacher. He knows the US political system very well and would like to compare from what age Germans are integrated in the political system. Your parents ask you to send him an email. Use M1 and the map on p. 121, M5, for information.

Dear Joshua,

Thank you for your last email, which was a great help for my school project. My parents told me that you are interested in how younger people can participate in our political system. So, in return, I'd like to give you some material on this topic.

Elections take place on four levels: the European, federal, state, and communal levels. The voting age has just been lowered to 16 on the European level, but you have to be 18 to elect our parliament ("Bundestag") on the federal level. The voting age on the state and communal levels depends on where you live. Every state makes its own rules, but most states allow voting on the state level from 18 and on the communal level from 16 years onwards.

The many different rules cause some confusion among teenagers, but I hope I have summarized it to your satisfaction.

All the best,

Ellen

---

1   Your 17-year-old English exchange student Sue wants to know whether she could vote if she were German. Use M1 and the map on p. 121, M5, to give her a short explanation.

2   Compare your answer from task 1 with the answer given in the webcode/QR code to the right.

3   Compare the content, length, style and register of the uses of mediation in 1 (above) and 2 (webcode/QR code). Give reasons for the differences.

4   Choose two terms from the box on the left (p. 72) and explain the different meanings of each term in Germany, the United Kingdom, and the United States.

INTERNET

WES-116955-341
Example 2 for mediation

3.5 Public and civil proceedings – who is responsible?

civil (or private) law
Zivil- bzw. Privatrecht
criminal law
Strafrecht
public law
Öffentliches Recht
suspect
Verdächtige/-r

VOCABULARY

to try sb.
jmdn. vor
Gericht stellen
to overburden
überlasten
lawyer
Anwältin/Anwalt
judge
Richter/-in
to distinguish
unterscheiden
public prosecutor's office
Staatsanwaltschaft
to investigate
untersuchen
criminal charge
Strafanzeige
to initiate proceedings
Gerichtsverfahren einleiten
defendant
Angeklagte/-r
(im *Strafprozess*)/
Beklagte/-r
(im *Zivilprozess*)
defence lawyer
Verteidiger/-in
verdict
Urteil
plaintiff
Kläger
complaint
Klage
settlement
Vergleich

M 1 Civil or criminal court?

Case 1:
It is summer, the weather is wonderful and Mr Meyer's son (17) barbecues every other weekend in the family's garden. The neighbours, Mrs and Mr Blum, are annoyed by the smell and ask Mr Meyer to talk to his son. Mr Meyer refuses and says that there is no problem, they should be more tolerant of the youngsters. A little later, the Blums decide to file a complaint with the court.

Case 2:
Ms Lazar (18) has always been very committed to questions of the environment. Thus, it is not surprising that she starts to take part in climate protests. One day, she is at a protest in Berlin and glues her hand to the street to block the road. Eventually, she is removed by the police and a little later, she faces a lawsuit and has to pay a fine.

Text by the author

M 2 Public and civil law in Germany

Imagine if a single court or only one type of court tried all crimes in a state. That would hopelessly overburden the state, as well as the lawyers and judges, who would have to know
5 all the laws and could not specialize. It would make the legal system disorganized and inefficient.

In Germany, we distinguish between two major areas of law: public law and civil law (or
10 private law).

Public law Public law regulates the relations between the state and its citizens. This includes criminal law, which is set out in the Criminal Code. The principle of subordination
15 of the citizen to state authority applies here, as only the state may prosecute and punish criminal offences (there is a state monopoly on the use of force). The public prosecutor's office represents the state. With the help of
20 the police, it investigates criminal charges and, if necessary, initiates proceedings where it faces the defendant and his defence lawyer. In the end, the court passes a verdict.

Public Law

The public interest is affected.

state

citizen

Private Law (Civil Law)

It is about interests of private individuals and organizations.

citizen ◄► citizen

47591EX © Westermann

Furthermore, public law regulates relations between state bodies, such as the federal gov- 25
ernment and the federal states, as well as between states, for example in European law.

Civil law, on the other hand, regulates the relations between citizens, for example, in the Civil Code. Here, two equal parties face each 30
other: plaintiff and defendant. Civil proceedings only come about when an affected party files a complaint. The court examines the case and passes a verdict. Sometimes the proceedings end in a compromise, which is called a 35
settlement.

Text by the author

M3 Course of civil proceedings

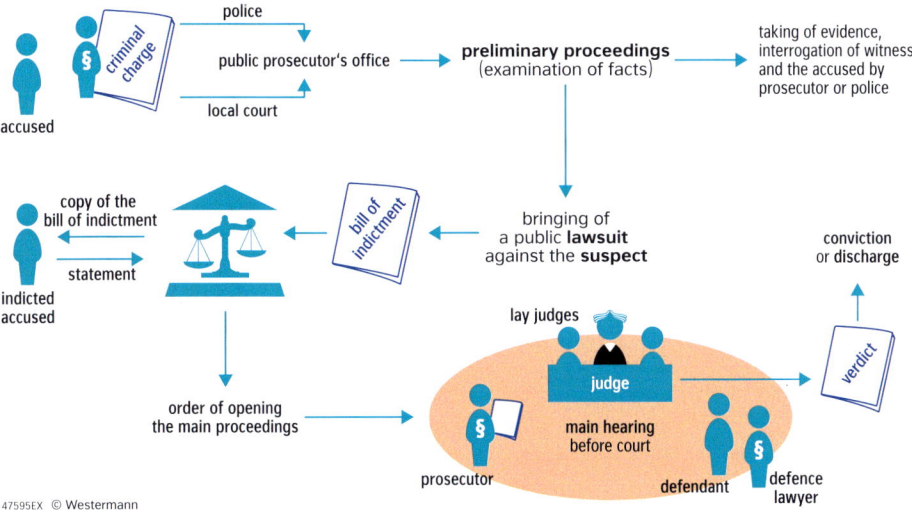

presentation of the asserted claim

request for decision by the court

complaint

plaintiff / defendant

local court or regional / state court

copy of complaint

defendant

statement of defence; motions, statements, evidence

early first appointment

or

written preliminary proceedings

statement of defence; motions, statements, evidence

At first instance, a **local court** is responsible for claims up to a volume of € 5,000. It is concerned with specific legal matters such as family law issues, residential housing matters, tourism related claims, etc.

A **regional court** is concerned with claims in excess of € 5,000. Commercial and corporate disputes are decided by a special judicial panel of three professional judges and two lay judges.

judge

lawyer §

oral (main) hearing

lawyer §

verdict

entitlements, claims, damages, decisions

plaintiff   defendant

47594EX © Westermann

M4 Course of criminal proceedings

accused

criminal charge §

police

public prosecutor's office

local court

preliminary proceedings (examination of facts)

taking of evidence, interrogation of witnesses and the accused by prosecutor or police

copy of the bill of indictment

statement

indicted accused

bill of indictment

bringing of a public **lawsuit** against the **suspect**

conviction or discharge

order of opening the main proceedings

lay judges

judge

prosecutor

main hearing before court

verdict

defendant

defence lawyer

47595EX © Westermann

VOCABULARY

statement of defence
Klageerwiderung
motion
Antrag
evidence
Beweis
local court
Amtsgericht
regional/state court
Landgericht
lay judge
Schöffin/Schöffe (Laienrichter/-in)
oral (main) hearing
mündliche Hauptverhandlung
accused
Beschuldigte/-r
indicted accused
Angeschuldigte/-r
preliminary proceedings
Ermittlungsverfahren
prosecutor
Staatsanwältin/ Staatsanwalt
bill of indictment
Anklageschrift
conviction
Verurteilung
discharge
Freispruch

INFO

Presumption of innocence
is a legal principle that every person accused of any crime is considered innocent until proven guilty.

§ 157 Code of Criminal Procedure
[…] [T]he "indicted accused" is an accused person against whom public charges have been preferred, and the "defendant" is an accused person or indicted accused in respect of whom a decision has been taken to open the main proceedings.

1 Identify who the disputing parties are in the two cases (M1).
  Take a guess: which code might be applicable?

2 Compare the civil and the criminal law in Germany (M2). Create a table for both code types and focus on the following aspects: Who initiates the proceeding? Who are the disputing parties? What is the aim of the proceeding?

3 a) **Partner jigsaw:** Focus either on M3 or M4 and explain the respective proceedings.
    ▸ Useful phrases (C), pp. 204 – 205
  b) Complete the table of task 2 with your findings in task 3.

4 **Extra:** Explain whether a person could face a civil and criminal proceedings for the same crime.

3.6 Youth Protection Act – too restrictive?

M 1   The scope of the Youth Protection Act

M 2   What is allowed by the Youth Protection Act?

The Youth Protection Act (JuSchG)

permitted   ● = Restrictions } are cancelled in the case of
not permitted   Time Restrictions } accompaniment by a parent or guardian.

Parents are not obliged to allow everything which is allowed
by law. They carry the responsibility until the age of majority.

		Children under 14 years of age	Young persons under 16 years old	under 18 years old
§4	**Presence in public houses**	●	●	until midnight
	Presence in late-night bars, night clubs or comparable licensed establishments			
§5	Presence in public dancing establishments, including **discos** (exceptional permits may be granted by the responsible authorities)	●	●	until midnight
	Presence at dancing events organized by recognized youth welfare organizations, in artistic activity or for the keeping of traditions	until 10 p.m.	until midnight	until midnight
§6	**Presence in public gambling halls,** taking part in games with the possibility of winning			
§7	**Presence in events and institutions which endanger youth** (The responsible authority may impose age and time limits as well as other conditions.)			
§8	**Presence in places which endanger youth** (The responsible authority can take measures to counter the danger.)			
§9	**Sale / consumption of beer, wine, sparkling wine, beverages mixed with beer, wine or something similiar** (Exception: permitted for 14- and 15-year-olds when accompanied by a person authorized with personal custody of the child [parents])			
	Sale / consumption of other alcoholic beverages or foodstuff, e.g. spirits			
§10	**Sale / consumption of tobacco products, e-cigarettes / e-shishas** (also nicotine-free)			
§11	**Cinema visits:** only if the film and opening credits are released "without any age restriction / from 6 / from 12 / from 16 years". (Children under 6 years of age may only attend with a parent or guardian. Important: their presence is only permitted if the film has no age restrictions. Exception: "films suitable for those aged 12 and above"; their presence is permitted from the age of 6 years onwards when accompanied by a person authorized with personal custody of the child [parents]).	until 8 p.m.	until 10 p.m.	until midnight
§12	**Sale of films or games** (on DVD, video etc.): only in accordance with the release indicators: "no age restriction / from 6 / from 12 / from 16 years upwards".			
§13	**Playing on electronic monitor playing devices** without the possibilty of winning: only in accordance with the release indicators: "no age restriction / from 6 / from 12 / from 16 years upwards".			

Source: Jugendschutztabelle englisch, DREI-W-VERLAG GmbH, Essen (modified)

M3 Youth protection in various areas of life

VOCABULARY

to impair sth./sb.
etw. behindern,
jmdm. schaden
integrity
Makellosigkeit,
Unbescholtenheit,
Integrität
objective
Ziel

The Youth Protection Act strengthens and protects children and adolescents by tying products, places, and media consumption, which are seen as harmful to children's health, to certain age groups. In this way, the law supports parents in raising their children responsibly. In terms of media, it aims at protecting from content that impairs development and is harmful to young people. It also protects from risks to the integrity of children and young people arising from media use. In addition, the law promotes orienting children, young people, parents, and educational professionals in media education and competence.

The individual regulations of the law are directed exclusively at persons of legal age, such as traders, event organizers and their employees. They are not directed at children and young people, because that is who the law is protecting here.

The Youth Protection Act focuses on three areas of content: protecting minors in public places (e.g. amusement arcades, discotheques, cinemas, and restaurants), in tobacco and alcohol consumption, and in media consumption.

Was bedeutet Jugendschutz?, Berlin: Bundesarbeitsgemeinschaft Kinder- und Jugendschutz e.V. (BAJ), https://jugendschutz-aktiv.de/de/juschg-bedeutung [23 Feb 2024] (translated and modified)

M4 Alcohol abuse by young people in Germany

Hospitalization due to alcohol intoxication
Number of young people aged between 10 and 24 hospitalized with acute alcohol poisoning

Legend: 15- to 19-year-olds / 20- to 24-year-olds / 10- to 14-year-olds

Source: Statistisches Bundesamt, Krankenhausstatistik 2021   47584EX © Westermann

1 **Think–Pair–Share:**
  a) List products, habits, and places which might have a harmful effect on young persons. Draw a table and list them on the left. The pictures (M1) may help you.
  b) Use the right column and list possible negative consequences from such products and places.

2 a) Analyse M2 and find out which products, habits, and places from your table (task 1) the Youth Protection Act allows for young people.
  b) **Extra:** Would you change anything? Give reasons, why (not)?

3 State the objective and the addressees of the Youth Protection Act (M3).

4 Assess the effectiveness of the Youth Protection Act regarding alcohol abuse by minors in Germany (M4).

5 **Inside-outside circle:** Discuss: The Youth Protection Act – too restrictive or sensible?

  ▸ Useful phrases (A), pp. 202–203

3.7 Juvenile criminal law – a necessary addition to criminal law?

M 1 **Most criminal offences committed by adolescents (14 to under 18 years) in Germany in 2022**

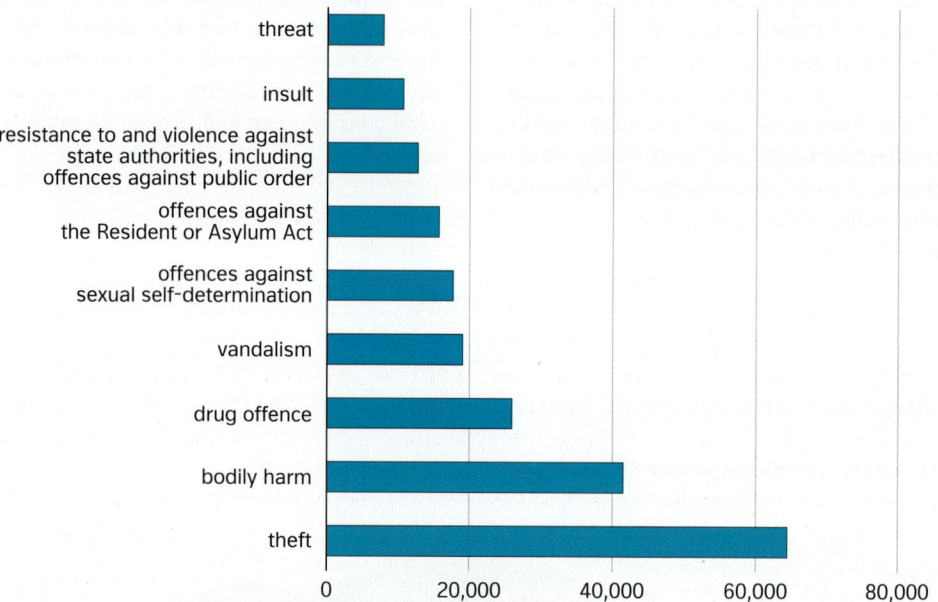

Source: Polizeiliche Kriminalstatistik 2022, Tab. 20: Tatverdächtige nach Alter und Geschlecht,
Berichtszeitraum: 1 Jan 2022 bis 31 Dec 2022, Wiesbaden: Bundeskriminalamt, 2023 (translated)

47585EX © Westermann

M 2 **Number of young criminal suspects in Germany in 2022**

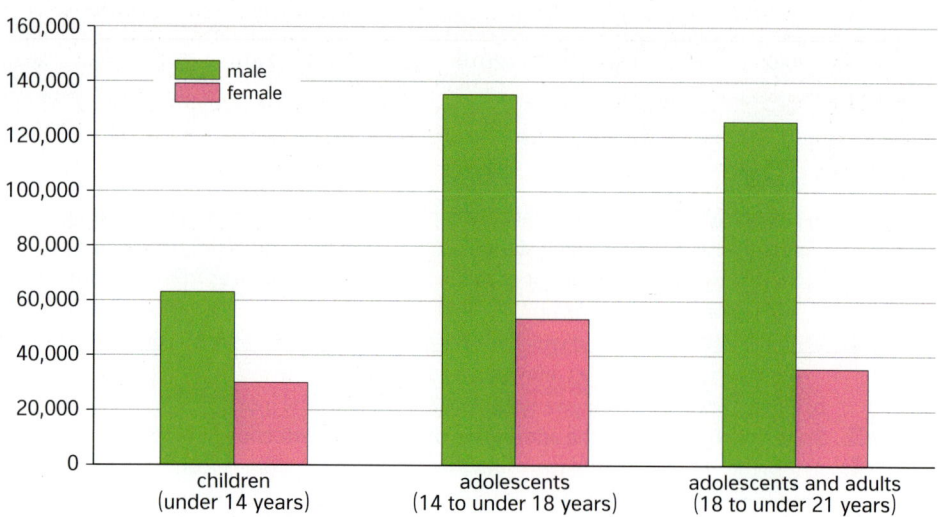

Source: Kriminalstatistik 2022, Ausgewählte Informationen Bund: Straftaten insgesamt,
Berichtszeitraum: 1 Jan 2022 bis 31 Dec 2022, Wiesbaden: Bundeskriminalamt, 2023 (translated)

47586EX © Westermann

M 3 ## Some possible causes of juvenile delinquency

The term "juvenile delinquency" refers to a large variety of behaviour of children and adolescents. Those actions are not **approved** by society and some kind of **admonishment**, punishment, or **preventive** and corrective **measures**
5 can be consequences. Juvenile delinquency refers to the failure of children and youth to meet certain **obligations** expected of them. [...]
Juvenile crime is not naturally born in chil-
10 dren, but it is largely present in them because of the surroundings that they are brought up in, their **absurd actions**, or simply lack of discipline and proper education. The following are some causes of juvenile delinquency. [...]
15 **Family problems:** For the full and harmonious development of their personality, children should grow up in a family environment, in an atmosphere of happiness, love and understanding. The family has more influence when
20 the child is young, as the child reaches adolescence, the **peer group** becomes increasingly important as an influence on behaviour.
Children learn basic concepts about good and bad from their family, they make their values
25 and set the norms of society. Thus, a family is a **socialization** school for the children. Parents and **siblings** have a great role in shaping the personality of the child. [...] [For example] frequent parents fighting, lack of trust and confidence
30 among the parents, criminal parents, psychological problems in parents, sibling rivalry, or unequal treatment between children may become reasons behind juvenile delinquency. [...]
In such a case, the child **feels deprived** and in-
35 **ferior** among friends. There is a chance that children may adopt depression and anger from parents or elder siblings. [...]

In many families and religious societies, parents or elder siblings are involved in various
40 social problems like gender, age, or racial discrimination, as well as child labour, etc. Some parents do not take care of their elders, and it is a known fact that such children who see their parents disrespecting their elders, never
45 respect their parents and elder siblings.
A parenting style has a large impact on the behaviour of children. **Autocratic** parents are sometimes very harsh, and they punish their children for small issues. Children start dis-
50 respecting such parents and may become violent. Such children start behaving harshly with others.

Inefficient education infrastructure: Due to poor education infrastructure, classrooms are
55 very small. Fewer teachers are available. The classrooms concentrate many children in a small area for a major part of their day. **Misconduct** in school ranges from rudeness to teachers to vandalism, **assault**, drug use, and
60 alcohol abuse. Other problems are the use of **obscene language**, cheating, lying, **petty theft**, weapon possession, etc. Many schools themselves handle most of the misconduct through relatively well-developed discipline and ob-
65 serving policies. [...]
Peer groups: The peer group is an informal network of individuals of similar age and generally formed spontaneously in areas where children readily meet and interact. Habits of
70 children and their friends such as stealing, gambling, consuming alcohol, and smoking are generally found among such peers.
[Other factors include the **neighbourhood** and **unemployment**.]

Hemant Laxman More, Juvenile Delinquency, in: The Legal Quotient, 26 Apr 2023, https://thelegalquotient.com/criminal-laws/juvenile-justice-act/juvenile-delinquency/1364/ [1 June 2023] (modified)

VOCABULARY

to approve
zustimmen, gutheißen
admonishment
Ermahnung, Warnung
preventive
vorbeugend
measure
Maßnahme
obligation
Verpflichtung
absurd actions
absurde/törichte Taten
peer group
Gleichaltrigengruppe
socialization
Sozialisierung
silbings
Geschwister
to feel deprived
sich sozial benachteiligt fühlen
inferior
unterlegen
autocratic
hier: autoritär
misconduct
schlechtes Benehmen
assault
Körperverletzung
obscene language
vulgäre Sprache
petty theft
kleiner Diebstahl (Bagatelle)

INFO

Socialization
is the process by which people, especially children, are made to behave in a way that is acceptable in their society (see chap. 1.3, pp. 22–23).

---

1 Add the various forms of criminal offences (M1) to your concept map from the beginning of the unit. Find out what they mean in German.

2 **Think–Pair–Share:** Guess at what age most of delinquent acts and crimes are committed and compare your guess with M2.

3 Analyse the chart (M2). ▸ METHOD Statistics, pp. 20 – 21

4 Create a flowchart (or fishbone diagram) to explain the multiple origins of juvenile delinquency (M3). ▸ METHOD Visualization, pp. 136 – 137

INFO

§ 26 Criminal Code: abetting
Whoever intentio-
nally induces another
to intentionally
commit an unlawful
act (abettor) incurs
the same penalty as
an offender.

§ 185 Criminal Code: insult
The penalty for insult
is imprisonment for a
term not exceeding
one year or a fine
and, if the insult is
committed publicly,
in a meeting, by dis-
seminating content
(section 11 (3)) or by
means of an assault,
imprisonment for a
term not exceeding
two years or a fine.

§ 223 Criminal Code: bodily harm
(1) Whoever physic-
ally assaults or
damages the health
of another person
incurs a penalty of
imprisonment for a
term not exceeding
five years or a fine.
(2) The attempt is
punishable.

§ 242 Criminal Code: theft
(1) Whoever takes
movable property
belonging to another
away from another
with the intention of
unlawfully appropria-
ting it for themselves
or a third party incurs
a penalty of impri-
sonment for a term
not exceeding five
years or a fine.
(2) The attempt is
punishable.

M 4   Four cases – four delinquent acts?

a) Mia and Ella (16 and 15) argue with Charlotte and Malea (both 16) in the schoolyard. When Charlotte insults Mia's mother, who is seriously ill, Mia blows a fuse. Ella and Malea try to calm her down. Yet she hits Charlotte so hard that she must be treated in hospital a little later. Mia apologizes, but Charlotte still reports it to the police.

c) Fernando (18) recently noticed that one of his classmates owns a new electric scooter and regularly rides it to school. One morning he confronts the classmate and wants to know how he can afford such a thing. After his classmate answered truthfully that the scooter was a gift from his parents, Fernando takes the scooter away from him and simply rides off with it. The schoolmate is completely perplexed and asks a passerby for help. Together they call the police. Half an hour later, Fernando slams on the brakes at the fellow student's feet and then notices the police officers. "Thanks for the loan, mate – that was fun!". His classmate looks at the police officers in shock and protests that he did not agree to this "loan". When they ask him if he wants to make an official report to the police, he says "no".

b) Daniel (16) kept urging his buddy to finally pocket two of the sports magazines they love so much without paying for them. Tim (14) keeps resisting but is afraid that Daniel will eventually look for other friends and then treat him the way they usually treat others. When he remembers the last situation with a boy from the parallel class whom they keep taking money from, Tim feels sick. He puts the sports magazines in his pocket. Just as they are about to leave the kiosk, the shopkeeper detains the two and a little later, the police are already on the scene.

d) Lucy (13), Hannah (15) and her sister Clara (19) realize that it is election time again. They find the posters boring and do not like some of the politicians. They arrange to meet one evening to "spice up" the election posters with thick black permanent markers. One politician gets a beard. The other politician gets black lips and dark circles under her eyes. Clara even takes one poster into her bag so she can throw it away somewhere. While they are having fun, a local resident observes the three and calls the police. Before the girls even notice the siren of the approaching car, two policewomen are standing before them and taking their personal details. During the questioning, Clara admits that she felt this was an exciting experience and she did not think about what she was doing or about the consequences. She also wanted to be a cool older sister for Hannah.

Finding a juvenile guilty is not easy!
Since young people are still developing, they need special protection. As a result, the criminal justice system must apply juvenile criminal law based on the Juvenile Justice Act (Jugendgerichtsgesetz) to offences committed by young people who are at least 14 years old at the time of the offence but not yet 18 years old. Adolescents who are at least 18 but not yet 21 are also subject to the provisions of juvenile criminal law if they were still socially or mentally at the level of a juvenile at the time of the offence. The offences are the same as in general criminal law, but there are differences in the procedure and legal consequences (punishment).

Text by the author

M 5 Punishment in juvenile criminal law

Punishment in juvenile criminal law has an educational purpose. It aims first at educating the young person to prevent further offences and at rehabilitation. Therefore, punishments often include community service in a social institution. It is also important to note that the court is a different one in juvenile criminal law: a separate juvenile court decides the criminal liability of the offender.

Moreover, the main hearings are not open to the public.
Furthermore, juvenile criminal courts consider the rights of parents and guardians during the proceedings. They may be present during the hearings and have the chance to make statements about the offence. They may also employ a lawyer to defend their child in juvenile court.

Warnings	Juvenile detention	Juvenile penalty
■ Most lenient means of punishment ■ Offenders have to apologize to victims, work for or pay a sum of money to a charitable institution. ■ Focus on feeling, compassion, and remorse	■ More severe punishment ■ Punishment of arrest during leisure time ■ Punishment of short detention to get an impression of a "real" detention for a short time; this only applies for a maximum of 4 days. ■ Punishment by arrest is the harshest level and can last for up to 4 weeks.	■ Most severe punishment ■ Offender stays in custody for a minimum of six months to a maximum of 10 or to 15 years if criminal law is applicable to the adolescent (on probation if necessary).

Information taken from: The juvenile criminal law/juvenile criminal law attorney, Kerpen: Baumfalk – Rechtsanwaltskanzlei/Patrick Jan Baumfalk, https://kanzlei-baumfalk.de/en/anwalt-fuer-jugendstrafrecht/ [14 June 2023] (modified)

M 6 Juvenile criminal law or (general) criminal law?

Indications for applying the criminal law	Indications for applying juvenile criminal law
■ a certain amount of life planning ■ ability to make independent judgements and decisions ■ the ability to take a long-term view of life, not focussing just on the moment ■ ability to support emotional judgements rationally ■ a serious attitude to work ■ a certain independence towards other people	■ insufficient development of the personality ■ helplessness (which is often hidden behind defiance and arrogance) ■ naïve and untrusting behaviour ■ living for the moment ■ a strong need to be led by others ■ playful attitude to work ■ tendency to daydream and be adventurous ■ lack of connection with peers

Adapted from: Jugendstrafrecht bei Heranwachsenden, Hamburg: SCHNEIDER || MICK. Rechtsanwälte Strafverteidiger PartmbB, https://www.strafverteidiger-hamburg.com/jugendstrafrecht/jugendstrafrecht-heranwachsenden/ [4 Mar 2024] (translated and modified)

1 Jigsaw: Analyse the different cases (M4): find out who is involved, and which criminal offence might be at stake, which law might be relevant and whether anybody may expect a punishment according to the respective law.

2 Discuss in class which punishments you as judges would impose on the juveniles from M4. Consider criteria that affect your decisions (M5 and M6).

INFO

§ 248b Criminal Code: unauthorised use of vehicle
(1) Whoever uses a motor vehicle or a bicycle against the will of the person authorised to use it incurs a penalty of imprisonment for a term not exceeding three years or a fine, unless the act is subject to a more severe penalty under other provisions.
(2) The attempt is punishable.
(3) The offence is prosecuted only upon request.
(4) Motor vehicles within the meaning of this provision are vehicles which are driven by machine power, terrestrial motor vehicles only to the extent that they are not rail-bound vehicles.

§ 303 Criminal Code: criminal damage
(1) Whoever unlawfully damages or destroys an object belonging to another incurs a penalty of imprisonment for a term not exceeding two years or a fine.
(2) Whoever, without being authorised to do so, substantially and permanently alters the appearance of an object belonging to another incurs the same penalty.
(3) The attempt is punishable.

3.8 Punishment – necessary or harmful for an offender's future?

M1 What life is like after the punishment

Nearly 90 % of juvenile offenders say they want to return to school after release, but only one-third do, the U.S. Department of Education reports. Several factors contribute to the gap, such as the inability to transfer academic credits from detention to a school, little or no guidance, and the poor quality of education inside a facility, experts say.

Starting when he was 10, Blake Casper spent 18 months removed from his home, jumping between foster care, group homes and eventually detention centers in Nebraska.

After he was released from his last placement at the Youth Rehabilitation & Treatment Center in Kearney, he returned to his middle school in Lexington, Nebraska in January 2011.

"Everyone knew the story of where I'd been," Casper said of his return to his small town.

Casper said he felt he was treated differently by his peers and teachers. He recounted being more strictly disciplined than his classmates after getting in fights – which happened several times during middle school. Eventually, he was expelled.

"The big message I learned from it was that moving forward, my actions were going to be judged 10 times harder than everybody else's," said Casper, 23. "It was more of a growing moment for me." […]

Courts can require inmates to see a psychologist after release because incarceration can lead to anxiety, post-traumatic stress disorder, depression and substance abuse, among others, experts say.

"There's no way that I was fully rehabilitated, or even back to normal," Casper said. "I still had a lot of issues to work out."

Sorell Grow/Jeff Uveino/Nicole Sroka/James Wooldridge, 'A lifelong trajectory': Three men navigate reentry after incarceration, Carnegie-Knight News21, 21 Aug 2020, https://kidsimprisoned.news21.com/life-after-incarceration-reentry/ [14 Mar 2024]

M2 Theories of punishment – an overview from the USA

a) Deterrence

[…] There has been much debate over whether deterrence works. Proponents claim that punishment deters if it is administered with celerity […], certainty, and severity. A distinction needs to be drawn between general versus specific deterrence. General deterrence uses the person sentenced for a crime as an example to induce the public to refrain from criminal conduct, while specific deterrence punishes an offender to dissuade that offender from committing crimes in the future. Critics point to the high recidivism (committing crimes again) rates of persons sentenced to prison as evidence of the lack of effectiveness of specific deterrence. Critics also note that there are limits to the impact of general deterrence. Some crimes, such as crimes of pas- sion and crimes committed while under the influence of drugs, can't be deterred because their perpetrators don't rationally weigh the benefits versus the costs (which include punishment) before breaking the law. Finally, research evidence suggests that the deterrent effect of punishment is weak.

b) Incapacitation

A popular reason for punishment is that it gets criminals off the streets and protects the public. The idea is to remove an offender from society, making it physically impossible (or at least very difficult) for him or her to commit further crimes against the public while serving a sentence. Incapacitation works as long as the offenders remain locked up. There is no question that incapacitation reduces crime rates by some unknown degree. The problem is that it is very expensive. Incapacitation carries high costs not only in terms of building and operating prisons, but also in terms of disrupting families when family members are locked up.

c) Rehabilitation

"Let the punishment fit the criminal" expresses the rehabilitative ethic. Rehabilitation calls for changing the individual lawbreaker through correctional interventions, such as drug-treatment programs. [...] But evaluations of correctional treatment show it doesn't consistently prevent or reduce crime. Why has rehabilitation failed? **Funding** has been inadequate, so the full effectiveness of rehabilitation hasn't been tested. Furthermore, certain criminals – such as perpetrators of nonviolent crimes and first-time offenders – are more likely to be successfully rehabilitated than **repeat offenders** and violent criminals.

d) Retribution

"Let the punishment fit the crime" captures the essence of retribution. Proponents advocate [...] fairness and proportionality. Retributivists aim to **dispense punishment** according to an offender's moral blameworthiness (as measured by the severity of crimes of which the offender was convicted). Ideally, the harshness of punishments should be **proportionate** to the seriousness of crimes. In reality, it is difficult to match punishments and crimes, since there is no way to objectively calibrate the moral **depravity** of particular crimes and/or the painfulness of specific punishments. Retribution is a backward-looking theory of punishment. It looks to the past to determine what to do in the present.

Theories of Punishment, in: CliffsNotes, Redwood City, CA: Learneo, Inc., https://www.cliffsnotes.com/study-guides/criminal-justice/sentencing/theories-of-punishment [12 Mar 2024] (modified)

VOCABULARY

incapacitation
hier: Außer-Gefecht-Setzung
retribution
Vergeltung
to dispense punishment
hier: eine Strafe erteilen
funding
Finanzierung
repeat offender
Wiederholungstäter/-in
proportionate
proportional, verhältnismäßig
depravity
Verwerflichkeit

1 **a)** List personal milestones you are going to make in your public and private life in the next years (such as getting an ID card, turning sixteen or eighteen, etc.).
   b) Now imagine two people 14 years old who go to a detention centre and are released two and five years later. Talk with a partner about what difficulties these people might face. Consider the milestones from task 1 a).

2 **a)** Summarize the experiences described in M1 which made Blake Casper's re-entry into society more difficult after his release.
   b) **Jigsaw:** Outline the main points about punishment and present the results to your group (M2). **MORE HELP**

3 Discuss how efficiently a punishment functions for the offender and for society. Think also about the type of punishment which is most sensible for a crime. Give reasons. **MORE HELP**

3.9 The rule of law – a "gateway" for all opinions and public desires?

M1 Breach of law or legal?

Case 1: Someone makes a critical and public statement about a head of state of another country. The head of state asks the federal government to punish the person with a prison sentence.

Case 2: A policeman wants to save the life of a child and threatens the suspected kidnapper with horrific torture. The (actually) guilty kidnapper sues the policeman.

Case 3: One political party drafts a bill to make citizens follow a certain dress code in public. From now on, too much skin, tattoos, piercings, and body mods should not be visible.

Text by the author

M2 Characteristics of the state under the rule of law

"Is the state allowed to do that?" This is the core idea of the rule of law, because it is about boundaries that even the state is not allowed to violate, so that its citizens can live freely and according to democratic principles. [5]
Probably the two most important characteristics of a constitutional state are legal certainty and equality under the law. Legal certainty means that every state measure requires a legal basis. Legislation is bound by the constitution, [10] the administration and the judiciary by law. In Germany, the constitution is the Basic Law. Legal certainty protects against arbitrary state action. Equality under the law means that the same laws apply to all citizens and that they [15] have to be treated equally in court (see Article 3 Basic Law).
Besides, three other features are significant: there is legal control, which states that if a pub- [20] lic authority violates someone's rights, she/he may go to court (Article 19 (4) Basic Law). Therefore, citizens can defend themselves against alleged unlawful interventions by the state. The courts have to hear the case independently. [25] The separation of powers makes certain that state power does not remain in one hand. That is why the legislative power (the parliament), the executive power (the government) and the judicial power (e.g. the Federal Constitutional [30] Court) are in different responsible hands. Citizens have rights that cannot be taken away. It is only possible to restrict freedom by passing laws in exceptional cases. Fundamental and human rights defend citizens against arbitrary [35] state action and protect private individuals; fundamental rights also protect other citizens.

Adapted from: Was ist ein Rechtsstaat. Das Rechtsstaatsprinzip, Stuttgart: Landeszentrale für politische Bildung Baden-Württemberg, https://www.lpb-bw.de/rechtsstaat#c65790 [2 Oct 2023] (translated and modified)

Separation of powers

§   legislative   executive   judicial

47592EX © Westermann

Fundamental and human rights in the Basic Law

first 19 articles
of the Basic Law   →   **fundamental rights**

articles that apply
to all human beings   →   **human rights**

47593EX © Westermann

M3   Art. 79 (3) Amendment of the Basic Law

(3) Amendments to this Basic Law affecting the division of the Federation into Länder, their participation in principle in the legislative process, or the principles laid down in Articles 1 and 20 shall be inadmissible.

₅

M4   Art 19 (2) Basic Law

(2) In no case may the essence of a basic right be affected.

M5   Lady Justice

1   Decide whether the cases in M1 are legal or break German laws.
Find the relevant passages in the Basic Law (webcode/QR code). **MORE HELP**

2   Explain the five principles of the rule of law (M2) in your own words and add them to your concept map from the beginning of the unit.

3   **a)** Analyse M3. Focus on what it aims at and what it should prevent.
▸ METHOD Law, pp. 68–69

   b) Assess the significance of Art. 79 (3) as well as Art 19 (2) of the Basic Law (M3, M4). Consider German history as well.

4   Describe and analyse the allegory of Lady Justice (M5): which elements of the rule of law are represented? ▸ Useful phrases (B), pp. 203–204

5   Verify the following statement: "In our constitutional state, everyone has the freedom to express their opinion – but only as long as it is based on our Basic Law." Use your acquired knowledge from this chapter.

3.10 Fundamental and human rights – indispensable and applicable to everyone?

M 1 What if …

… you lost fundamental rights you are used to in Germany? Use two six-sided dice. Roll the dice and check the number. It represents one of the exemplary basic rights that are being *temporarily* abolished. Discuss in the group what would change in the country and what consequences this could have for you.

Variation: With each roll of the dice, the fundamental rights are *permanently* removed from the game. If you roll a number that was already on the dice, you keep rolling until you get a new number.

Protection of human dignity — **7**		Occupational freedom — **9**
Equality under the law — **6**	Inviolability of the home — **3**	Right to asylum — **10**
Freedom of expression — **8**	Right to life and physical integrity — **4**	Freedom of assembly — **11**
Privacy of correspondence, post, etc. — **5**	Freedom of movement — **2**	Right to vote — **12**

Text by the author

M 2 Do rights apply to everyone?

Art. 2 [Personal freedoms]
(1) Every person shall have the right to free development of his personality insofar as he does not violate the rights of others or offend against the constitutional order or the moral law.

Art. 8 [Freedom of assembly]
(1) All Germans shall have the right to assemble peacefully and unarmed without prior notification or permission.

In the Basic Law, there is a difference between rights that **?** has and rights that only apply to **?** citizens (or partly to other EU citizens).

M3 Does the Basic Law apply here?

a) I was born in Germany, but people always ask me where my home is or where I actually come from. My answer: I was born in Berlin, so I'm German. But the controls are even worse. No matter where I go, if someone is checked, it's me. It must be because of my black hair and slightly darker skin. I don't think that's okay!
(Gina, 16)

b) My teacher doesn't allow me to go to school with my wonderful fishnet shirts because they are offensive, as I would show too much skin. She also says that my holey tights are not an appropriate outfit for school. I tried to explain to her that this is my style, but she didn't care at all. I feel this restricts my personal development.
(Ariana, 15)

c) During the pandemic, there were hardly any places where people could still meet. People were really lonely. That's why my friends and I met in the park and even kept our distance. Nevertheless, the police asked us to vacate the place. Well, if that wasn't an attack on our freedom!?
(Mika, 13)

d) I have been living in Germany for two years now. Next year there are national elections and I want to vote for a party that represents my interests very well. A friend told me now that I will not be able to vote. Why is that? I'm living here and I benefit and suffer from the choices made by politicians. I should have the right to say who makes the decisions for me …?
(Yosef, 18)

Text by the author

1 **a)** Play the game (M1) and follow the instructions.
   b) Create a personal top 5 list of the most important rights. Explain what has influenced your decision the most.
2 **a)** Complete the definition in M2 with the help of Art. 2 and 8.
   b) Create a table with a few examples of the two different types. Check articles 1, 2, 3, 4, 5, 9, 11, 12 and 20 (4). ▶ webcode/QR code Basic Law, p. 85
3 **a)** As young experts on the Basic Law, you have been sent some complaints by students from all over Germany (M3). Analyse the cases and study relevant articles of the Basic Law to find out if the cases might be relevant for a real complaint. Write short replies in English for an international magazine. ▶ Useful phrases (C), pp. 204 – 205
   b) **Extra:** Choose one or two cases and write short letters to the students. Explain whether a court is likely to hear the cases. ▶ METHOD Law, pp. 68 – 69

Gap text: are you ready for court?

Basic Law | constitution | contractual capacity | criminal capacity | entitled to | human rights | juvenile delinquent | law | legal age | legal order | parental permission | peace, obligation, order, and legal security | public law, civil law, criminal law | rule of law | suspect | Youth Protection Act

1) The entire legal system creates a **?**.
2) One precisely formulated text which explains what is or is not allowed is called a **?**.
3) If you have the right to get something you are **?** something.
4) The functions of the law are **?**.
5) The highest German law is the **?**. It is our **?**.
6) For some purchases or actions, teenagers need **?**.
7) In Germany, at the age of 18, you are of **?**.
8) The fact that you can be punished for violations against the Criminal Code is called **?**.
9) The ability to make a contract with somebody is called **?**.
10) In Germany, you distinguish between several types of law, e.g. **?**.
11) A legal text that aims at safeguarding young people in Germany is called **?**.
12) A young person who has committed a crime like vandalism is called a **?**.
13) A person the police think has committed a crime is called a **?**.
14) A guiding constitutional principle a state follows to respect the citizens' rights and legal security is called **?**.
15) Rights that apply to all human beings not just to citizens of one nation are **?**.

Find the right expression: legal terms and phrases

a) A law is **applicable | indispensable**.
b) Something is **against the law | no one is above the law**.
c) To **inflict | impose | mete out** a punishment.
d) Somebody **commits | perpetrates** a crime.
e) An offender must pay a **penalty | fine**.
f) The police **arrest | imprison | incarcerate** someone.

I) If you steal something from a shop, that is **?**. You will be charged because **?**.
II) A criminal is a person who **?** a crime.
III) In Germany, laws are **?** even to children.
IV) The police **?** a suspect, and a court may then **?** such a person.
V) A court of law can **?** a punishment if it finds you guilty of a crime.
VI) An offender who is found guilty by law may have to pay a **?**.

1 Find the right terms for sentences 1) to 15) and copy the sentences into your folder.
2 Choose the right expression a) to f) to complete the sentences I) to VI).
Focus on the expressions printed in bold type to make a decision.
3 Return to your concept map from the beginning of this unit. Check if it is complete.
Optional: Redesign and reorganize the concept map with what you have learned in this unit.

The American jury – (un)biased?

Adult U.S. citizens representing all races, religions, occupations, and ethnic backgrounds can become jurors. In some states, Americans are called for jury duty, in others lists of li-
5 censed drivers and registered voters are combined to select them. Moreover, in some states Americans can volunteer for service. Those who are selected receive a summons, which is an official demand to report for jury
10 duty on a specific date.

When they arrive at the courthouse, citizens report to a central location where jury trials are scheduled to begin. The jury panel is always larger than the number of persons
15 needed for the final jury. For example, in certain criminal trials, 32 or more potential jurors come into the courtroom, they take an oath, which means that each member swears to tell the truth, and they are questioned by
20 lawyers (and sometimes the judge). This process is called *voir dire*, a French phrase that means "to speak the truth".

The *voir dire* process helps the judge and attorneys to choose jurors who have not pre-
25 judged the facts of the case and who are as fair and impartial as possible, to ensure a just trial. It is important that jurors not know the lawyers or each other. It is also important that they not have strong opinions about the
30 issue – or premature views about how a case should be decided. If a juror shows one of these criteria, then one of the lawyers may challenge the juror for cause, and the judge will usually allow the juror to be removed (or
35 excused) from service on the jury. Additionally, each side in a case has the right to challenge a certain number of jurors without giving any reason. These are called *peremptory challenges*.
40 Once the jury is selected, the judge explains the jury process. After that, the lawyers pre-

sent the case. There are generally two lawyers involved in the trial – one for each side – but in more complex cases, there might be many more lawyers participating. The law-45 yers bring in witnesses and present evidence – through witnesses and documents – so that the jury can determine the facts and what they mean.

The judge presides over the trial, ensuring 50 that it proceeds properly and fairly, and sometimes stopping the action to preserve fairness. After the lawyers have presented their entire case, the judge instructs the jury on its obligations and on the factual issues 55 that the jury must decide. The jury then goes to a separate room in the courthouse to deliberate, that is to discuss the issues before them and to reach a decision.

After carefully considering the evidence pre-60 sented during the trial, the jury reaches its verdict. In most cases, jury verdicts must be unanimous. Unanimous verdicts may not be required in civil cases; many states allow verdicts of fewer jurors to stand in some circum-65 stances. If the required number of jurors cannot agree on a verdict of whether the suspect is guilty or not, the judge declares a mistrial, which means that the case must be tried again unless it is withdrawn.70

Jury in a jury box.

Based on: HANDOUT 1 for students, The Jury in the United States and Iowa, Iowa Judicial Branch, https://www.iowacourts.gov/static/media/cms/Background_information_4C3E68CF3C2F1.pdf [26 Mar 2024] (modified)

VOCABULARY

to volunteer
sich freiwillig melden
to schedule
planen
oath
Eid
premature
vorschnell
to challenge sb. for a cause
jmdn. für eine Sache anfechten
to preside
den Vorsitz führen
unanimous
einstimmig
partisanship
Parteilichkeit
prejudice
Vorurteil

HOT SPOT

In the USA, the term "**race**" is used more as a sociocultural and political (self) categorization. You will e.g. find it on official forms and in spoken language. It is also connected to antiracist protests and measures. In Germany the term "**Rasse**" has a biological meaning and therefore is problematic as there are no human "Rassen" – this idea itself is based on racism. The term can still be found in the Basic Law (Art. 3), but there are discussions about replacing it.

INFO

German lay judges
At a local court, the team consists of two lay judges and one professional judge. In a district court, there are two lay judges for every two to three professional judges. Not only may they have a say on whether someone is guilty or not, they may also question the witnesses and the defendant and take part in determining the penalty.

1 **a)** Describe the process of becoming a juror in the U.S.
   b) Explain how lawyers and judges try to avoid partisanship and/or prejudice.
2 Compare the American jury's impact on the verdict with that of a German lay judge.
3 Assess the concept of a jury and that of a lay judge regarding their efficiency and legitimacy. **MORE HELP**

4

Cartoon: Tim Verhoeven

INFO

student body president
American term for student school representative = Schülersprecher/-in

Democracy in school

1 Analyse the cartoon at the top left. ▸ METHOD Cartoons, pp. 26–27
2 Think about what the students in the drawing below could be talking about.
3 Compare the photos above and state how school has changed over time.
4 Think about your school day(s) – who makes decisions? **MORE HELP**

4.1 Democracy in school?

M1 Statements on electing a class representative

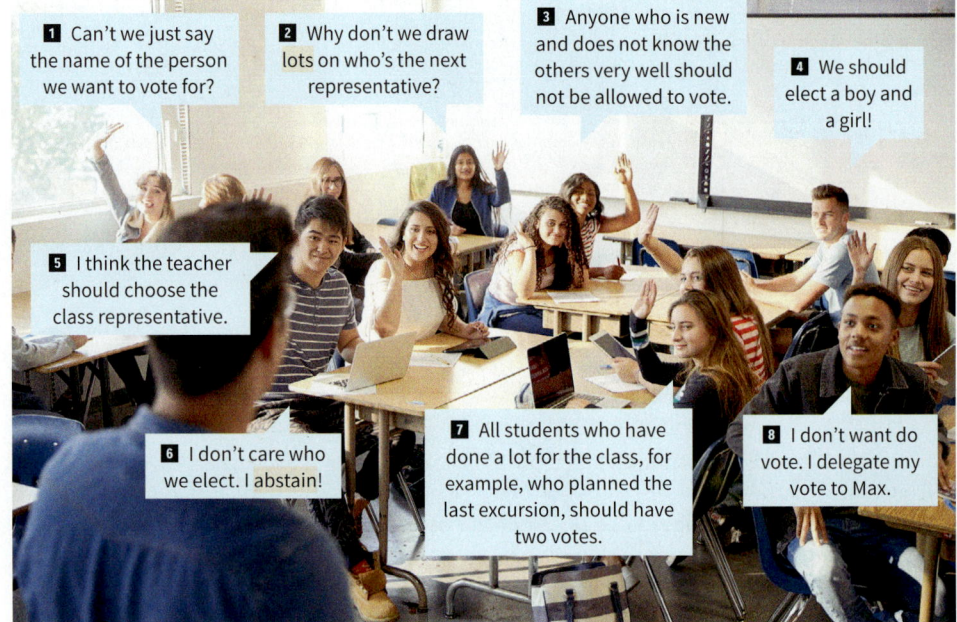

1. Can't we just say the name of the person we want to vote for?
2. Why don't we draw lots on who's the next representative?
3. Anyone who is new and does not know the others very well should not be allowed to vote.
4. We should elect a boy and a girl!
5. I think the teacher should choose the class representative.
6. I don't care who we elect. I abstain!
7. All students who have done a lot for the class, for example, who planned the last excursion, should have two votes.
8. I don't want do vote. I delegate my vote to Max.

M2 Rules for democratic elections

There are rules for democratic elections in Germany. Article 38 (1) of the Basic Law states: "Members of the German Bundestag shall be elected in general, direct, free, equal and secret elections." These are electoral principles. State and local elections in Germany have the same principles. But what exactly do they mean?

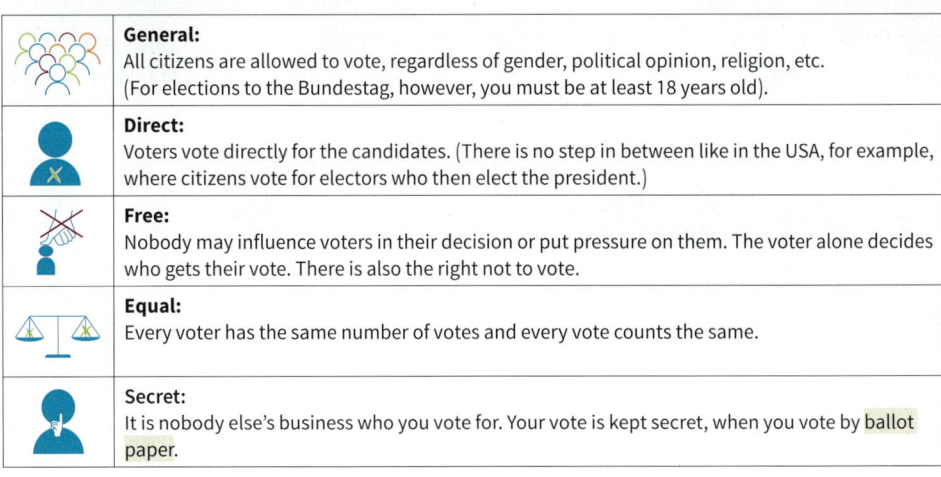

	General: All citizens are allowed to vote, regardless of gender, political opinion, religion, etc. (For elections to the Bundestag, however, you must be at least 18 years old).
	Direct: Voters vote directly for the candidates. (There is no step in between like in the USA, for example, where citizens vote for electors who then elect the president.)
	Free: Nobody may influence voters in their decision or put pressure on them. The voter alone decides who gets their vote. There is also the right not to vote.
	Equal: Every voter has the same number of votes and every vote counts the same.
	Secret: It is nobody else's business who you vote for. Your vote is kept secret, when you vote by ballot paper.

Text by the author

м3 Skills and qualities of a class representative

A class representative ...

can communicate clearly

has a friendly tone

has a strong sense of fairness

?

appears self-confident

has the courage to stand up to teachers

is self-critical

prevents arguments in class

has good marks at school

?

presents her/his opinion clearly

? ?

has a lot of friends in class

м4 Tasks of the student representation

2 Aufgaben der SV (aus dem SV Erlass Nordrhein-Westfalen)

2.1 Im Rahmen des Schulgesetzes wirkt die SV durch ihre Organe an Entscheidungen der Schule mit.

5

2.2 Außer der Mitwirkung am Entscheidungsverfahren und der Teilnahme an Konferenzen gehört zur Mitwirkung […] insbesondere:

2.2.1 Die Förderung von fachlichen, kultu-

10 rellen, sportlichen, politischen und sozialen Interessen der Schülerinnen und Schüler. Hierzu gehören insbesondere: Arbeitskreise über selbstgewählte Themen einschließlich solcher über politische Fragen, Forumsge-

15 spräche und Vortragsveranstaltungen […], Arbeitsgemeinschaften, Fach- und Neigungsgruppen.

2.2.2 Das Recht, Probleme des schulischen Lebens sowie Beschwerden allgemeiner Art aufzugreifen, sie mit den am Schulleben Beteiligten zu diskutieren und sie über die Schule den Schulaufsichtsbehörden vorzutragen.

20

2.2.3 Das Recht, im Einzelfall eine Schülerin oder einen Schüler ihrer Schule auf deren oder dessen Wunsch bei der Wahrnehmung ihrer oder seiner Rechte gegenüber Schulleitung und Lehrkräften, insbesondere bei Ordnungsmaßnahmen und Beschwerdefällen zu beraten und zu unterstützen.

25

2.2.4 Das Recht zur Abgabe von Erklärungen an die Öffentlichkeit im Rahmen des schulpolitischen Mandats. Derartige Erklärungen können nur abgegeben werden, wenn ein entsprechender Beschluss des Schülerrats vorliegt.

30

INTERNET

WES-116955-411
Collection of links to the regulations of various federal states

1 Comment on the statements (M1) and give reasons for your opinion.

2 Name principles that should be valid for the election of the class representative.
MORE HELP

3 Decide whether the statements (M1) and your principles (task 2) fit with the rules for democratic elections (M2).

4 a) Make a list of possible tasks for the class representative.
b) Rank the listed tasks from most important to least important.

5 **Think–Pair–Share:** Assess how important the skills and qualities in M3 are to fulfil the tasks of a class representative as part of the student representation (M4).
You can also check the regulations in your federal state.

6 Do you think it is important to have a class representative? Discuss this question.

▸ METHOD Debate, pp. 48 – 49

4.2 School uniforms – a way to improve interaction at school?

VOCABULARY

rational
vernünftig
legitimate
berechtigt, legitim
objectives
Ziele
neatness
Ordentlichkeit
distraction
Störung
disruption
Unterbrechung
torn
zerrissen

M 1 "Non-uniform day today"

Cartoon: Clive Goddard, 2009

M 2 School uniforms in the USA

Washington District of Columbia Municipal Regulations (DCMR)
District of Columbia Public Schools 5-B 2408 DCMR

B2408   *DRESS CODES/UNIFORMS*
         […]
B2408.2 The local school dress code or uniform policy shall be as follows:
         (a) Clearly defined;
         (b) Not be gender specific;
         (c) Designed to support rational and legitimate school objectives including, but not
             limited to, the following:
             (1) Neatness and cleanliness;
             (2) Elimination of distractions and disruptions to the education process;
             (3) Health and safety considerations; and
             (4) Respect for the rights of others;
         (d) Include the following principles:
             (1) Excessively dirty and/or torn clothing may not be worn in school;
             (2) Students shall, when present in areas where the possibility of injury to the
                 student or to others exists, such as near rotating machinery, power tools, or
                 chemicals, wear appropriate protective clothing, gloves, eye goggles, and/or
                 other devices needed for health and safety; […].

District of Columbia Register Vol. 56 – No. 33, 14 Aug 2009, NE, Washington, DC: District of Columbia Public Schools,
https://dcps.dc.gov/sites/default/files/dc/sites/dcps/publication/attachments/DCMR-Chapter-24-Title-5-Final-
Rulemaking-2009.pdf [9 Jan 2024]

M3 School uniforms – some pros and cons

Pros of school uniforms	Cons of school uniforms
1. When students don't wear school uniforms it can be easy to spot kids with the most – and least – economic **privilege** based on what they wear to school.	1. Keeping a child in school uniforms may be more expensive for parents than buying regular clothes. Often, uniforms are only available from a limited number of **suppliers** and the lack of competition keeps prices high.
2. Uniforms may increase student focus. Many proponents of uniforms argue that when students don't have clothing to notice, comment on or respond to, they can spend more mental energy on learning.	2. Uniforms limit students' self-expression. Teenagers, in particular, are famous for needing to express their emotions and their tastes in music, fashion and art through clothing, hair and piercings.
3. Uniforms may also build community in a school as students of all ages bond over the outfits they all associate with their school days.	3. Some uniforms may seem to students and parents as sexist. For example, if a uniform requires girls to wear skirts and pants are not allowed.
4. In areas where students may be gang-involved, uniforms can increase safety by preventing students from wearing clothing that declares – intentionally or not – gang affiliation.	4. If a school has a uniform policy, it generally tries to enforce that policy by **monitoring** students' clothing and punishing students for violating uniform requirements.
…	…

Amelia Josephson, The Pros and Cons of School Uniforms, New York, NY: SmartAsset, 21 Mar 2023, https://smartasset.com/insights/the-pros-and-cons-of-school-uniforms [6 Sep 2023] (modified)

VOCABULARY

privilege
Vorteil, Privileg
supplier
Anbieter
to monitor
überwachen
measure
hier: Messung
proponent
Befürworter/-in

M4 Current findings on school uniforms

Despite the belief of many parents and teachers, school uniforms don't seem to have any effect on young students' behavior or attendance overall, a new national study found. But
5 students who attended schools requiring school uniforms did report lower levels of "school belonging" in fifth grade than did students in schools without uniforms. [...]
"A lot of the core arguments about why
10 school uniforms are good for student behavior don't hold up in our sample," said Arya Ansari, lead author of the study and assistant professor of human sciences at The Ohio State University. "We didn't see much difference in our behavior **measures**, regardless of 15 whether the schools had a uniform policy or not." [...]
Proponents of school uniforms have argued that, among other things, they promote better attendance and a stronger sense of communi- 20 ty, which results in less bullying and fighting. To test that, the researchers used data from the Early Childhood Longitudinal Study, which followed a nationally representative sample of 6,320 students from kindergarten through the 25 end of fifth grade.

Jeff Grabmeier, School uniforms don't improve child behavior, study finds, Columbus, OH: The Ohio State University, 20 Dec 2021, https://news.osu.edu/school-uniforms-dont-improve-child-behavior-study-finds/ [9 Jan 2024]

1 Analyse the cartoon (M1). **MORE HELP** ▸ METHOD Cartoons, pp. 26 – 27
2 Explain in German the regulation on school uniforms in Washington D.C. public schools to your German friend who does not speak English very well (M2).
▸ METHOD Mediation, pp. 72 – 73
3 **Fishbowl:** Debate introducing a school uniform at your school (M3, M4).
▸ Useful phrases (A), pp. 202 – 203

4.3 How democratic is school?

M1 At your school …

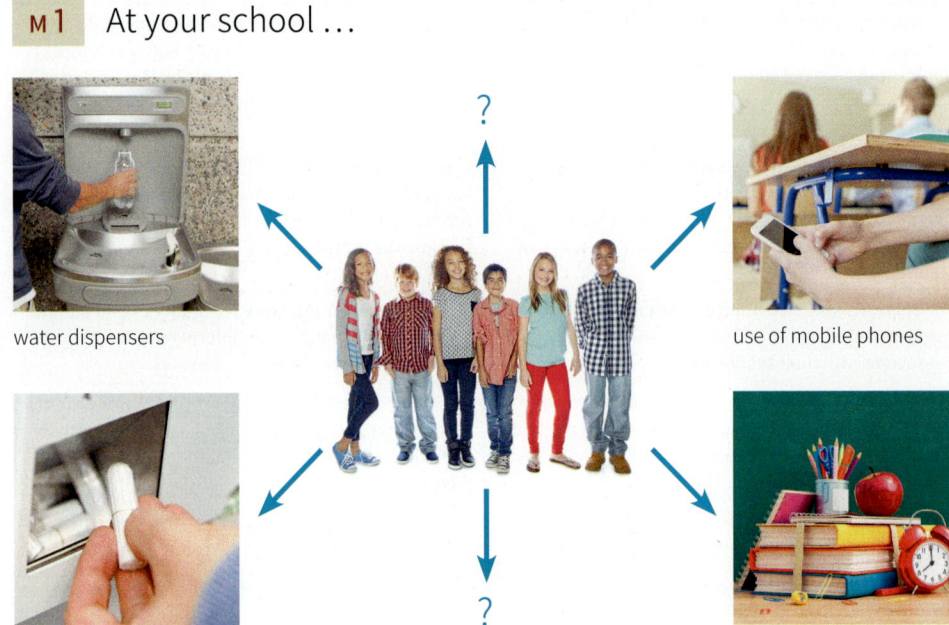

water dispensers

toiletries

use of mobile phones

start of school

M2 Democratic representation in the school system

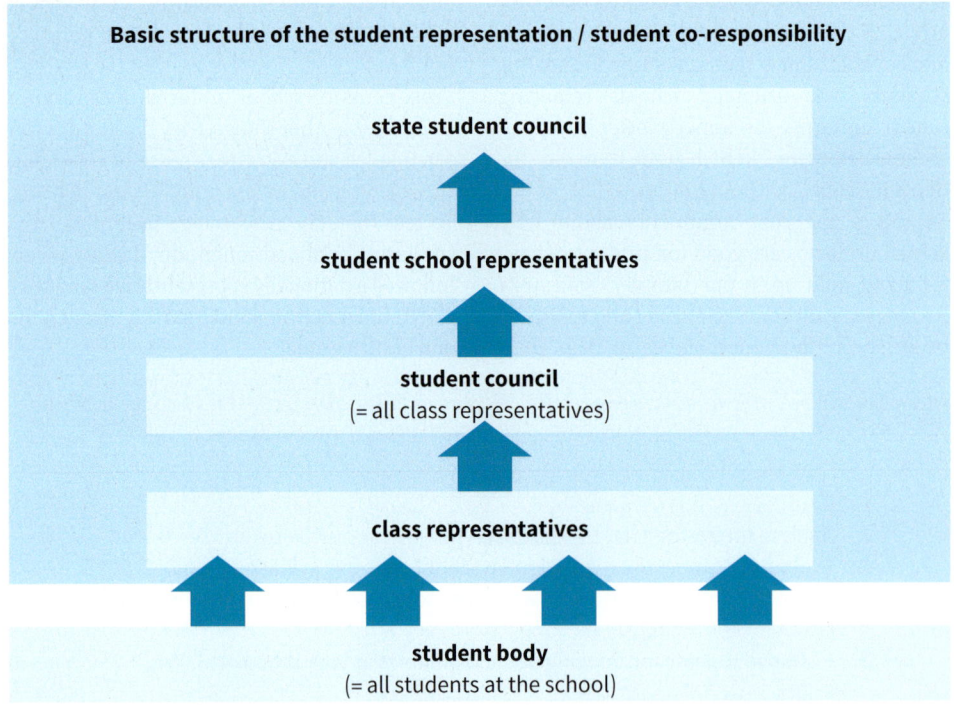

Basic structure of the student representation / student co-responsibility

state student council

student school representatives

student council
(= all class representatives)

class representatives

student body
(= all students at the school)

м3 Baden-Württemberg student advisory council calls for air filter systems for classrooms

Der Landesschülerbeirat in Baden-Württemberg fordert die Anschaffung von Luftfilteranlagen für Klassenräume. Die Sprecherin des Beirats, Elisabeth Schilli, sagte dazu [...]: „Dadurch würde
5 man auch dem Lüftungsproblem entgehen, das ja auch noch nicht ganz geklärt ist – wie das funktioniert, wenn es Minusgrade hat." Die derzeit geltende Maskenpflicht für Schüler ab der fünften Klasse hält sie nicht für das optimale
10 Mittel zur Bekämpfung der Pandemie.
Die bereits kritisierte fehlende Verfügbarkeit von Luftfilteranlagen sieht Schilli weniger als Problem an – mehr den hohen Preis. Doch auch dies lässt die Schülervertreterin als Absage für
15 solch eine Lösung nicht gelten: „Allerdings muss man hier auch sehen, dass es sich nicht um eine Investition bis zu den Weihnachtsferien handelt, sondern dass uns die Pandemie noch eine Weile begleiten wird" [...].
20 Helfen könnte aus Sicht Schillis zudem „ein rollierendes System, bei dem ein Teil der Klasse zu Hause bleibt und der andere Teil da ist". Dank des Sofortausstattungsprogramms der Landesregierung seien die Schulen dafür ausgerüstet.
25

red/dpa/lsw, Landesschülerbeirat fordert Luftfilteranlagen für Klassenräume, in: Stuttgarter Zeitung online, 22 Oct 2020, https://www.stuttgarter-zeitung.de/inhalt.schulen-in-baden-wuerttemberg-landesschuelerbeirat-fordert-luftfilteranlagen-fuer-klassenraeume.4996d3c3-a228-4b28-b22d-cb85cf963c1c.html [6 Sep 2023]

м4 Hessian state student council demands reform of rules for hot days

Eine Reform des Hitzefrei-Erlasses fordert der Landesschülerrat [in Hessen]. Am Montag hat er dazu eine zweimonatige Unterschriftensammlung für eine Petition an den Landtag gestartet.
5 Ziel ist, dass auch Schüler der Berufsschulen und Oberstufen bei großer Hitze nicht mehr in ihren Klassenräumen brüten müssen. Auch sollen die 2009 abgeschafften Temperaturrichtwerte wieder eingeführt werden. Der-
10 zeit liegt es alleine im Ermessen der Schulleiter, ob es zu heiß ist, um zu lernen.
Die Schülervertreter wollen auch mehr Flexibilität – etwa die Möglichkeit, bei Hitze die Unterrichtsstunden von 45 auf 30 Minuten zu
15 verkürzen. Die gesetzlichen Regelungen müssten dem spürbaren Klimawandel angepasst werden [...].
Die konkreten Forderungen stehen in der Petition: Bei Temperaturen von mehr als 24 Grad kostenlose Getränke ab der Mittagspause für
20 alle. Verzicht auf Hausaufgaben oder andere Unterrichtsformen, wenn um 11 Uhr das Thermometer mehr als 24 Grad in der Sekundarstufe 1 zeigt beziehungsweise 26 Grad für die Älteren. Kürzere Stunden oder Unterrichts-
25 ende nach der 5. Stunde bei mehr als 26 Grad respektive 28 Grad. [...]
Das Kultusministerium sieht keinen Anlass, die auf Eigenverantwortlichkeit der Schulen basierenden Regelungen zu ändern [...]. Weder
30 Staatliche Schulämter noch die Verbände, der Landeselternbeirat oder der Landesschülerrat hätten bisher eine Erweiterung des Erlasses [...] angeregt.

Jutta Rippegather, Hitzefrei auch in Hessens Oberstufe, in: Frankfurter Rundschau online, 30 Sep 2019, https://www.fr.de/rhein-main/hitzefrei-auch-hessens-oberstufe-13054911.html [6 Sep 2023]

1 a) **Think-Pair-Share:** What would you like to change at your school? Collect ideas and rank them in your class. You can use M1 as a starting point.
b) Find out which of your ideas could be realized and how.
2 Describe the basic structure of democratic representation in the school system (M2) and check out the specific structure at your school.
3 Assess how effectively the state student council advocates its concerns (M3, M4).
MORE HELP

4.4 The school conference – who decides?

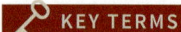
M1 Should children be banned from using mobile phones in the classroom?

Anne Longfield, Children's Commissioner for England: Many have seen the debate framed by France's decision to ban mobile phones in schools [...]. There is a pretty good
5 argument for all schools to go smartphone-free. I have never argued the internet is a bad thing, it's a fabulous resource for children but the fact is that it wasn't designed with them in mind, and overuse or misuse of it presents
10 some clear problems for children. [...]

Carolyn Roberts, [headteacher in London]: [...] [Children] may have their phones with them, but they have to be on silent and out of the way. They can use them at breaks. If they become a problem, they're confiscated. We 15 want to teach them self-moderating behaviour and how to live with a phone without it dominating their lives.

Anne Longfield/Carolyn Roberts, Should children be banned from using mobile phones in the classroom?, in: The Guardian online, 1 July 2018, https://www.theguardian.com/commentisfree/2018/jul/01/children-ban-mobile-phones-in-classroom-school-debate [6 Sep 2023]

M2 "More headteachers should ban mobile phones in school"

"I admire headteachers who do not allow mobile phones. More schools should follow their lead." Students should not be allowed their mobile phones during school hours, the British culture
5 minister, Matt Hancock, has said. He suggested more headteachers should confiscate mobile phones from children at the start of the day, as he warned mobiles can have a "real impact" on students' achievements. The minister is concerned social media use can expose 10 children to "risks" – including cyberbullying. He said "I believe that very young children don't need to have access to social media. They are children after all. They need to be able to develop their social skills in the real 15 world first." ▸ Social media, p. 46 – 47

Eleanor Busby, More headteachers should ban mobile phones in school, says minister, in: Independent, 20 June 2018, https://www.independent.co.uk/news/education/education-news/mobile-phones-ban-school-headteachers-twitter-snapchat-matt-hancock-a8407356.html [6 Sep 2023] (modified)

M3 The school conference

The school conference is a very powerful committee at school. It decides on many important matters or must at least be consulted – for example, regarding the school programme,
5 the start of school, the financial budget, new partnerships or the name of the school.
The tasks of the school conference vary from state to state, as does its composition (and sometimes its name). Depending on the fed-
10 eral state there is a different number of teachers, parents, and students in the conference: in some states, for example, teachers, students, and parents are equally represented, while in others teachers make up one half and students and parents the other half. The role of the 15 headteacher also differs, she or he often chairs the conference. In some cases, other groups are also represented.
The school conference meetings are not public as confidential information is exchanged. 20

Text by the author

How to run a role-play

Role-play – what is it good for?

In a role-play, you take on the role of another person. To do this, you first put yourself in their shoes. How does the person think and feel? What are the person's views? How do they behave towards others?

Through role-playing, you can experience the behaviour of others, observe it, and then discuss it.

How do we do it?

Usually, a role-play has three phases:

Phase 1: Preparation

- Discuss together the initial situation and find views and wishes which belong to the roles. You can design a role card for each role based on the model on the right.
- Tip: You could adapt the roles to the composition of the school conference at your school.
- Divide the class into groups. Each group gets a role (card) and thinks about arguments, behaviour, and strategies, etc. for their role.

ROLE CARD:	
Name: Mrs Müller	
Function:	parent representative
Position:	against a general mobile phone ban
Interests and goals:	accessibility of her children
Strategies for achieving interests:	seeking a compromise with the teachers

- Each group chooses one person to play the role.
- Those of you who do not play a role are observers. Agree on specific observation tasks. Observe, for example, whether the role-play is realistic and how to assess each character's the behaviour.

Phase 2: Performance

- The role-players play the scene without interruption.
- The observers watch carefully and take notes.

Phase 3: Evaluation

- First, the players leave their roles and briefly say how they felt in it.
- Then talk about what you noticed (most) during the role-play. The observers contribute their notes here. You can also talk in groups first and then share your results with the class.
- Afterwards, you can repeat the role-play. If you like, you can change roles now. It makes sense, for example, for students from the observation group to take on a role now.

1 Compare the attitudes on banning mobile phones at school (M1, M2).
2 Explain the function and the tasks of the school conference (M3).
3 **Extra:** Find out which model of the school conference applies in your federal state (webcode/QR code).
4 Hold a school conference debate (METHOD, pp. 99–101) on the pros and cons of banning mobile phones at school. ▸ Useful phrases (A), pp. 202–203
5 **Milling around:** Evaluate the institution of the school conference. Would it be better if the headteacher made all decisions alone? **MORE HELP**

Topic: Does a ban on mobile phones make sense?

Imagine the following situation: Your school's regulations do not yet have any rules on the use of mobile phones. However, some teachers want to ban mobile phones from the school grounds. The school conference must now decide.

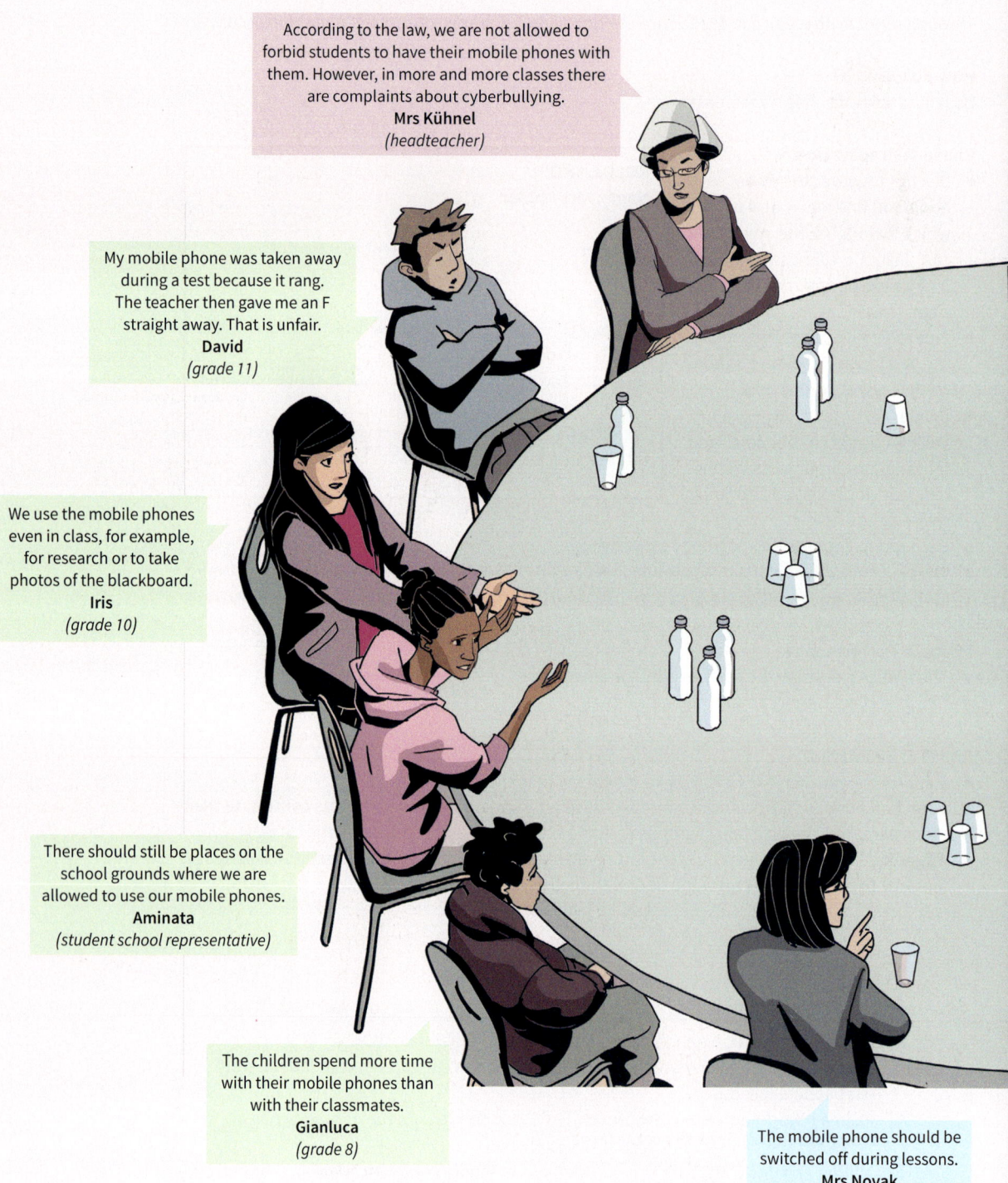

According to the law, we are not allowed to forbid students to have their mobile phones with them. However, in more and more classes there are complaints about cyberbullying.
Mrs Kühnel
(headteacher)

My mobile phone was taken away during a test because it rang. The teacher then gave me an F straight away. That is unfair.
David
(grade 11)

We use the mobile phones even in class, for example, for research or to take photos of the blackboard.
Iris
(grade 10)

There should still be places on the school grounds where we are allowed to use our mobile phones.
Aminata
(student school representative)

The children spend more time with their mobile phones than with their classmates.
Gianluca
(grade 8)

The mobile phone should be switched off during lessons.
Mrs Novak
(parent council chair)

4.5 Rights and duties at school – are they fair?

M1 Jakob suspended

After hitting a fellow student, Jakob must see the headteacher, who suspends him for three days. The headteacher says he cannot tolerate Jakob's action and must punish him severely. Jakob is upset and asks his parents to help him from being suspended. 5

Text by the author

Schulordnung Rheinland-Pfalz
§ 96 Anwendung von Ordnungsmaßnahmen
(1) Ordnungsmaßnahmen können nur ausgesprochen werden, wenn andere erzieherische
5 Einwirkungen nicht ausreichen. Als erzieherische Einwirkungen kommen insbesondere in Betracht: Gespräch, Ermahnung, Verpflichtung zur Wiedergutmachung angerichteten Schadens, Verpflichtung zur Übernahme von
10 Arbeiten für die Schul- oder Klassengemeinschaft, Nacharbeiten von Versäumtem, zeitweise Wegnahme von Gegenständen, Entschuldigung für zugefügtes Unrecht und Überweisung in eine andere Klasse [...].
15 **§ 97 Maßnahmenkatalog**
(1) Es können folgende Ordnungsmaßnahmen [...] getroffen werden:
1. Untersagung der Teilnahme am Unterricht der laufenden Unterrichtsstunde durch die
20 unterrichtende Lehrkraft,

2. schriftlicher Verweis durch die Schulleiterin oder den Schulleiter,
3. Untersagung der Teilnahme am Unterricht des laufenden Unterrichtstages oder an sonstigen bis zu einwöchigen Schulveranstaltungen 25 durch die Schulleiterin oder den Schulleiter,
4. Untersagung der Teilnahme am Unterricht bis zu drei vollen Unterrichtstagen oder an über einwöchigen sonstigen Schulveranstaltungen durch die Klassenkonferenz [...], 30
5. Untersagung der Teilnahme am Unterricht für vier bis sechs Unterrichtstage durch die Klassenkonferenz [...] im Einvernehmen mit der Schulleiterin oder dem Schulleiter,
6. Androhung des Ausschlusses [...] durch die 35 Klassenkonferenz [...] im Einvernehmen mit der Schulleiterin oder dem Schulleiter. Das Benehmen mit dem Schulausschuss ist herzustellen [...].

M2 Where does the mark come from?

Janna is confused about her mark in geography. In the class test and in her presentation she got a satisfactory mark. Mr Yilmaz, her geography teacher, tells her that she did not hand in the homework and gave her a failing 5 mark for that. Last lesson he asked her a couple of questions that she could not answer and noted her answers were not sufficient.

Text by the author

§ 7 Verordnung des Kultusministeriums Baden-Württemberg über die Notenbildung
(1) Grundlage der Leistungsbewertung in einem Unterrichtsfach sind alle vom Schüler
5 im Zusammenhang mit dem Unterricht erbrachten Leistungen (schriftliche, mündliche und praktische Leistungen). [...] Der Fachlehrer hat zum Beginn seines Unterrichts bekanntzugeben, wie er in der Regel die verschiedenen Leistungen bei der Notenbildung 10 gewichten wird.
(2) Die Bildung der Note in einem Unterrichtsfach ist eine pädagogisch-fachliche Gesamtwertung der vom Schüler im Beurteilungszeitraum erbrachten Leistungen. 15

M3 Christian is sick and tired of school

Christian is in 8th grade at a Gymnasium – already for the second time. Last year he had to stay down a year. Now he is sick and tired of school and skips classes. For one week no
5 one realized it but now it got out. He and his parents must see the headteacher. Christian says that he does not want to go to school anymore. His parents are okay with that, he knows what is best for him. The headteacher
10 disagrees.

Text by the author

Schulgesetz für das Land Nordrhein-Westfalen (SchulG NRW)
§ 34 Grundsätze
(2) Die Schulpflicht umfasst in der Primarstu-
5 fe und in der Sekundarstufe I die Pflicht zum Besuch einer Vollzeitschule.
§ 35 Beginn der Schulpflicht
(1) Die Schulpflicht beginnt für Kinder, die bis zum Beginn des 30. September das sechste
10 Lebensjahr vollendet haben, am 1. August desselben Kalenderjahres.
§ 37 Schulpflicht in der Primarstufe und in der Sekundarstufe I
(1) Die Schulpflicht in der Primarstufe und
15 der Sekundarstufe I (Vollzeitschulpflicht) dauert zehn Schuljahre, am Gymnasium mit achtjährigem Bildungsgang neun Schuljahre. […] Sie endet vorher, wenn die Schülerin oder der Schüler einen der nach dem zehnten
20 Vollzeitschuljahr vorgesehen Abschlüsse in weniger als zehn Schuljahren erreicht hat.
§ 41 Verantwortung für die Einhaltung der Schulpflicht
(1) Die Eltern melden ihr schulpflichtiges Kind bei der Schule an und ab. Sie sind dafür
25 verantwortlich, dass es am Unterricht und an den sonstigen verbindlichen Veranstaltungen der Schule regelmäßig teilnimmt, und statten es angemessen aus. […]
(3) Lehrerinnen und Lehrer, Schulleiterinnen
30 und Schulleiter sind verpflichtet, Schulpflichtige, die ihre Schulpflicht nicht erfüllen, zum regelmäßigen Schulbesuch anzuhalten und auf die Eltern sowie auf die für die Berufserziehung Mitverantwortlichen einzu-
35 wirken.

INTERNET

WES-116955-451
Collection of links to the regulations of various federal states

M4 US judge grants German homeschooling family asylum

Homeschooling has been illegal in Germany for most of the 20th century. But a decision in the United States granting asylum to a German homeschooling couple has revived an on-
5 going debate on the freedom of education.
An American judge on Tuesday granted asylum to a German couple who wanted to homeschool their children […]. The decision came from immigration judge Lawrence O. Burman
10 in Memphis, Tennessee. Judge Burman said the German government violated Uwe and Hannelore Romeike's "basic human rights" […].
The parents identify themselves as evangelical Christians and say religion was the primary reason why they chose to homeschool
15 their children. Hannelore Romeike said public education can never be neutral. […] While religious homeschoolers are often covered in the media, they don't represent all German homeschooling families, said Dagmar Neubronner, a
20 publisher and therapist in Bremen […]. After asking to get permission from German courts to homeschool her children, she says, she was threatened with fines and jail time.

HOT SPOT

compulsory =
mandatory =
obligatory =
necessary
versus
homeschooling =
voluntary schooling
at home

Andrew Bowen, Homeschooling debate, Bonn: Deutsche Welle, 27 Jan 2010, https://www.dw.com/en/us-judge-grants-german-homeschooling-family-asylum/a-5174919 [6 Sep 2023]

1 Explain the legal situation for the cases (M1–M3) in groups and present your findings.
2 Give reasons for your opinion: Do you find the rules fair?
3 **Inside-outside circle:** Discuss the pros and cons of homeschooling starting from M4.
MORE HELP ▸ Useful phrases (A), pp. 202–203

4.6 Conflicts – can there be a win-win situation?

M1 An argument

The bell rings, it's the long break. The students of 8b and 8c like to spend their break playing table tennis against each other. Two boys, John (8b) and Leo (8c) get into an argument over who won the game. First the boys only ⁵ scream at each other but then John grabs Leo's shirt and it rips. Immediately all the other students in class 8c attack John. The teachers who are on duty interrupt the fight. They send both classes back to their rooms and question ¹⁰ John and Leo about the incident. Both boys are still angry, and the dispute is not yet settled. John's classmate Sarah whispers to her friend Claire: "That's just the tip of the iceberg. John is only angry at Leo because Leo is now to- ¹⁵ gether with John's ex-girlfriend Susan".

Text by the author

M2 The iceberg model

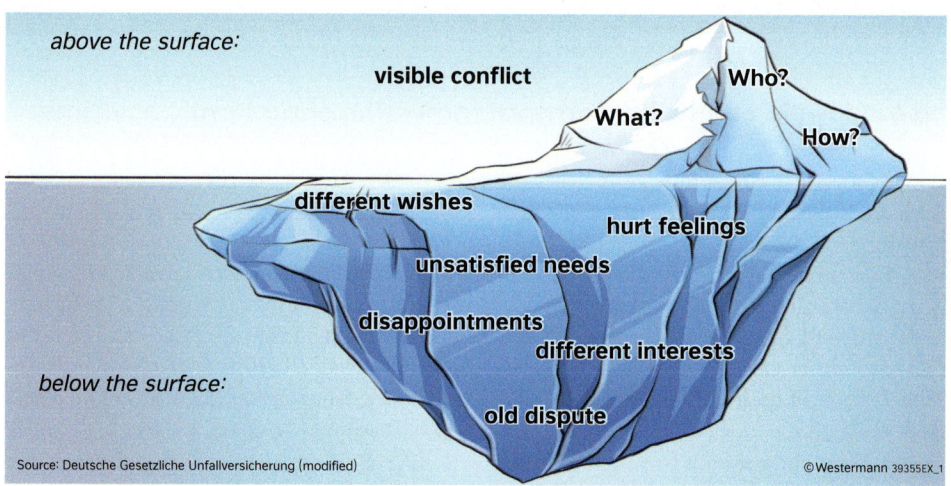

above the surface:
visible conflict   **Who?**
                What?   **How?**
different wishes
                        hurt feelings
        unsatisfied needs
    disappointments
                different interests
below the surface:
        old dispute

Source: Deutsche Gesetzliche Unfallversicherung (modified)   ©Westermann 39355EX_1

1 **Think-Pair-Share:** Develop possible solutions to the conflict (M1).
2 Explain the iceberg model (M2) and apply it to the conflict in M1. **MORE HELP**
3 **Chose a task:**
   a) Explain to your German friend who does not speak English very well how the process of a mediation works (M3). ▸ METHOD Mediation, pp. 72 – 73
   b) Carry out the mediation between John and Leo (M1) using M3.
4 Verify whether your solution (task 1) is a collaborating win-win situation (M4).

M3 Process of a mediation

1. **Introduction**
   - Mediators introduce themselves to the disputants, ask for the disputants' names, and explain the process, including
   5 confidentiality.
2. **Sharing perspectives**
   - Each disputant tells his/her story of what happened.
   - Disputants share their interpretation of
   10 what happened and how the conflict made them feel.
3. **Getting more information**
   - Mediators ask open-ended questions to clarify and verify.
   15 Mediators ask, "Is there anything else that we need to know?"
4. **Defining the problem**
   - Mediators paraphrase and restate each disputant's account.
   20 Mediators guide disputants to come to an agreement about what the problem really is.
5. **Brainstorming solutions**
   - Disputants brainstorm possible solutions.

   - Mediators ask disputants to talk about which solutions the disputants are willing 25 to agree on and which ones are not agreeable.
   - Mediators ask disputants to talk about how each possible solution will affect the disputants' relationship with each other. 30
6. **Choosing solutions**
   - Disputants decide together how they will proceed.
   - Disputants come to an agreement on which solutions are the best. 35
   - Mediators ask if the disputants are satisfied and if they need anything else from the mediation.
7. **Closing**
   - Mediators thank the disputants for 40 participating and remind them, if necessary, of confidentiality.
   - Mediators mention that if the disputants need help in the future, the mediation process is always available to them. 45

Maureen F. Block/Barbara Blazej, Resolving Conflict with a Peer Mediation Program. A Manual for Grades 4–8, University of Maine/University of Southern Maine, 2005, https://umaine.edu/peace/wp-content/uploads/sites/173/2016/03/PEER_MEDIATION_FINAL_11.pdf [9 Jan 2024]

M4 Conflict management

Source: Thomas-Kilmann conflict mode instrument, 1974   47510EX © Westermann

4.7 The class council – solving your problems on your own?

KEY TERMS

class council
Klassenrat

VOCABULARY

PE (physical education)
Sportunterricht
assembly
Versammlung
chairman/ chairwoman
Gesprächsleiter/-in
timekeeper
Zeitwächter/-in
rule monitor
Regelwächter/-in
recorder
Protokollant/-in
to take the minutes
das Protokoll führen

M1 Demands in class 8c

We demand a different seating plan!

We want a different biology teacher.

We need more group tasks.

We want more PE!

We should decide on the class trip destination, not the teacher!

M2 What is the class council?

The idea comes from the classroom assembly, a concept developed by Célestin Freinet, a French pedagogue in the early 20th century. The class council is a democratic forum at
5 school. Students and teachers in one class discuss problems according to set rules. The goal is to find solutions together. They can also suggest ideas and discuss them as a class community. It is important that they all listen to each
10 other, then discuss and assess the suggestions made by the members. They chose a chairman/ chairwoman who leads the debate. He or she organizes votes and summarizes the results. There is also a timekeeper who limits the
15 speaking time of each speaker. The rule monitor makes sure that everybody sticks to the set rules. The recorder takes the minutes and summarizes the important results of the debate. The offices can rotate during a school year. Every student can put topics on the agenda. A 20 bulletin board in the classroom is useful for collecting topics. The teachers don't have privileges and must follow the same rules as all the students. The overall goal is to find compromises which everyone agrees with. If that is not 25 possible, a vote takes place, and the majority solution is put into action. The council writes the rules, so each class council has its own rules. It is recommended that rules on how to behave and how to speak are established. 30

Text by the author

M3 Cases for the class council?

Seven of us were not there the last time when you discussed where to go on hiking day. We would have voted for the amusement park and not for visiting the castle. That's not fair!

The vote for the class trip was 14 votes for the zoo and 7 for the bike trip. But 7 more abstained. What should we do now?

1 Discuss the suggestions (M1) in class: Are they realistic?
2 **Partner presentation:** Summarize the principles of the class council (M2).
3 Discuss how the class council can deal with both problems (M3).

How to hold a class council

Class council – what is it good for?

- The students state their concerns and work together to find solutions.
- Everyone is allowed to express their concerns in class. No one is left alone with their wishes or problems.
- Conflicts are solved together, to improve the class climate.

How do we do it?

Phase 1: Preparation

- Rules of conversation are agreed upon and recorded in writing, for example:
  - No one interrupts; anyone who wants to say something speaks up.
  - We talk to each other, not about each other.
  - Each person is allowed to finish.
  - No one is insulted.
  - There is no talking about people who are absent.
  - A simple majority is enough to decide a vote.
- Suitable topics for the class council are collected, either secretly or publicly, according to the pattern shown below.
- Tasks are distributed:
  - The chairman/chairwoman **gives the floor** and names the topics.
  - The recorder notes the topics of discussion and the results of the voting.
  - The rule monitor ensures that the rules of the discussion are observed.
  - The timekeeper checks that a topic is not discussed for too long.

VOCABULARY

to give the floor
das Wort erteilen
motion
hier: Antrag

Phase 2: Procedure

- The class makes a circle of chairs.
- The chairman/chairwoman opens the class council.
- The recorder reads the minutes of the last class council aloud; the group decides whether the agreements have been kept.
- The concerns are presented and discussed according to a predefined order and **motions** are voted on. The recorder writes down the results in the minutes.
- The tasks for the next class council are distributed.
- The chairman/chairwoman ends the class council.

Reflection: Exchange your impressions at the end: How was it? What could be better?

Our topics for the next class council:		
I think that …	I suggest that …	I don't think it's good that …

4.8 Democratic schools – better schools?

M1 How aliens see it …

Cartoon: Kevin Muir, 20 August 2019

M2 The Sudbury philosophy

Sudbury school students have total control over what they learn, how they learn, their educational environment and how they are evaluated. They choose their curriculum.
5 They choose their method of instruction. They choose, through a democratic process, how their environment operates. They choose with whom to interact. They choose if, how and when to be evaluated – often they choose
10 to evaluate themselves. This is radically different from any other form of education and this is what differentiates a Sudbury school. Why does a Sudbury school give this level of responsibility to the student? It is because
15 Sudbury educators believe that children are capable of assuming this level of responsibility. It is not a type of pedagogical tool used to motivate the students. The responsibility is real; the students absolutely have the ultimate say in their education. Giving real responsibil- 20 ity to the students allows them to gain experience making decisions and handling the consequences of their choices. In this way, the students gain experience and maturity.

Much of the current effort in education is 25 spent attempting to motivate students to learn. A Sudbury school doesn't spend any time attempting to motivate students; we believe that they are inherently motivated. We believe this because all the evidence of childhood develop- 30 ment supports it. Anyone who has observed a baby attempting to take his or her first steps or learn to talk can clearly see this. They struggle and fail and continue to struggle and fail until they finally – on their own – get it right and 35 start walking and talking. If not suppressed, this inherent motivation to grow and develop does not die when the child reaches school age.

*The Sudbury Model of Education, Kingston, NY: Hudson Valley Sudbury School, https://hvsudburyschool.com/
the-sudbury-model-of-education/ [6 Sep 2023]*

M3 Learning without rules – can it work?

As with [...] many other educational [...] school concepts, the Sudbury School has also been heavily criticized in some cases. Many parents and teachers fear that children are not moti-
5 vated to learn without rules and duties or that they are simply overwhelmed by the freedom of choice.

Another point of criticism is the lack of comparability of learning performance with that
10 at conventional schools: As learning at Sudbury schools takes place without a curriculum, lesson structure or class tests, it is difficult to objectively assess learning progress. However, the school has carried out studies on its graduates, according to which around 80 % 15 of graduates went on to attend college or university after graduating from the Sudbury School. It is very likely – and this is true of most [alternative] schools – that the Sudbury model does not work for every child. But for 20 those who struggle in mainstream schools, it may be the path to a more satisfying adult life.

Freiheit über alles: Sudbury Schulen, in: JAKO-O, Bad Rodach: HABA Sales GmbH & Co. KG, https://www.jako-o.com/de-de/magazin/kinderbetreuung-schule/schule-lernen/alternative-schulkonzepte/sudbury-schule [6 Sep 2023] (translated/modified)

HOT SPOT

In German, schools with alternative concepts are often referred to as "**Reformschulen**". In British and US English, the term "**reform school**" has a different meaning, as a penal or correctional school for teenagers (especially in the past).

M4 An alternative approach: FREI DAY

Am FREI DAY beschäftigen sich Kinder und Jugendliche mit aktuellen gesellschaftlichen und ökologischen Herausforderungen, die sich an den Global Goals der Vereinten Nationen orien-
5 tieren. Sie finden Antworten auf selbstgewählte Zukunftsfragen: Wird es in 30 Jahren noch Bäume geben? Was führt zu Konflikten, Terror und Flucht? Warum gibt es Rassismus? Oder was können wir gegen Armut tun? Sie finden
10 nicht nur Antworten auf diese Fragen; sie entwickeln gemeinsam mit anderen Schüler*innen konkrete Lösungen für die gesellschaftlichen und ökologischen Herausforderungen in ihrer Nachbarschaft und setzen diese als eigenes
15 Projekt selbstständig in ihrem Kiez um. Dabei recherchieren, planen und tüfteln sie selbst, wie sie ihre Projektideen in die Tat umsetzen können. Lehrer*innen treten in den Hintergrund und nehmen eine begleitende Rolle ein.

Am FREI DAY entwickeln Schüler*innen Hoff- 20 nung und Zuversicht für ihre Zukunft, da sie sich als selbstwirksam und handlungsfähig erleben. [...] Am FREI DAY können sie aktiv werden und ihre Umgebung selbst gestalten. Sie lernen, neue Perspektiven einzunehmen, ent- 25 wickeln ihre Problemlösefähigkeit und die Bereitschaft für Veränderung und Innovation.

Lösungen für Zukunftsfragen finden, Berlin: Schule im Aufbruch gGmbH, https://frei-day.org/der-frei-day/lernformat/ [9 Jan 2024]

INTERNET

WES-116955-481
Film clips about Sudbury Valley School and FREI DAY

WES-116955-482
Link to the 17 Sustainable Development Goals (SDGs)

1 Analyse the cartoon (M1). ▸ METHOD Cartoons, pp. 26 – 27

2 **Partner quiz:** Explain the concept of democratic schools using the example of Sudbury school (M2).

3 **a)** Summarize the criticism about Sudbury schools (M3).
   b) Would you like to attend such a school? Give reasons. ▸ Useful phrases (A), pp. 202 – 203

4 Evaluate the concept of FREI DAY (M4): would you like to have such a day at your school?

5 "Democratic schools – better schools?" Discuss this question. **MORE HELP**

Word cloud: world of school

compulsory schooling
homeschooling
school
iceberg model
mediation
suspension
representation
conflict management
compromise
win-win situation
school law & regulations
freedom of choice
social interaction
election
democracy
student representation
school conference
school uniform
rights & duties
headteacher
class representative
student council
class council

Gap text: democratic representation at school

At German secondary schools (e.g. Gymnasium, Realschule, etc.) every class elects one or more **1** to represent the interests of the class in the **2**.

Additionally, all the members of the student council elect the **3** to represent the interests of all the school's students.

Members of the **4** are also part of the **5** together with the parents, the teachers and the head-teacher, where they can influence important school decisions.

There is even a higher level of student representation: the **6**, where students can network with students from other schools and try to actively influence political decisions on the state level.

1 Explain the terms of the word cloud and connect them to their chapter topics.

2 Name the missing terms 1 to 6 in the text about democratic representation at school.
MORE HELP

Only a "puppet government"?

"Let's face it, we're nothing but a puppet government."

Cartoon: Dave Carpenter, 26 April 2010

VOCABULARY

staff
Belegschaft, Personal,
hier: Lehrkörper
to dare (to) do sth.
es wagen/sich trauen,
etw. zu tun
to reprimand sb.
jmdn. tadeln
to put in place
hier: in die Schranken
weisen
board
Gremium
transcript
hier: Zeugnis
principal
Schulleiter/-in
faculty
Lehrkörper
school district
Schulbezirk
flaw
Fehler, Schwachstelle
decathlon
Zehnkampf

Student council: effective or unnecessary attention?

In fiction, student council is seen as "serious business" with unparalleled freedom and special privileges. Student council members' power is so great that no member of the **staff**
5 will **dare reprimand** them for their overpowering actions. Rarely will they be **put in place** by their peers.

However, this is fiction and in reality, the student council has no power. Its members fight
10 hard for a spot on the **board** only to put on their **transcripts**, such as "Student Council President". All the power lies in the hands of the **principal**, **faculty**, and the **school district**. Student council in itself is a popularity con-
15 test, making those who did not get elected feel cheated of a spot they truly deserved. There are no criteria to justify those qualified for the positions because there are no qualifications. In order to make student council elections fair
20 and productive, there have to be criteria for those who apply. They should not be voted into positions by their peers but by the professional hierarchy above students – the teachers […].

25 Researchers have found that [a] majority of student councils had little to no budget to work with. Also, the biggest **flaw** in the concept is that communication is not regular and effective. Student councils can keep stu-
30 dents from wanting to be involved in democracy later in life. It is a popularity contest where the quiet, realistic students become sidelined.

If student representation in schools is the
35 goal, there are many different ways of achieving it. For example, join a club, become a team mascot, participate in some form of academic **decathlon**, contribute something beneficial to both the school and student body. Schools pay
40 lip service to the term "student council", action would be more appreciated. The lack of resources and communication hinder the possibilities and magnificent ideas of "what could be".

Amber Kakkar, Student Council: Effective or Unnecessary Attention?, in: Medium, o. O., 13 June 2019, https://medium.com/@askambz/student-council-effective-or-unnecessary-93761237d4a2 [26 Feb 2024] (modified)

1 Analyse the cartoon. ▸ METHOD Cartoons, pp. 26–27
2 Compare the American students council's power with that of the German student council.
3 Comment on the proposal to have the student council elected by the teachers.

1

2

3

4

5

6

7

8

Local politics

9

10

11

12

1 Which things in local politics concern you as a teenager?
Rank your personal TOP 3 tasks of your local government.
MORE HELP

2 Discuss your results in class.

5.1   Does my municipality concern me?

M1   Functions of local government*

Municipal tasks		Assigned tasks
Required tasks Local government must do these tasks but decides *how* to do so.	**Voluntary tasks** Local government decides *whether* and *how* to do these tasks.	**Instructional and ordering matters** Local government does these tasks for the federal and state governments, there is *no local decision-making.*
Examples	**Examples**	**Examples**
schools and kindergartens	sport sites and public pools	organization of elections
local streets and foothpaths	public parks and recreation areas	identity cards, passports
water and energy supply	theatres, museums, and other cultural facilities	registry office
sewage and waste disposal	public transport	social benefits (e.g. social assistance, housing benefits)
fire brigade	youth centre	vehicle registration

*In this table no distinction is made for the different types of local governments.
47478EX © Westermann

M2   German administrative structure

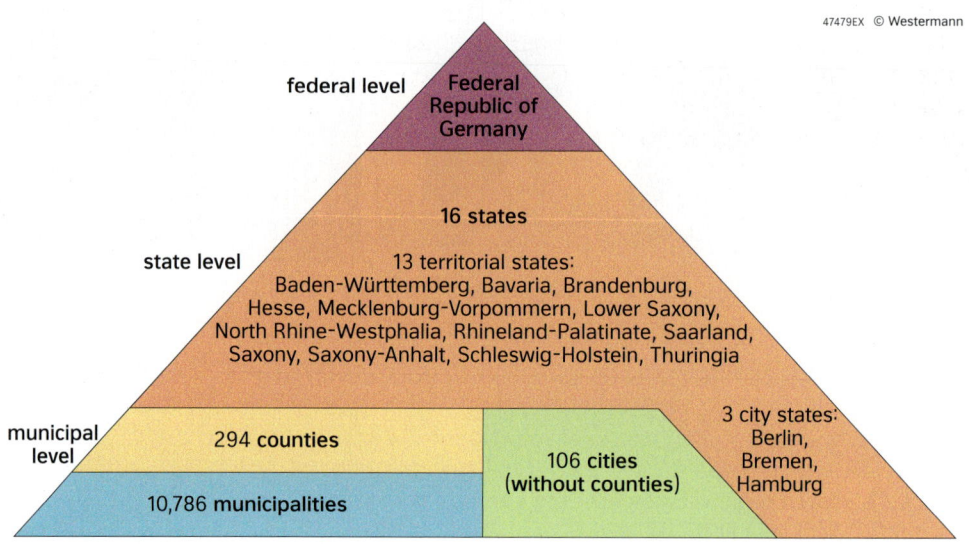

47479EX © Westermann

federal level — Federal Republic of Germany

state level — 16 states
13 territorial states:
Baden-Württemberg, Bavaria, Brandenburg, Hesse, Mecklenburg-Vorpommern, Lower Saxony, North Rhine-Westphalia, Rhineland-Palatinate, Saarland, Saxony, Saxony-Anhalt, Schleswig-Holstein, Thuringia

municipal level — 294 **counties** | 106 **cities (without counties)** | 3 city states: Berlin, Bremen, Hamburg
10,786 **municipalities**

(simplified representation)
Data: Statistisches Bundesamt (Destatis), Wiesbaden, 31 Mar 2003 (Landkreise und kreisfreie Städte); 31 Dec 2022 (Gemeinden)

M3 Basic law, Article 28 (2): Municipal autonomy

(2) Municipalities must be guaranteed the right to regulate all local affairs on their own responsibility, within the limits prescribed by the laws. [...] The guarantee of self-govern-
5 ment shall extend to the bases of financial autonomy; these bases shall include the right of municipalities to a source of tax revenues based upon economic ability and the right to establish the rates at which these sources shall be taxed.
10

M4 The principle of subsidiarity

Subsidiarity is an important principle in Germany (and in the European Union). It means that a public task should always be carried out by the authority closest to the problem in
5 question. Only if a lower level cannot do the task should a higher level take over. In this way, problems should always be solved as close to the citizens as possible. For example, a municipal authority, not a federal authority, should repair a streetlight if it is broken.
10

Text by the author

M5 Should public libraries be open on Sundays?

The Association of German Cities asks permission for public libraries to open on Sundays. Municipalities should decide themselves whether to open their libraries on Sundays.
5 This would let more people use them. The federal government needs to change the Working Time Act so that municipalities can regulate this themselves.
Helmut Dedy, Executive Director of the Asso-
10 ciation of German Cities, says that libraries are the German cultural and educational institutions that are visited the most, but they are also the only ones that are not open on Sundays. That is different from public pools, cinemas, and concert halls, which are all open on 15 Sundays.
A lot of people, especially single parents and people with long working hours, cannot go to libraries during opening hours on weekdays. Thus, they can only go there on Saturdays. 20 Dedy says that many cities know that their citizens would like the libraries to add to their opening hours. Therefore, the federal government should let cities open their public libraries on Sundays as well. The federal gov- 25 ernment intends to do this but has not yet changed the law.

„Sonntagsöffnung von Bibliotheken bundesweit ermöglichen", Berlin: Deutscher Städtetag, vertreten durch Helmut Dedy, 4 Dec 2023, https://www.staedtetag.de/presse/pressemeldungen/2023/arbeitszeitgesetz-sonntagsoeffnung-bibliotheken-ermoeglichen [22 Apr 2024] (translated and modified)

1 Assign the pictures on pp. 112–113 to the municipal tasks (M1).
2 **Think-Pair-Share:** Describe the administrative structure of Germany (M2).
3 **Extra:** Draw the administrative stucture (M2) for your own municipality.
4 Verify how independent municipalities are and how they can govern themselves (M3, M4). **MORE HELP**
5 Summarize the regulations on opening hours for public libraries and the position of the Association of German Cities on this issue (M5).
6 Discuss if municipalities in Germany should have the right to open libraries on Sundays. ▸ Useful phrases (A), pp. 202–203

5.2 Decisions in the municipality – tough choices?

🔑 KEY TERMS

administration
Verwaltung
citizen
Bürgerin/Bürger
city council/
municipal council
Stadtrat/
Gemeinderat
faction
Fraktion (einer Partei)
(Lord) Mayor
(Ober-)Bürger-
meisterin/
(Ober-)Bürgermeister

VOCABULARY

to demand
fordern
loan
Kredit
deficit
Verschuldung
budget
Haushalt
home for the elderly
Altenheim
taxes
Steuern
swing
Schaukel
seesaw
Wippe

M1 Headlines from the Neustadt local newspaper

Outdoor pool facing the end? Planned renovation in question

City council says keeping the public outdoor pool is too expensive

Mayor Schmitt: "We have to offer free-time activities for the people!"

"We cannot afford a renovation and our neighbouring town has a pool as well." (Municipal councillor Franka Mayer)

Local rescue swimmers association demands a place for swimming lessons for kids to prevent fatal accidents

M2 Municipal council meeting: outdoor pool debate

At yesterday's meeting of the Neustadt city council several council members demanded that the plans to renovate the local outdoor pool must be cancelled. They said that the
5 costs were now much higher than last year because of rising prices for building materials and not having enough construction workers. There was a lively debate among the different council factions and mayor Schmitt. He is in favour of renovating the pool as he says it is a 10 good attraction for citizens to use in their free time. He stated that a loan of €3.5 million would also be a good investment for future generations. A majority of the council members claimed that such an investment is not possible 15 now because the city has a deficit in its budget.

Text by the author

M3 Other demands from citizens of Neustadt

Mrs Haller, headteacher of a local school: Our school needs a new roof if we want our children to sit in a dry classroom.

Mr Kowalski, pensioner: The home for the elderly needs renovation which will cost hundreds of thousands of euros.

Mr Romano, owner of a local business: The business park is growing. We must build new roads and set up a good infrastructure. Then new companies will come and pay a lot of taxes.

Mrs Weyer mother of three children: I think we should put new swings and a new seesaw in the local playground.

1 Describe the situation of the outdoor pool in Neustadt using the headlines (M1).
2 Summarize the discussion in the city council (M2). ▸Useful phrases (C), pp. 204 – 205
3 State what other demands there are and give reasons for what you would invest in (M3).
4 Explain who decides on the outdoor pool and other requests of citizens (M4)
5 Illustrate how people (especially teens) can participate in local politics (M4).

M 4 Who is who?

committees

committee for finances

committee for elections

committee for youth affairs

committee for accounting

municipal administration

...

appoints

often: chairs or is member

leads

controls

municipal council

faction A | faction B | faction C | ...

if succesful: binding
if not succesful: council decides

mayor / Lord Mayor

can decide to hold

citizen's referendum

youth participation
depending on municipality, e.g. youth parliament / council

elect

if succesful

citizen's petition

elect

initiate / support

elect

teenagers

citizens

47480EX © Westermann

The **municipal council** (in larger cities: **city council**) represents the people in a municipality. In most federal states the members of the municipal council – known as councillors – are
5 elected for 5 years (except: Bavaria: 6, Bremen: 4). The size of the council depends on the size of the town. Smaller town councils, for example, have 8 members, while the Cologne city council has 90. The councillors often be-
10 long to parties (e.g. CDU, SPD, Greens, Liberals, etc.) and form factions in the council. The councillors usually work voluntary alongside their regular jobs, although in larger cities there are often full-time councillors.
15 To work efficiently, the councillors sit on different **committees** that have fewer members. These committees specialize in certain topics and prepare for discussions at the council meetings. Final decisions are made by the
20 council.
One of the most important tasks of the council is to set the municipal budget which **determines** how much money it can spend. Another important task is to control the mayor and the
25 administration.

The **mayor** (in larger cities: **Lord Mayor**) is the head of the municipality. She or he is elected directly by the citizens. The mayor's term of office varies between 5 and 10 years, depending on state regulations. She or he 30 represents the municipality in public and leads the administration, which puts the council's decisions into effect.

Municipal **citizens** can elect their council and mayor (or Lord Mayor) if they are 16 or 18 years 35 old, depending on state regulations (see p. 121, M5), if they are German or EU-citizens, and if they have lived in the municipality for more than three months. They **participate** not only indirectly in elections but also directly if they 40 initiate or support a **citizens' referendum** or vote in a **citizens' referendum** itself. Some municipalities (especially smaller towns and villages) hold regular **assemblies** to discuss important current affairs. People can also organize 45 a **citizens' initiative** to campaign for a cause.
Teenagers also have a say in many municipalities. They can have their own representation in an elected youth parliament or youth council. The youth representatives can, for 50 example, organize their own projects or **advise** the municipal council in the affairs of children and teenagers, such as a new skater park or local youth centre.

Text by the author

M5 Municipal administration: Who is responsible?

An example of the structure of a larger city administration

(Lord) Mayor: head of administration						
General administration	**Finances**	**Law, security and order**	**Schools and culture**	**Social issues and youth**	**Building and environment**	**Economy and transport**
Internal organization	Financial administration	Residents' registration office	School authority	Social welfare office	Urban development	Economic development
Municipal staff	Tax office	Office of public order	Cultural office	Youth welfare office	Building regulations office	Tourism
Audit office		Legal office	City library	Elderly care	Building authority	Road construction and maintenance
Press office	City treasury	Registry office	Adult education centre	Housing office		
Equal opportunities office		Fire brigade	Municipal archives		Parks and cemeteries	Public transport

47481EX © Westermann

M6 Where can I …?

a) I would like to find out more about the history of the city.

b) We want to get married soon.

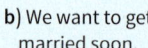

d) We would like to know what new cycle lanes are planned.

c) I moved here from Frankfurt a week ago and need to register.

e) I would like to open a start-up company.

f) My friends will visit and I want to find out about activities for them.

M7 The Neustadt budget plan

Income and expenses (in thousand euros)

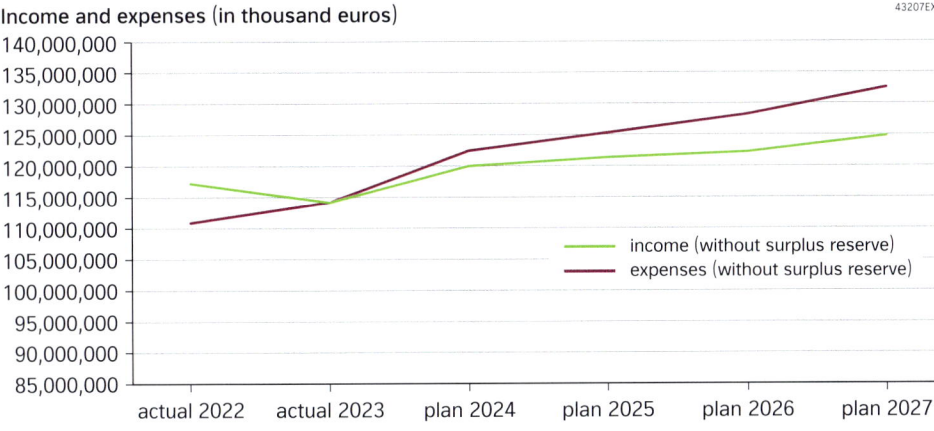

43207EX

— income (without surplus reserve)
— expenses (without surplus reserve)

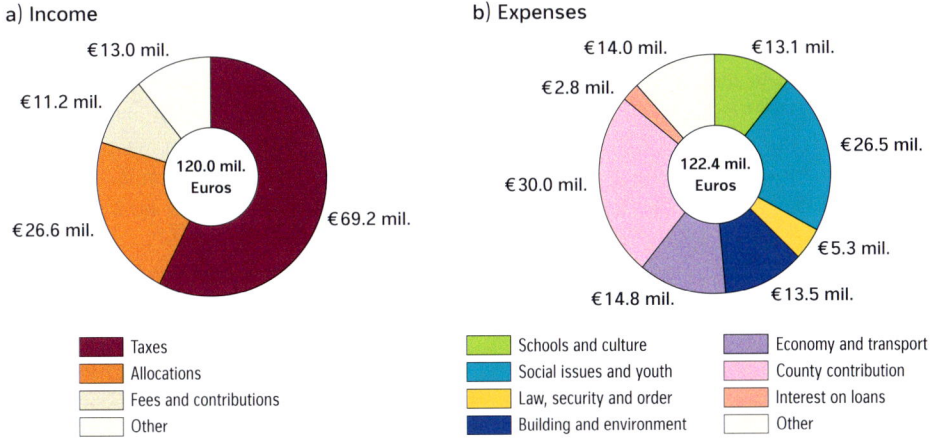

a) Income

€13.0 mil.
€11.2 mil.
120.0 mil. Euros
€26.6 mil.
€69.2 mil.

Taxes
Allocations
Fees and contributions
Other

b) Expenses

€14.0 mil.
€2.8 mil.
€13.1 mil.
€26.5 mil.
€30.0 mil.
122.4 mil. Euros
€5.3 mil.
€14.8 mil.
€13.5 mil.

Schools and culture
Social issues and youth
Law, security and order
Building and environment
Economy and transport
County contribution
Interest on loans
Other

Taxes include income tax (paid by working residents), business tax (paid by businesses), property tax (paid by property owners, e.g. homeowners), sales tax (paid when buying goods and services) and dog tax (paid by dog owners).

Allocations are financial resources from the federal, state, or county government, for example, for the construction of schools or roads. Some regular allocations are paid annually and others are paid only for a specific purpose.

Citizens pay **fees** for certain services, such as parking fees or entrance fees for swimming pools.

Contributions are required for using public facilities, such as for road renewal in front of a property or connection to the sewage system.

Interest is paid on a **loan**, after borrowing money from a bank.

1 Assign the concerns of the people (M6) to the right department of the administration (M5).

2 **Extra:** Every municipality is different: Research how the administration in your municipality is organized by visiting the town hall with your class.

3 Describe the city's budget plan (M7).

4 **Placemat:** Develop ideas on how the municipality can improve its finances.
MORE HELP

5.3 Can citizens influence local decisions?

KEY TERMS

citizens' initiative
Bürgerinitiative
citizens' petition
Bürgerbegehren
citizens' referendum
Bürgerentscheid
municipal elections
Kommunalwahlen
political participation
politische Teilhabe,
Partizipation

VOCABULARY

to apply
Antrag stellen
issue
Sachfrage,
achverhalt
requirements
Anforderungen
justification
Begründung
majority
Mehrheit
proportion
Anteil

M1 Political participation in the municipality

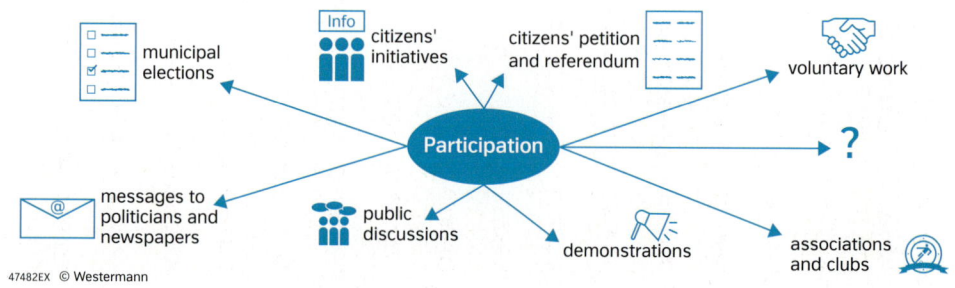

municipal elections

citizens' initiatives

citizens' petition and referendum

voluntary work

Participation

messages to politicians and newspapers

public discussions

demonstrations

associations and clubs

?

47482EX © Westermann

M2 The citizens' petition and citizens' referendum

In all federal states, citizens can act directly in local politics with the help of citizens' petitions and citizens' referendums.

A citizens' petition applies for a referendum on an issue. The goal of the petition is to col-[5]lect signatures to hold a referendum. All citizens who want to hold the referendum sign up on lists. If enough signatures are collected, the referendum can be held and the citizens vote on the issue. In most federal states, municipal [10] councils can also put a question to the citizens for a referendum.

Only citizens who can vote in local elections are allowed to participate in citizens' petitions and referendums. Depending on the federal [15] state, there are further legal requirements. Generally, many issues are excluded from a petition and referendum, often when they deal with municipal financial, budgetary and personnel matters. [20]

The question for the petition must be stated clearly, and it must usually be answered with "yes" or "no". A justification must also be included. The quorum – the number of signatures required for a citizens' petition – is de-[25]fined by the federal state.

If enough signatures are collected within the given time and all other formal requirements are met, the municipal council may adopt the initiative's request. If this does not happen, a [30] referendum is held.

A referendum is successful if a majority of voters agrees with the matter and this majority represents a certain proportion of all those who are allowed to vote. This quorum differs [35] depending on the federal state. A successful referendum has the same effect as a council resolution, so the administration must put it into practice in the same way.

Bürgerbegehren und Bürgerentscheid, in: Wegweiser Bürgergesellschaft, Bonn: Stiftung Mitarbeit, https://www. buergergesellschaft.de/mitentscheiden/buergerbeteiligung-in-stadt-land/buergerbeteiligung-in-der-kommune/ buergerbegehren-und-buergerentscheid [24 Nov 2023] (translated and modified)

M3 A citizens' initiative for the Neustadt outdoor pool

An initiative in Neustadt is campaigning for the renovation of the outdoor pool. The citizens argue that having an outdoor pool is not only a good free-time activity but it is also impor-tant for the kids. They have been losing their [5] swimming skills and accidents are increasing …

Text by the author

м4 Voter turnout in German elections

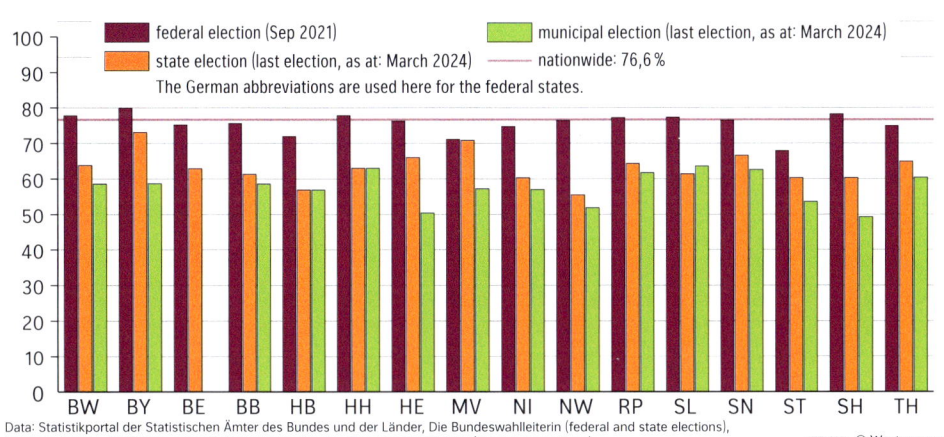

- federal election (Sep 2021)
- state election (last election, as at: March 2024)
- municipal election (last election, as at: March 2024)
- nationwide: 76,6%

The German abbreviations are used here for the federal states.

Data: Statistikportal der Statistischen Ämter des Bundes und der Länder, Die Bundeswahlleiterin (federal and state elections), Landeswahlleiter, Statische Landesämter, Landeszentralen für politische Bildung (municipal elections)

47512EX © Westermann

м5 At what age can you vote in local elections?

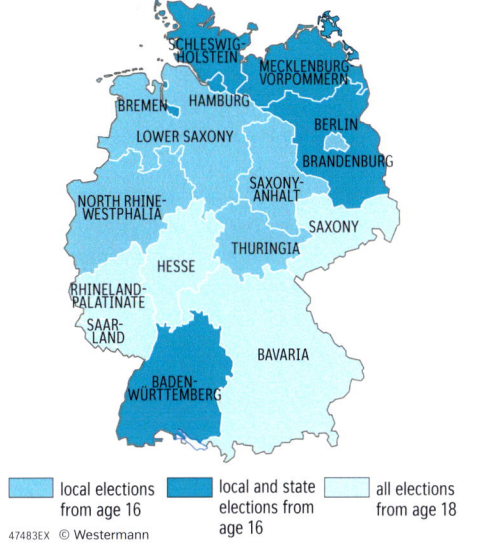

- local elections from age 16
- local and state elections from age 16
- all elections from age 18

47483EX © Westermann

м6 Some arguments on voting rights for young people

In favour of voting rights for under 18 years old	Against voting rights for under 18 years old
Most political decisions also affect young people. That is why they should also be allowed to vote.	There are plenty of opportunities for young people to get involved in politics, even if they cannot vote.
The young people of today are the adults of tomorrow. Therefore, having young people vote strengthens democracy at its roots.	Young people are easier to manipulate and more receptive to extreme positions than adults.
When young people are allowed to vote, their interest in politics will increase and they will become better informed.	Many young people are simply not interested in politics and are poorly informed.
…	…

Text by the author

---

1 Describe the different forms of political participation (M1).

2 **Think–Pair–Share:** Use M2 to describe what the citizens' initiative (M3) could do.

3 **Extra:** Find out the requirements for petitions and referendums in your federal state (number of signatures, deadlines, quorums, etc.).

4 Discuss the pros and cons of more direct political participation. **MORE HELP**

5 a) Analyse the chart (M4). ▸METHOD Statistics, pp. 20 – 21
   b) **Extra:** Think about reasons why fewer people are voting in local elections (M4).

6 a) Describe the map and find out when you can vote (M5).
   b) "16, 18 or what?" Hold a debate on the right voting age. Use M6 and find more arguments. ▸ METHOD Debate, pp. 48 – 49

How to simulate a municipal council meeting

VOCABULARY

agenda
Tagesordnung
residents' meeting
Einwohner-
versammlung
consultation
Beratung
resolution
Beschussfassung
chamberlain
Kämmerer (Leiter der
Finanzverwaltung)
to abstain
sich enthalten

While the citizens' initiative is campaigning to save the outdoor pool, some residents living near the pool would be quite happy if it closed: They feel often disturbed by the noise there in summer. In addition, some visitors "lose" their rubbish on the way to and from the pool. In the local newspaper, other residents also ask whether the pool is needed and say other issues are more important. The issue is now back on the council's agenda. First, a residents' meeting will give people a chance to tell their different opinions. The council will then decide on the issue. Therefore, the simulation has two phases.

Preparation

Form a group for each role. Read your role card carefully. Think about arguments you can use to convince others in the residents' meeting (only speakers from residents' interest groups) or in the council meeting (only representatives of the factions and mayor). Then decide which of you will play the role. Everyone else takes notes on their observations and gives feedback to the players afterwards.

Phase 1: Residents' meeting

The mayor has organized a public residents' meeting on the subject of "Renovation of the outdoor pool – yes or no?". He knows that the topic is controversial and has asked the speakers from various interest groups to give their opinions.
The councillors are also present. However, they do not take part in the debate, but only get an idea of what people think about the issue.

Phase 2: Council meeting

The council meeting starts after the residents' meeting. There is only one topic on the agenda: "Renovation of the outdoor pool: consultation and resolution".
So that the council knows what the renovation will cost, the chamberlain (head of financial administration) gives a report on the financial situation at the beginning.
A vote is taken at the end of the council meeting: The mayor formulates a resolution as a yes-no question. He is not allowed to vote himself. (You may change this after talking with your teacher.) Everyone with a green role card votes yes or no by raising their hands. It is also possible to abstain. The resolution is adopted if there are more votes in favour than against. If there is a tie, it is rejected. The speakers of the various interest groups pay attention to the council meeting. However, they do not take part in the discussions.

Reflection

After the simulation, all players briefly describe how they felt in their roles. The observers use their notes to give the players feedback. Discuss which position seemed the best and why. If necessary, collect ideas on what you would do differently next time to improve the simulation.

ROLE CARD: MAYOR

You chair both the residents' meeting and the council meeting. At first you say a few words of welcome and briefly introduce the topic. During the discussion, you give the floor to the speakers. If someone talks too long or gets off topic, tell them. You are responsible for running the meeting smoothly. At the council meeting, you first give the chamberlain the floor. Second, you give each faction the opportunity to present their opinion. Third, you open the debate between the council members. Finally, you put the question to the vote of the council and state the result. You are not allowed to vote yourself. You then bring the meeting to a close.

ROLE CARD: CITIZENS' INITIATIVE "PRO POOL"

You are the spokesperson for the citizens' initiative "Pro Pool". The outdoor pool is very important to you. You also lead the local swimming club and so are very interested in the renovation. You are concerned that many children cannot swim properly. What will it be like if they have to travel for kilometres to the nearest town just to learn to swim?

ROLE CARD: CITIZENS' "ASSOCIATION FOR SAVINGS"

You are chairman of the "Association for Savings". It was founded before the council decided to build the new town hall, which meant higher taxes to pay for the loan. Your aim is now to keep the debt from growing, which could lead to more taxes. Higher taxes burden the citizens and discourage companies from investing.

ROLE CARD: FACTION CENTER PARTY

There is no question that it's great for Neustadt to have the outdoor pool. But you do not think it is right to make cuts elsewhere or take out loans to pay for it. After all, the municipality will have to do more in the coming years, for example, to make the infrastructure for businesses better. So, you think that the renovation of the outdoor pool is unfortunately not possible now.

ROLE CARD: FACTION FREE LIST

In your eyes, the outdoor pool is very important for the municipality. Some businesses also benefit from it, especially the restaurants and hotels for tourists. However, you are very critical of other loans and you also reject tax increases. Instead, you can imagine other savings; the public library, for example, has fewer visitors than the outdoor pool.

ROLE CARD: CHAMBERLAIN

You are responsible for the municipality's finances. You provide information about the financial situation at the beginning of the meeting. The municipality's main source of income is taxes, mostly income tax from residents and business tax from local companies. Unfortunately, the municipality is already in debt because the new town hall was expensive. Renovating the pool would create a big hole in the budget. The municipality would probably have to take out a loan, which it would have to pay back with interest. Alternatively, cuts could be made elsewhere, perhaps at the public library.

ROLE CARD: POOL NEIGHBOURS

You are the spokesperson for the neighbours of the outdoor pool. You are often quite annoyed by the pool. Swimming is all well and good, but all that noise during nap time? In addition, you and the others neighbours have to collect all the rubbish from the street that visitors to the outdoor pool throw around.

ROLE CARD: TOURIST OFFICE

You are the head of the tourist office. You feel responsible for making sure that Neustadt offers tourists as much as possible. The outdoor pool is a good tourist attraction, especially for families on holiday. If the pool disappeared, fewer people might come to Neustadt. And fewer tourists mean less income from tax revenue for the municipality.

ROLE CARD: FACTION VOTERS PARTY

The outdoor pool is not only popular for swimming, for many people in Neustadt it is also a favourite meeting place in summer. Some senior citizens like to play chess or boules there, for example. Children and young people can spend their free time at the pool. You think it would be okay to take out a loan for this. After all, growing tourism will bring in more revenue in the long term. So, you are in favour of the renovation.

ROLE CARD: ENVIRONMENTAL PARTY

You think exercise in fresh air is a good thing. But you could do that without an outdoor pool. The amount of rubbish is also a thorn in your side. You are concerned about the energy that an outdoor pool needs; for example, you think that the heated whirlpools are unnecessary. So, you have doubts as to whether the renovation is necessary.

5.4 The decision-making process in the municipality – a never-ending cycle?

M1   The policy cycle: decision-making never stops

In every political community there are challenges and problems to solve. Elected politicians are especially responsible for this, as they make the political decisions. However,
5 there are also many other factors and actors that influence the political decision-making process, whether citizens that make political demands or the media that report on problems.
10 The policy cycle is a model to understand this complex process better. It divides the political decision-making process into different stages. At the same time, it shows that there are rarely "eternal" solutions for problems. Often a
15 problem seems different after a time because the situation has changed.

Text by the author

1 Problem recognition / Agenda setting
Problemwahrnehmung / Themensetzung

At the beginning of the cycle, there is a problem that attracts public attention. This often happens through the media. Citizens' initiatives, political parties or interest groups can also try to put a problem on the political agenda.

5 Evalution / Reactions
Bewertung / Reaktionen

After a time, the results of the decision become clear. The decision-makers then evaluate it as positive or negative. The citizens can also react: While some may see the decision positively, others criticize it harshly.
If the decision is mainly positively, it will remain in place and the policy cycle will end.
If the decision is viewed more critically, the cycle begins again.

6 End
Beendigung

2 Debate

Auseinandersetzung

The problem is then discussed publicly, and solutions are suggested. Political parties play a special role here, trying to win people over in favour of their solutions. At this stage, there are often conflicts of interest.

Policy Cycle

3 Decision-making

Entscheidungsfindung

Finally, the responsible political institution (such as the municipal council) decides. The decision is often a compromise of different solutions.

4 Implementation

Umsetzung / Implementierung

The responsible institutions (e.g. the municipal administration) then put the decision into practice.

1 **Think–Pair–Share:** Analyse the outdoor pool problem (pp. 116 –123) with the help of the policy cycle (M1).

2 Illustrate possible new problems if the outdoor pool is (not) renovated.

5.5 Youth parliament – a success story?

M1 Voices from teens

"I wish there was a really good music festival here."

"I would like to see the playground renovated."

"We should fight for more money for kids in shelters."

"It is high time that we get a youth centre where we can spend our free time."

"The outdoor pool has to stay open!"

M2 What is a youth parliament?

We are the youth parliament

The youth parliament – also nicknamed "Ju-Pa", which is short for its German name "Jugendparlament" – represents Monheim's youth at local policy level. It is elected every
5 two years. Boys and girls aged 12/13 to 19/21 years are entitled to vote for its members and stand for election.

The mission of the youth parliament is to:
- give all young people a voice and act on
10 their behalf,
- ensure that young people can participate and are involved in political and administrative planning and decision-making processes,
- raise awareness for young people's needs,
- promote understanding between people with different nationalities, ethnic roots, cultures and denominations,
- contribute to political education.

We are the Youth Parliament, Monheim am Rhein: Büro des Jugendparlaments, https://jupa.monheim.de/english/ [7 Sept 2023]

M3 Youth parliament requests four cycle lanes

a) Es ist die Jugend, die in Leipzig besonders gern und oft mit dem Rad fährt. Es überrascht also nicht, wenn das Jugendparlament jetzt einen Antrag an den Stadtrat stellt, dass mehrere Straßen im Musikviertel zu Fahrradstraßen umgewidmet werden sollen. Hier befinden sich auf engstem Raum mehrere Hochschulen, täglich sind hier tausende Studierende mit dem Rad unterwegs. Es könnte ein Anfang sein, die Stadt wirklich fahrradfreundlich zu machen. 10

Leipzig hat rund 45.000 Studierende und auch die Schülerzahlen sollen sich bis 2030 verdoppeln", stellt der Jugendbeirat, der den Antrag für das Jugendparlament einreicht, in der Begründung fest. "Die Mehrheit dieser jungen Menschen bewältigt ihre täglichen Wege auf dem Fahrrad. [...]" 15

Ralf Julke, Jugendparlament beantragt vier Fahrradstraßen für das Musikviertel, in: Leipziger Zeitung online, 29 Jan 2018, https://www.l-iz.de/wirtschaft/mobilitaet/2018/01/Jugendparlament-beantragt-vier-Fahrradstrassen-fuer-das-Musikviertel-204065 [7 Sep 2023]

b) Das Musikviertel in Leipzig soll Fahrradstraßen bekommen. Das hat nach Medienberichten der Stadtrat in seiner Sitzung gestern mit großer Mehrheit beschlossen. Das Jugendparlament hatte einen entsprechenden Prüfantrag gestellt. Jetzt wird also geprüft, ob die Beethovenstraße, die Straße des 17. Juni, die Wächterstraße und die Wilhelm-Syfferth-Straße die Klassifizierung Fahrradstraße bekommen. Radfahrer haben in Fahrradstraßen absoluten Vorrang. Sind Autos zugelassen, dürfen sie höchstens 30 km/h fahren. Das Nebeneinanderfahren ist für Radfahrer erlaubt. 10

Musikviertel in Leipzig soll Fahrradstraßen bekommen, Leipzig, Radio Leipzig, 17 May 2018, https://www.radioleipzig.de/beitrag/musikviertel-in-leipzig-soll-fahrradstrassen-bekommen-536694/ [25 May 2024]

M4 Youth parliament decides to quit

Penzberg – Der Entscheidung des aktuellen Jugendparlament, sich aufzulösen, war erwartet worden. [...] Der einstimmige Beschluss der sieben anwesenden Jungparlamentarier am Montagabend hatte aber auch einen zweiten Teil: Es soll im Sommer einen Wahltermin für ein neues Jugendparlament geben. Zumindest soll versucht werden, dann mehr Erfolg zu haben. Der Grund für das Aus: Für die Wahl im Januar gab es nur sieben Kandidaten. Für den ursprünglichen Wahltermin im November waren es sogar noch weniger gewesen. Jungparlamentarier Max Link sagte in der Sitzung am Montag, es hätte etwas gebracht, in die Schulklassen zu gehen und über das Jugendparlament zu erzählen. Das geschah aber nicht, anders als vor zwei Jahren bei der Gründung des Jugendparlaments, als genug Kandidaten zur Verfügung standen. „Es ging zeitlich nicht", sagte Pauline Link. 20

Wolfgang Schörner, Jugendparlament beschließt eigenes Ende, in: Merkur online, 23 Jan 2018, https://www.merkur.de/lokales/weilheim/penzberg-ort29272/jugendparlament-in-penzberg-beschliesst-eigenes-ende-9552073.html [7 Sep 2023]

VOCABULARY

einen Antrag stellen
to file a motion
Fahrradstraßen
cicle lanes
umwidmen
to repurpose
Hochschulen
universities
Jugendbeirat
youth advisory board
etw. auflösen
to dissolve sth./
to close down
einstimmiger Beschluss
unanimous decision
Wahltermin
election date
proposal
Vorschlag

1 Name reasons why kids and teens might want to act politically. You can start with M1.
2 Explain what a youth parliament / youth city council is (M2).
3 Summarize M3 a) and b) for your American exchange student and tell him if the proposal was successful. (Remember: He has never heard of a youth parliament.)
  ▸ METHOD Mediation, pp. 72 – 73
4 **Extra:** Do research about your municipality – does it have a youth parliament?
5 Discuss if youth parliaments are a success story, or not (M3, M4). **MORE HELP**
6 **Chose a task:**
  a) Design a flyer to help find new members for the youth parliament.
  b) Collect ideas for topics that you think a youth parliament could deal with.

5.6 Are you interested in politics?

M1   A survey

How interested are you in political issues?
at national level   ☐ VERY MUCH   ☐ A LITTLE BIT   ☐ NOT AT ALL
at local level   ☐ VERY MUCH   ☐ A LITTLE BIT   ☐ NOT AT ALL

What political/social/economical topics are you interested in? _____

How often do you inform yourself about political issues?
                                    ☐ EVERY DAY   ☐ ONCE A WEEK   ☐ LESS OFTEN

Where do you inform yourself? _____

Are you happy
with national politics?   ☐ VERY MUCH   ☐ A LITTLE BIT   ☐ NOT AT ALL
with local politics?   ☐ VERY MUCH   ☐ A LITTLE BIT   ☐ NOT AT ALL

What changes would you like to see so that the interests of young people are considered in politics more? _____

Are you worried about the future? ☐ VERY MUCH   ☐ A LITTLE BIT   ☐ NOT AT ALL

What political/social/economical topics worry you now? _____

Text by the author

M2   What do young people think about politics? A study

43205EX

a) Interest in politics (in %)

How interested are you in politics?
14- to 24-year-olds

| 22 | 42 | 29 | 7 |

formal high education

| 35 | 47 | 16 | 2 |

formal medium education

| 15 | 49 | 31 | 5 |

formal low education

| 15 | 36 | 38 | 11 |

very interested   not interested at all

People my age are interested in politics.
14- to 24-year-olds

| 7 | 36 | 47 | 8 |

formal high education

| 11 | 46 | 35 | 7 |

formal medium education

| 6 | 35 | 47 | 10 |

formal low education

| 4 | 30 | 55 | 8 |

applies fully   does not apply at all

Survey population: German-speaking population between ages 14 and 24, missing values to 100 per cent: don't know, number replying: 2,124
Source: Vodafone Stiftung Deutschland gGmbH (Hrsg.), Hört uns zu!, Jugendstudie 2022, Düsseldorf, March 2022, p. 4

b) Informing about politics (in %)

Interest in federal elections

I regularly inform myself about political parties
and politicians in the election campaign.

| 17 | 36 | 33 | 14 | 14- to 24-year-olds[1] |
| 22 | 38 | 28 | 12 | eligible voters[2] |

I am interested in the election campaign
of political parties and politicians.

| 27 | 34 | 26 | 13 | 14- to 24-year-olds[1] |
| 32 | 33 | 24 | 11 | eligible voters[2] |

I am interested in how the election turns out.

| 57 | 28 | 11 | 4 | 14- to 24-year-olds[1] |
| 68 | 23 | 7 | 2 | eligible voters[2] |

applies fully   does not apply at all

How often do you inform yourself about political issues?

14- to 24-year-olds[1]

■ at least once a day
■ at least once a week
■ less often

| 31 | 29 |
| 40 | |

[1]Survey population: German-speaking population between ages 14 and 24, number replying: 2,124
[2]Survey population: German-speaking population between ages 18 and 24, number replying: 1,375
Source: Vodafone Stiftung Deutschland gGmbH (Hrsg.), Hört uns zu!, Jugendstudie 2022, Düsseldorf, March 2022, pp. 5, 9

c) Satisfaction with democracy and future prospects (in %)

43206EX

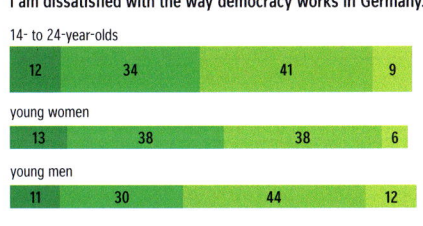

I am dissatisfied with the way democracy works in Germany.

14- to 24-year-olds
| 12 | 34 | 41 | 9 |

young women
| 13 | 38 | 38 | 6 |

young men
| 11 | 30 | 44 | 12 |

fully agree ——————————————— do not agree at all

I am worried about the future.

14- to 24-year-olds
| 43 | 43 | 12 | 1 |

young women
| 47 | 41 | 9 | 1 |

young men
| 38 | 44 | 15 | 2 |

fully agree ——————————————— do not agree at all

Survey population: German-speaking population between ages 14 and 24, missing values to 100 per cent: don't know, number replying: 2,124
Source: Vodafone Stiftung Deutschland gGmbH (Hrsg.), Hört uns zu!, Jugendstudie 2022, Düsseldorf, March 2022, pp. 13, 27

d) Wishes/demands on politics (in %)

What changes would you like to see so that the interests of young people are considered in politics more?

Legend:
- 14- to 24-year-olds
- formal high education
- formal medium education
- formal low education

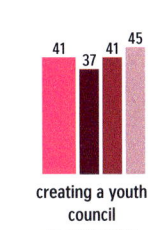
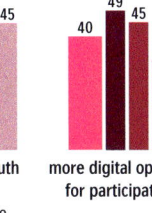

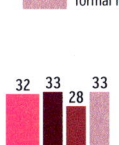
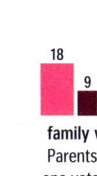
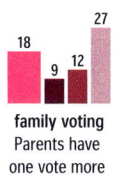

more young politicians	creating a youth council to advise the federal government	more digital options for participation	more participation beyond elections e.g. by citizens' referenda	voting at 16 years old	family voting Parents have one vote more for their children.
54 / 64 / 57 / 46	41 / 37 / 41 / 45	40 / 49 / 45 / 32	39 / 46 / 42 / 33	32 / 33 / 28 / 33	18 / 9 / 12 / 27

Survey population: German-speaking population between ages 14 and 24, number replying: 2,124
Source: Vodafone Stiftung Deutschland gGmbH (Hrsg.), Hört uns zu!, Jugendstudie 2022, Düsseldorf, March 2022, p. 28

M3 Ways for young people to participate

INTERNET

WES-116955-562
Links to information on some forms of participation

- Youth organizations of political parties (e.g. Green Youth, Young Socialists, Young Liberals, Young Union)
- youpaN – Youth panel for education about sustainable development
- youcoN – Youth conference for education about sustainable development
- Youth councils (e.g. Bavarian Youth Council) to foster interests of young people

- Youth forums (e.g. JugendPolitikTage from the Bundesministerium für Familie, Senioren, Frauen und Jugend)
- Y7 Summit (G7 Youth Summit) with international delegations of teenagers
- European Youth Parliament
- NGOs (e.g. Greenpeace, Friends of the Earth, Amnesty International, ...)
- Local clubs (in sports, music, culture, ...)

1 Conduct the survey in your class (M1).
2 Analyse the charts (M2) in groups and share your results with the class.
▸ METHOD Statistics, pp. 20–21
3 Compare your survey findings (M1) with those from the youth study (M2).
4 Illustrate ways how youths can participate in politics (M3).
5 **Extra:** Research in your municipality which of the organizations (M3) you have.
6 **a)** Write a short statement: Why I am (not) interested in politics in my municipality.
   b) Discuss your statements in class.

Matching excercise: municipal tasks

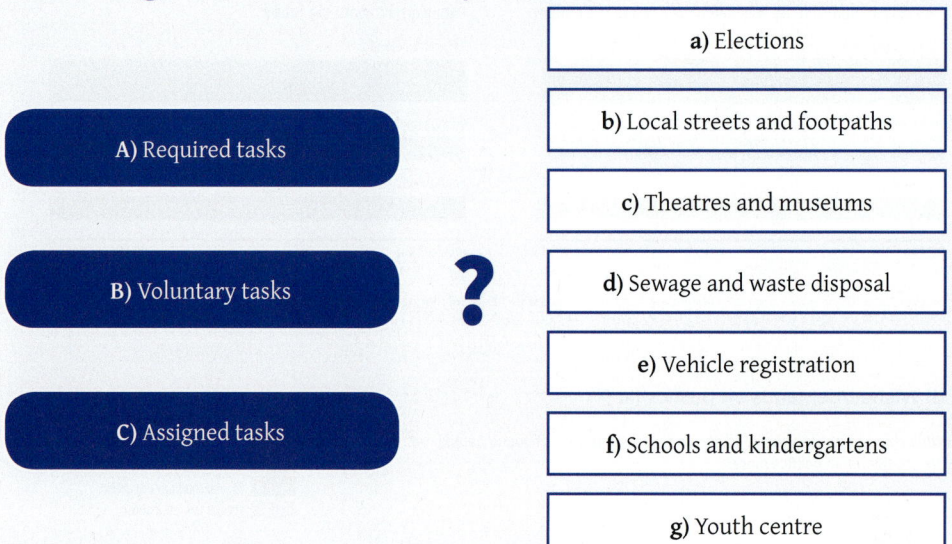

- **A)** Required tasks
- **B)** Voluntary tasks
- **C)** Assigned tasks

?

- **a)** Elections
- **b)** Local streets and footpaths
- **c)** Theatres and museums
- **d)** Sewage and waste disposal
- **e)** Vehicle registration
- **f)** Schools and kindergartens
- **g)** Youth centre

Matching excercise: who is responsible?

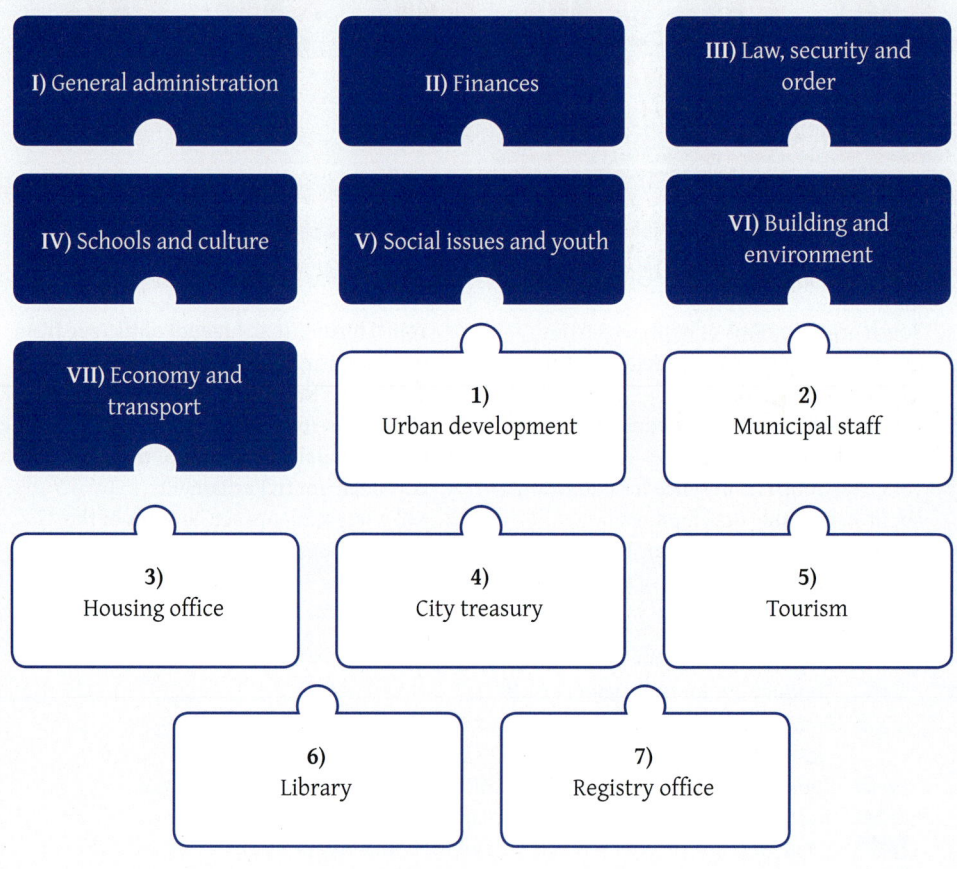

- **I)** General administration
- **II)** Finances
- **III)** Law, security and order
- **IV)** Schools and culture
- **V)** Social issues and youth
- **VI)** Building and environment
- **VII)** Economy and transport
- **1)** Urban development
- **2)** Municipal staff
- **3)** Housing office
- **4)** City treasury
- **5)** Tourism
- **6)** Library
- **7)** Registry office

1   Match the examples with the headings.

Administrative structure in Canada

INTERNET

WES-116955-571
Link to more
information about
local government
in Canada

Your local government

About your government in Canada

The City of Toronto is your local government, also known as municipal government. In Canada we have three levels of government: federal, provincial and municipal. Each level has different responsibilities and often work together. The City of Toronto provides services that have a direct impact on our daily lives.

Municipal

The **City of Toronto** is your local government and is responsible for:
water treatment, parks, libraries, garbage collection, public transit, land use planning, traffic signals, police, paramedics, fire services, sewers, homeless shelters, childcare, recreation centres and more. Powers are defined by the City of Toronto Act, 2006.

Provincial

The **Government of Ontario** provides services across the province and is responsible for:
health, education, driver and vehicle licensing, energy, human rights, natural resources, environment, social services and more. Powers are defined by the Constitution Act, 1867.

Federal

The **Government of Canada** provides services across the country and is responsible for:
national defence and Canadian Armed Forces, postal service, banking, immigration and citizenship, census, foreign affairs and international trade, agriculture and more. Powers are defined by the Constitution Act, 1867.

Getting involved in Toronto, Canada

Get involved

Now that you have an understanding of how local government works we want to tell you about the ways you can get involved.

Be informed:
- Watch Council and committee meetings
- Follow along with the agenda
- Subscribe to email updates
- Follow on social media
- View public notices
- Access information

Have your say:
- Contact your councillor
- Participate in a committee meeting
- Participate in the City budget
- Participate in a consultation
- Participate in a local poll
- Vote in local elections

Serve your city:
- Apply to serve on a City board
- Become a candidate

1 a) Analyse the administrative structure in Canada (chart above).
  b) Compare Canada's administrative structure with that of Germany.
2 Explain how citizens can get involved in local politics in Toronto (chart below).

1

2

3

4

5

6

Living in global contexts

"As a global community, we face a choice. Do we want migration to be a source of prosperity and international solidarity, or a byword for inhumanity and social friction?"

António Guterres (*1949, Portuguese politician, and secretary-general of the UN), Towards a new global compact migration, United Nations: Secretary-General, 11 Jan 2018, https://www.un.org [28 Nov 2023]

„Krise kann ein produktiver Zustand sein. Man muss ihr nur den Beigeschmack der Katastrophe nehmen."

Max Frisch (1911–1991, Swiss writer), cit. in: zitate.eu, Bad Vöslau: zitate.at gmbh, https://www.zitate.eu [28 Nov 2023]

"Where globalization means [...] that the rich and powerful now have new means to further enrich and empower themselves at the cost of the poorer and weaker, we have a responsibility to protest in the name of universal freedom."

Nelson Mandela (1918–2013, South African activist and politician), Address on receiving the Freedom Award, Johannesburg: Nelson Mandela Foundation, 22 Nov 2000, http://www.mandela.gov.za [28 Nov 2023]

"Globalization is a fact, because of technology, because of an integrated global supply chain, because of changes in transportation. And we're not going to be able to build a wall around that."

Barack Obama (*1961, former president of the USA), cit. in: Jessie Hellmann, Obama: We can't 'build a wall' around globalization, in: The Hill, o.O., 22.07.2016, https://thehill.com [28 Nov 2023]

"You come to my house according to my rules."

Georgia Meloni (*1977, Italian Prime Minister and chairwoman of the right-wing party Fratelli d'Italia), in: Chico Harlan/Stefano Pitrelli, Georgie Meloni's interview with The Washington Post, 13 Sep 2022, https://www.washingtonpost.com/ [28 Nov 2023]

„Wir können die Grenzen nicht schließen. Wenn man einen Zaun baut, werden sich die Menschen andere Wege suchen."

Angela Merkel (*1954, former chancellor of Germany), in „Anne Will" on 7 Oct 2015, cit. in: Annett Meiritz, Merkels ehrlichste Regierungserklärung, in: Spiegel online, 8 Oct 2015, https://www.spiegel.de [28 Nov 2023]

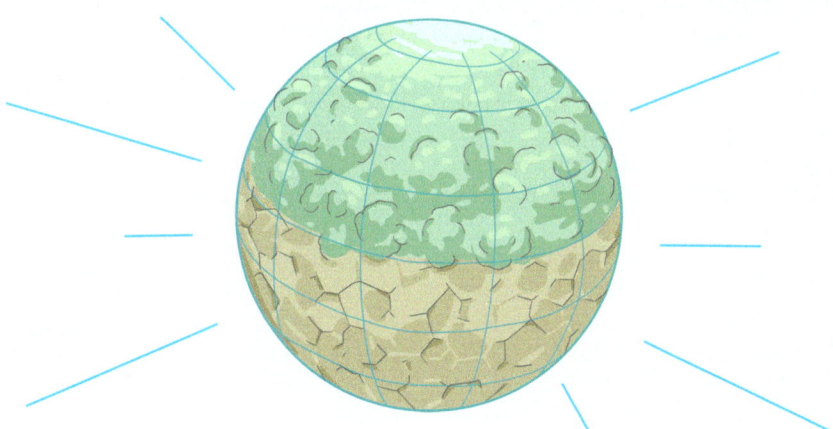

1 a) Describe the photos and explain the quotes. ▸ Useful phrases (C), pp. 203 – 204
   b) Find umbrella terms for political problems or aspects related to them.
2 The 21ˢᵗ century brings modern conveniences but also new political dangers and challenges. Create a visualization of what you know about this. Include the problems and aspects from task 1. You can start as shown above. **MORE HELP**

6.1 Migration – worth the effort?

M 1 Reasons for migration

M 2 Why do people leave their countries?

People have different reasons for leaving the place where they live. Some just move from one city to another in one country (internal migration) and others emigrate to a new coun-
5 try. Some plan to live in the new country just for a while (temporary migration), for example, until a situation gets better. However, sometimes the situation in their home country does not change and the temporary migration
10 becomes permanent.
If people flee their country of origin, they often do so because of war, persecution, and human rights violations. These people have no choice – they must leave (forced migration). Especial-
15 ly people who fear discrimination because of their ethnicity, religion, sexual orientation, or political opinion feel they have no choice and have to seek asylum in a new country. Starvation, extreme poverty, natural disasters, or a
20 combination of these are other reasons to emigrate.

Some people have a free choice: they move because they believe they will find better jobs in another country (labour migration). They might have qualifications (highly skilled labour mi- 25
gration) which the new country needs, or they hope to work without training (unskilled low-wage labour migration). Additionally, some people simply want to start or finish their education abroad (educational migration). 30
Finally, it is important to note the difference between legal migration and illegal migration. A legal migrant usually applies officially for a temporary or permanent stay. In Europe, however, people who are citizens of another EU 35 country need not apply. People who are forced to migrate from outside the EU must file an application for political asylum. Illegal migration includes those people who migrate secretly without official permission. Often, they 40 become victims of exploitation; they also might work illegally because they cannot work legally in the country.

Text by the author

M3 Reports on migration experiences

a) Ryyan Alshebl fled Suwaida in southern Syria at the age of 21. In 2015, he decided to leave Syria to escape military service. The journey was dangerous: he
5 first passed through Lebanon and then had to take a rubber dinghy to Lesbos, Greece. He later came to Germany. First he arrived in Karlsruhe, then moved to Calw and Althengstett. He learned Ger-
10 man and even became mayor of Ostelsheim in Baden-Wuerttemberg.

Pascal Eichner/dpa, Geflüchteter aus Syrien wird Bürgermeister, ZDFheute, Mainz: ZDF, 3 Apr 2023, https:// www.zdf.de/nachrichten/panorama/ryyan-alshebl-ostelsheim-baden-wuerttemberg-buergermeister-100. html [5 Mar 2024] (translated/modified)

b) "My father came in the early 1980s from Italy to Germany. He had a lot of experience with cars and wanted to work in the famous German car industry. Little did he know: since he had no docu-
5 ments to prove his experience, every attempt he made to become a mechanic was denied. As a result, he started working in Italian restaurants in Berlin. There he spoke mostly Italian and only two years later, he met my mother. Another two
10 years later, I was born. Until his death, he always worked as a chef to earn money for his family. Until I was sixteen, I was not sure whether I was Italian or German or both."

Text by the author

INFO

In **Syria**, there has been a civil war since 2011.

c) "I started school when I was 14 because there was no school for me," says the now 18-year-old Shamshidha. Together with her sister Yasmin [...] Shamshidha attends an informal school in the Malaysian capital Kuala Lumpur every day. [...] In Malaysia, where 150,000 refugees are registered, refugees have no legal status. The children of the Rohingya Muslim minority, who
5 fled to Malaysia from Myanmar more than 10 years ago, are not allowed to attend public schools.

Rohingya-Teenager auf der Suche nach dem Glück, Bonn: UNO-Flüchtlingshilfe e. V., https://www.uno-fluechtling-shilfe.de/hilfe-weltweit/fluechtlinge-erzaehlen/shamshidah-aus-myanmar [5 Mar 2024] (translated and modified)

M4 Push and pull factors

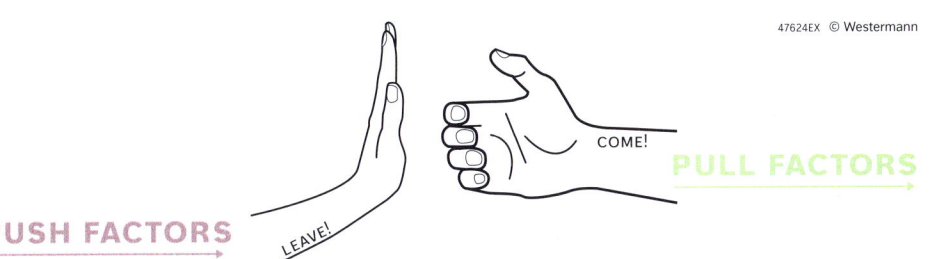

47624EX © Westermann

PULL FACTORS

COME!

PUSH FACTORS

LEAVE!

INFO

Push factors are unfavourable aspects about a place which make people go away from there.

Pull factors are beneficial aspects that make people want to move to a certain country.

1 **Think-Pair-Share:** Create a mind map about reasons which would make you personally leave the country and what could be difficult about it. Use the pictures for help (M1) and add ideas from your partner and class. ▸ METHOD Visualization, pp. 136–137

2 Identify types and further reasons for migration (M2). Add them to your mind map.

3 Analyse the reports and note the type of migration they show (M3). **MORE HELP**

4 **a)** Explain in your own words what push and pull factors are (M4).
b) Mark the examples in your mind map (task 1) as either push or full factors.
c) Extra: Categorize the push and pull factors as environmental, social, economic, and political factors.

5 Discuss the question "Migration – worth the effort?". ▸ Useful phrases (A), pp. 202–203

How to visualize content

Visualization – what is it good for?

Visualization is the illustration of content through a graphic and structured presentation. You can use visualization techniques both in your own learning and in a presentation. In this way you can:

- understand complicated content better, for example, in texts,
- present content in a way that is easier to re-member,
- show complex data more simply,
- educate both presenter and audience better,
- appear professional and confident, which can lead to better marks.

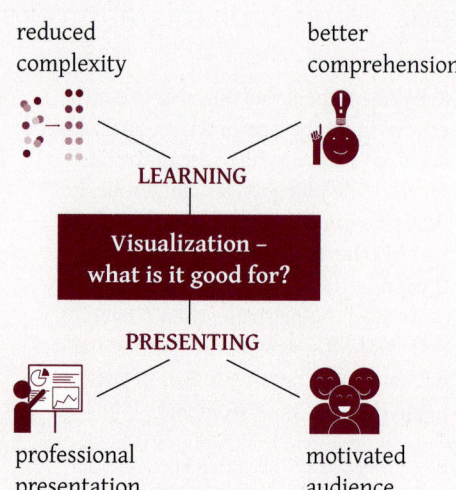

How do I do it?

Step 1: Brainstorm and cluster

- Write down all possible aspects that are related to your topic.
- Try to think of it from as many perspectives and angles as possible.
- After first collecting ideas, go through the individual points and group those with a similar gist. Cluster connected ideas with the help of a catchy keyword (highlighted in red in the above example).

Step 2: Choose a method of visualization

Decide on the type of visualization that best suits your object and your purpose.

Mind map

A mind map is a basic type of visualization that is often used when brainstorming. You can improve your mind map after the initial brainstorm with the help of keywords (see example above).

To create a mind map, write the topic in the centre. From there, you draw lines ("branches") on which you write subtopics/keywords. From the subtopics, you draw further lines on which you add related aspects. A well-structured mind map is a good tool to give an overview, so keep it short.

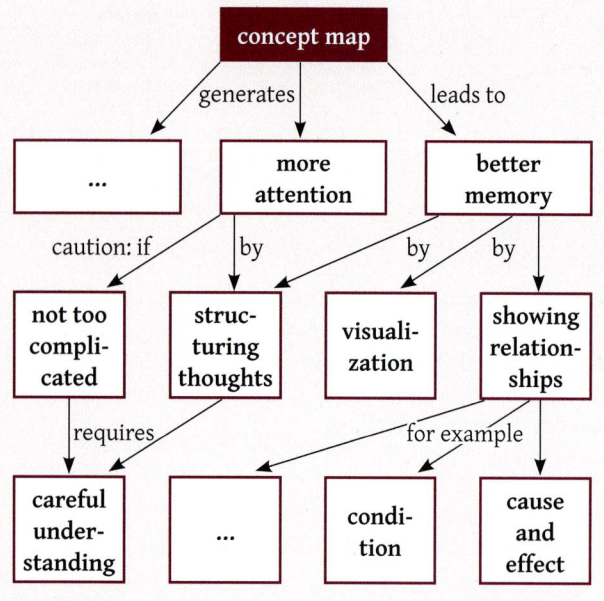

Concept map

This method is more extensive compared to a mind map because it names the connections between the mentioned items. The topic is not written in the middle, but at the top or the lefthand side. From there, the keywords are arranged in a logical sequence and connected with words that clarify the nature of the relationship.

Possible relations:

- cause and effect: lead to, create, induce, generate, provoke, cause, result
- condition: if … then, assume, require, depend on
- means to an end: while, as, through, by (use/means of), hence
- feature/definition: mean, marked by, characteristic of
- example: for instance/example, such as
- alternative: either … or

Flow chart

This method

- shows processes or data flow,
- can give step-by-step advice on how to handle a problem,
- gives a reference point in a project,
- can be used to document a process,
- can help to identify **bottlenecks**: if many arrows lead to the same point or if they always go back to it, then this shows that the process does not flow properly. You can use this information to look for a solution on this point.

First, identify inputs and outputs as well as cause and effects. Then arrange them in a logical sequence. You can show options (yes/no, either/or, …) and different courses of action.

Problem-solving flow chart

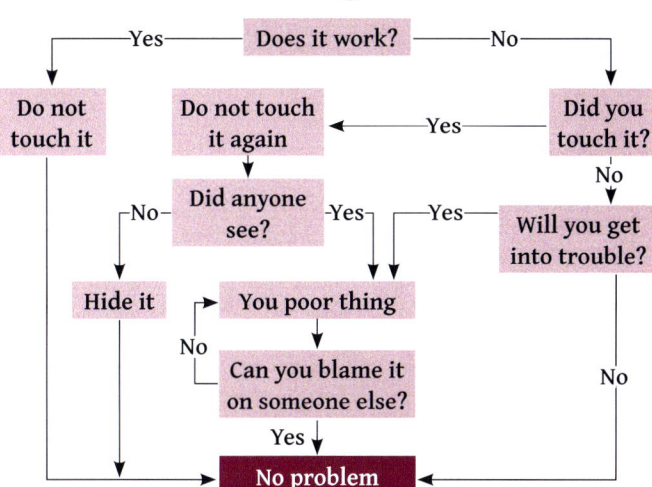

Fishbone diagram

This method analyses a problem with the help of cause and effect:

- The fish head represents the problem in question or the effect.
- The "bones" are the causes of the problem.
- Again, sort ideas into useful categories and find a keyword for each category. Frequently used categories/keywords are environment, economy, equipment, people, society.

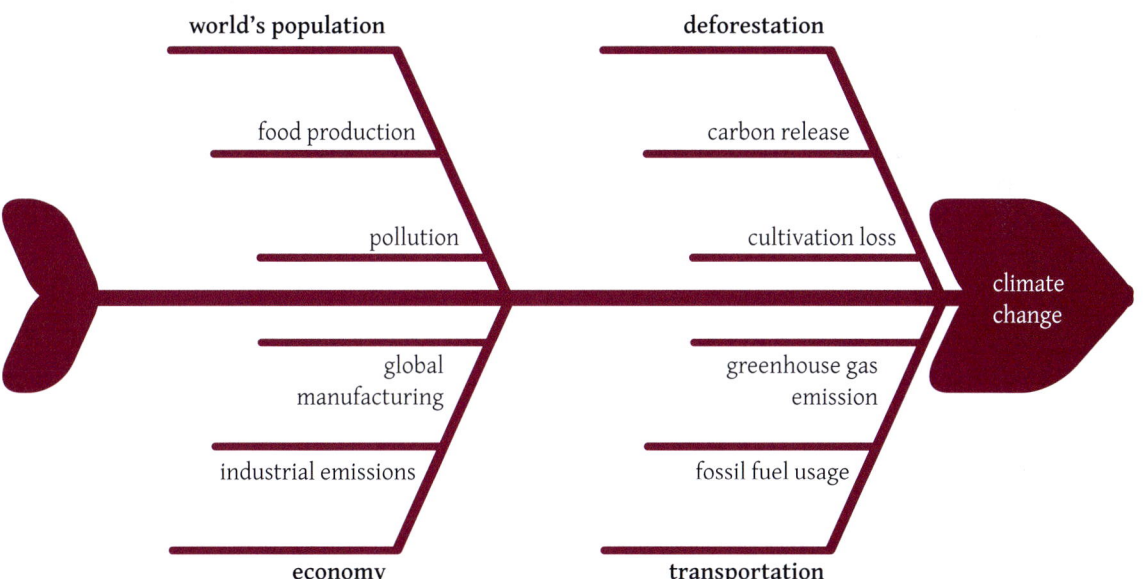

1 Compare the two types of presentation (text and mind map) under the heading "visualization – what is it good for" at the beginning of this double page.

2 You want to make a presentation on the effects of globalization. Brainstorm aspects that you must mention, then cluster your ideas. Decide which type of visualization fits this task best. Give reasons.

6.2 Integration – first off, the government's responsibility?

M 1   Everybody is welcome?

Cartoon: Gerhard Mester

M 2   Migration can benefit the world

Managing migration is one of the most profound challenges for international cooperation in our time. Migration powers economic growth, reduces inequalities and connects diverse societies. Yet, it is also a source of political tension and human tragedies. The majority of migrants live and work legally. But a desperate minority are putting their lives at risk to enter countries where they face suspicion and abuse.

Demographic difficulties and the impact of climate change on vulnerable societies are likely to drive further migration in the years ahead. As a global community, we face a choice. Do we want migration to be a source of prosperity and international solidarity, or a byword for inhumanity and social friction? [...]

Migrants take jobs that local workforces cannot fill, boosting economic activity. Many are innovators and entrepreneurs. Nearly half of all migrants are women, looking for better lives and work opportunities.

Migrants also make a major contribution to international development by sending remittances to their home countries. [...]

[S]tates need to strengthen the rule of law emphasizing how they manage and protect migrants – for the benefit of their economies, their societies and the migrants themselves. Authorities that create major obstacles to migration – or place severe restrictions on migrants' work opportunities – cause needless economic self-harm, as they impose barriers to having their labour needs met in an orderly, legal fashion. Worse still, they unintentionally encourage illegal migration. Aspiring migrants, denied legal pathways to travel, inevitably fall back on irregular methods. This not only puts them in vulnerable positions, but also undermines governments' authority. The best way to end the stigma of illegality and abuse around migrants is, in fact, for governments to put in place more legal pathways for migration, removing the incentives for individuals to break the rules, while better meeting the needs of their labour markets for foreign labour.

António Guterres, Migration can benefit the world. This is how we at the UN plan to help, in: The Guardian online, 11 Jan 2018, https://www.theguardian.com/commentisfree/2018/jan/11/migration-benefit-world-un-global-compact [4 Nov 2023] (modified)

M3 Different migration experiences with different outcomes?

a) Ahmet Özdemir is a child of Turkish migrants. He was born in Germany, near Aachen. At the age of 39, he looks back: is he really integrated in his country of birth? [...]
Even his primary school years were a rocky road [...]. Migrants
5 [...] were sorted, couldn't speak German – were different – and the looks from the German parents were often strange. "How – my child with so many migrant children in one class?" [...]
I felt like a wanderer between two worlds. A traveller who was
10 never accepted because of his origins. A traveller who didn't really know his homeland. Homeless on both sides. For the Germans, always the Turk who didn't want to integrate and was never regarded as a Turk by the Turks on holiday in Turkey. There we were the "German Turks". [...]
15 Life in Germany was always associated with obstacles for me. The stupid remarks, the unfair things said about me weren't always meant as harshly as they were said, they were often combined with a touch of irony, but they were still hurtful and clearly directed at me, as a foreigner, as a Turk.
20 [...] Two quotes are very central for me when it comes to the key to better coexistence in Germany. [...] For all those who consider the mother tongue of migrants unimportant, Wilhelm von Humboldt should be quoted here: "Language is, as it were, the outward appearance of peoples; their language is
25 their spirit and their spirit is their language; they can never be thought of as identical enough."
And to all young people who still have their lives ahead of them and who can decide which path to take, the recently deceased Richard von Weizsäcker recommends: "Do not allow
30 yourself to be driven into enmity and hatred against other people, against Russians or Americans, against Jews or Turks, against alternatives or conservatives, against black or white. Learn to live with each other, not against each other!" [...]
I am often asked whether I am integrated. My answer: I am
35 integrated when I am no longer asked such questions.

Ahmet Özdemir, Wie ein Migrantenkind Integration erlebte, in: Stern online, 1 May 2015, https://www.stern.de/politik/deutschland/ erfahrungsbericht--wie-ein-migrantenkind-integration-erlebte-6190796. html [2 Mar 2024] (modified/translated)

b) Nadia Nadim was born in 1988 in the city of Herat in Afghanistan. When she was eleven years old, her mother fled the country with her and her four sisters after
5 her father, a general in the Afghan army, was murdered by the Taliban. He had loved football and passed this passion on to his daughter, who started playing football as a young refugee in Denmark and scored
10 goals like no other.
"Football came into my life at a very difficult time," she says. "I had lost everything. I had lost my father and our home and had to flee to a completely foreign
15 country. I was still a child and couldn't understand what was happening around me. It was in the refugee centre that I fell in love with football when I saw children playing for the first time, including girls.
20 That awakened something in me, and I instantly fell in love with the sport. Looking back, I can say that football saved me. Football gave my life meaning."
Nadim's story is further evidence of the
25 power of football as an inclusive sport that can ignite great passion, break down barriers and unite the world. "Football allowed me to make sense of everything that was happening around me," Nadim
30 continues. "I learnt the Danish language quite quickly and experienced that barriers can actually be broken down. Football gave me self-confidence. It gave me joy."

Nadia Nadim: "Der Fussball hat meinem Leben einen Sinn gegeben", in: Inside FIFA, Zürich: FIFA, 22 July 2023, https://www.fifa.com/de/social-impact/ campaigns/football-unites-the-world/news/ nadia-nadim-der-fussball-hat-meinem-leben-einen- sinn-gegeben [2 Mar 2024] (modified/translated)

1 Analyse the cartoon (M1). ▸ METHOD Cartoons, pp. 26 – 27
2 List positive and challenging aspects of migration which are presented by Antònio Guterres (M2). Organize the information in a table.
3 Analyse the two migration experiences (M3): Do these migrants feel integrated into their societies? What factors seem to be important?
4 Discuss in class: Integration – first off, the government's responsibility?
   ▸ METHOD Debate, pp. 48 – 49

6.3 Diversity concepts at work – the path to economic success in the 21st century?

M1 Examples of job advertisements

© Deutsche Bahn

© Berliner Verkehrsbetriebe (BVG) / Die Botschaft

M2 Three layers of diversity

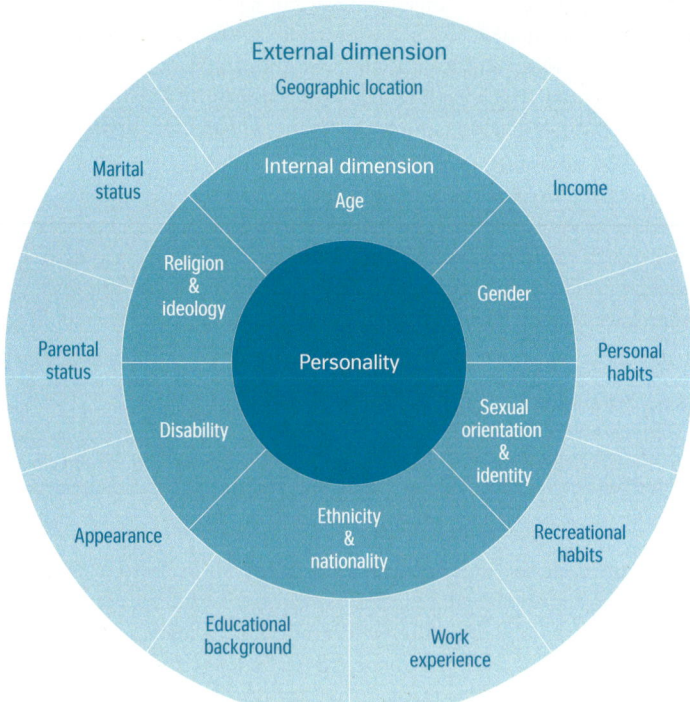

Source: Yassin Karay/H. Hallal/Christoph Stosch, "Diversity Charter" based on L. Gardenswartz and A. Rowe (2003),
Diverse Teams at Work. Society for Human Resource Management, May 2018

47625EX © Westermann

M3   Diversity and inclusion – essential for economic success

VOCABULARY

productivity
Produktivität,
Effizienz
to promote
fördern
retention
Erhaltung,
Beibehaltung
**to resource sth.
(with sth.)**
etw. (mit etw.)
ausstatten
to be accountable
verantwortlich sein

High levels of diversity and inclusion in the workplace are associated with greater productivity, innovation, and workforce well-
5 being, yet too little is being done to promote them, particularly among minority groups, meaning that enterprises, workers, and societies are missing out on con-
10 siderable potential benefits.

One-in-four people do not feel valued at work and those who do feel included are in more senior roles, according to a new report on diversity and inclusion
15 by the International Labour Organization (ILO).

High levels of equality, diversity and inclusion are associated with greater innovation, productivity and performance, talent recruit-
20 ment and retention, and workforce well-being. However, the report's survey found that only half of respondents said that diversity and inclusion were sufficiently identified and resourced in their workplaces' culture and
25 strategy. Only a third of enterprises currently measure inclusion, although doing so is essential for progress. [...]

Diversity and inclusion play a "critical role ... in the high performance of the workforce, businesses, economies and societies globally," 30 the report says. "If inclusion remains a privilege experienced only by those at senior levels, enterprises risk missing out on ... considerable benefits." [...]

The report outlines four key principles for 35 achieving transformational and sustainable change which are applicable globally and to all workforce groups and levels: diversity and inclusion should be a priority and part of strategy and culture; there must be diversity 40 in top management; senior leaders, managers and staff must be accountable as role models; and actions must apply throughout employment – covering recruitment, retention, and development.   45

INFO

**International
Labour Organization**
is a United Nations
agency to advance
social and economic
justice by setting
international labour
standards.

Diversity washing
This practice aims at
projecting a (public)
image of diversity
and acceptance for
financial gain only.

Greater progress on diversity and inclusion essential to rebuild productive and resilient workplaces, Genf: International Labour Organization (ILO), 6 Apr 2022, https://www.ilo.org/global/about-the-ilo/newsroom/news/WCMS_841085/lang--en/index.htm [25 Nov 2023]

1 a) Look at the images and explain whom and what they focus on (M1). Take notes.
   b) Explain why these campaigns might be necessary.

2 a) Choose some aspects of the chart (M2). Find examples and explain why they are important to think about when talking about diversity.
   b) Based on M2, develop criteria to include in a successful diversity concept.
   MORE HELP

3 Do research on the diversity concept of a company, brand, or institution and use your criteria from task 2 b). Present your findings in class. **MORE HELP**

4 a) First, create a table to list benefits which companies might expect if they follow the suggested principles from the report (M3).
   b) Then think about challenges or risks that could happen when the company's culture moves towards respect and tolerance for diversity.
   c) **Milling around:** Discuss the question: "Diversity concepts at work: changing world of work for the better or just diversity washing?"

6.4 Globalization – the driving force behind social and economic disparities?

M 1   Dimensions of globalization

Globalization makes the world a smaller place. It connects people all over the globe and lets them share ideas, goods, and services. Globalization acts like a network of giant bridges be- tween countries which allow people to travel, [5] trade, and communicate more easily. The il- lustration below shows where globalization takes place and what it has an impact on.

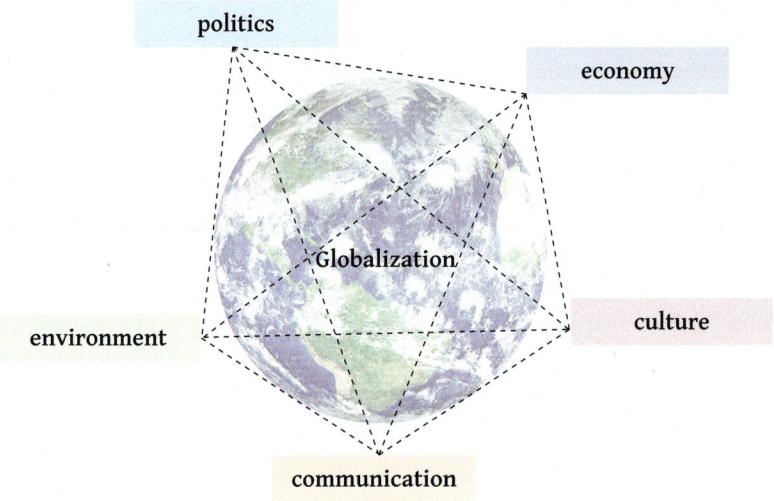

politics · economy · Globalization · culture · environment · communication

M 2   Extract from a speech delivered by Johannes Rau, former President of the Federal Republic of Germany

Johannes Rau
(1931 – 2006)
President of the
Federal Republic
of Germany
1999 – 2004

Es hat mit Globalisierung zu tun, wenn die Fir- ma, in der man arbeitet, plötzlich mit Betrie- ben aus Gegenden der Welt konkurriert, von denen man bisher kaum gehört hatte.
[5] Es hat mit Globalisierung zu tun, wenn sich junge Leute, die durch die Anden wandern, aus dem Internetcafé in Quito bei ihren Eltern in Oberursel melden und mal eben per E-Mail die ersten digitalen Fotos schicken.
[10] Es hat mit Globalisierung zu tun, wenn wir vom PC aus unseren Urlaub buchen und wenn Studenten sich nachmittags aus dem Internet Material aus Amerika für ihre Hausarbeit ho- len.

Es hat mit Globalisierung zu tun, wenn in dem [15] Auto, das wir kaufen, die Teile aus vielen Län- dern kommen, wenn also das „Made in Ger- many" manchmal nur noch für die Idee, für die Endmontage oder für den Namen steht.
Es hat mit Globalisierung zu tun, wenn Men- [20] schen in aller Welt am 11. September [2001] live miterleben mussten, wie das World Trade Center Tausende von Menschen unter sich be- grub.
Es hat mit Globalisierung zu tun, wenn aus ab- [25] gelegenen Berghöhlen ein Verbrechen ge- plant und gesteuert wird, das die ganze Welt erschüttert.

Berliner Rede 2002 von Bundespräsident Johannes Rau, Berlin: Bundespräsidialamt, 13 May 2002, https://www. bundespraesident.de/SharedDocs/Reden/DE/Johannes-Rau/Reden/2002/05/20020513_Rede.html [27 Nov 2023]

M3 Decisive factors of globalization

Fall of the Iron Curtain
World trade increased as the ideological conflicts between the East and West (temporarily) calmed down after 1989/90.

Improvements in transportation
Larger cargo ships make it possible to transport more and more goods between countries, which means that the price for transport decreases.

What will happen in the future?

Advancement of communication
The internet and the development of mobiles increase communication among people all across the globe.

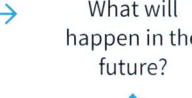
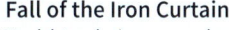

Freedom of trade
The deregulation of markets and reduction of customs duties (especially within the EU) facilitate trade.

Cheaper labour costs in LEDCs
Low social standards combined with high skill levels (for example, in India), let labour-intensive industries such as the clothing industry take advantage of cheaper labour costs.

INFO

Social standards
include both statutory regulations and all agreements between employee and employer organizations aimed at improving the situation of employees.

LEDCs
Less Economically Developed Countries

INTERNET

WES-116955-641
Links about fair trade

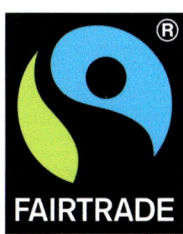

1 Complete the mind map in your folder with examples for each dimension of globalization (M1). You can complete this visualization with further examples from this and previous chapters within the unit.
▸ METHOD Visualization, pp. 136–137

2 In his speech from 2002, Johannes Rau explained what he thinks globalization is (M2). Use his examples to complete your mind map (task 1).

3 a) State the decisive factors of globalization (M3).
b) Choose a product and do research on where it is produced or processed and sold in the world. You can choose coffee, fast-food items, clothes, or other products.
c) **Extra:** Find more examples for your mind map.

4 **Extra:** Find out what the logo stands for (webcode/QR code). Explain whether the logo would influence you to buy a product or not, even if it is slightly more expensive.

M 4   # Are you getting the discount?

Cartoon: Alexandre Magnin, 20 Nov 2018

M 5   # Rana Plaza disaster 11 years on: What has changed?

[…] [T]he tragic collapse of the Rana Plaza garment factory building on the outskirts of Bangladesh's capital, Dhaka, killed 1,134 and wounded at least 2,500 people. […]

5 The Rana Plaza building had housed five garment factories that manufactured clothes for many international clothing brands in Europe and North America. Investigations would later reveal that besides shoddy construction, the
10 building had too many floors and too much heavy equipment for the structure to withstand. […]

Eleven years since the tragedy […] some reforms have been introduced to hold international brands accountable for worker safety,
15 even though violations persist. The groundbreaking Bangladesh Accord came into force in 2013, giving [trade] unions greater say while holding fashion brands legally accountable for
20 ensuring factories remained safe. Over 220 brands eventually signed on to the original accord, which ran until 2018 and has since been renewed as the "International Accord." […]

25 Still, not all is well when it comes to safety, say rights groups. "Occupational safety and health measures in these factories are very lax," said

Collapsed textile factory in Dhaka, Bangladesh, 25 Apr 2013

Diana Quiroz, a researcher who surveyed trade union leaders active in the garment sector in a few Asian countries, including Bangladesh. 30 Her research […] has shown that workers are forced to sit on the factory floor in the same position for hours and do repetitive tasks. […] Many workers also suffer from overwork, underpay and a lack of job security. […] The 35 workers earn on average €70 ($75) a month, much less than the about €284 needed for a decent living, according to the Bangladesh Institute of Labor Studies. […] Workers' rights bodies say global fashion brands […] should 40 commit to paying living wages and absorbing the higher labour costs.

Shristi Pal, Rana Plaza disaster 11 years on: What has changed?, Bonn: Deutsche Welle, 23 Apr 2024, https://www.dw.com/en/rana-plaza-disaster-11-years-on-what-has-changed/a-68900666 [29 May 2024]

M6 Findings on the transparency of purchasing practices

Living wages

47627EX © Westermann

Each year, the Fashion Transparency Index explores some key issues in more detail.
In 2023, the index examined decent work and purchasing practices. The main question was
what major brands and **retailers** are doing to improve conditions for workers within the companies
and their supply chains. One important issue was living wages and wage data in the supply chain.
The following statistics focus on a few details of that category.

28%
Disclose approach to
achieving living wages
for supply chain workers

2%
Publish no. of workers
paid by piece-rate

2%
Publish annual
progress towards
paying living wages

2%
Disclose whether piece-rate
and daily wage workers earn
at least **minimum wage**

1%
Publish no. of workers
being paid a living wage

5%
Report on **proportion**
of factory workers
who are paid at least
minimum wages

Source: Fashion Transparency Index 2023, 12 July 2023, pp. 88–89

M7 Ecological footprint of textiles

The Higg Index measures the sustainability of different materials.
The higher the value, the more ecological damage is created by making the product.

47628EX

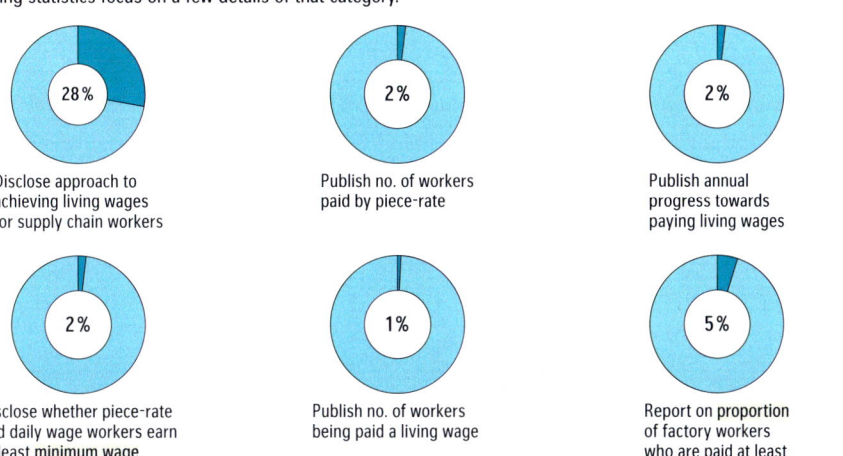

	Global warming	Water pollution*	Use of water	Use of fossil fuel	Chemistry	Total
Silk						1076
Alpaca wool						316
Cotton						101
Hemp fibre						95
Flax (linen)						88
Wool						79
Viscose						56

*Adding rich nutrients to water, leading to the growth of algae and loss of biodiversity
Data: Sustainable Apparel Coalition, June 2022 Source: Picture Alliance, Globus 015461 (translated and modified)

Globus 015461

---

1 Analyse the cartoon (M4). ▸ METHOD Cartoons, pp. 26–27

2 Summarize how much progress the garment industry has made in working
conditions according to the article (M5).

3 Analyse the pie charts (M6) on the transparency of wages in the garment industry.
MORE HELP ▸ METHOD Statistics, pp. 20–21

4 Analyse the chart (M7) on the ecological footprint of textiles.
Add examples to your mind map from p. 143, task 1. ▸ METHOD Statistics, pp. 20–21

5 **Graffiti:** Assess the consumer's, the company's, or the government's responsibility in
the process of globalization. **MORE HELP**

Six spotlights

In our complex world, it is important to listen to many different arguments to understand various points of view. However, too many arguments and points of view can become overwhelming. It also helps in a discussion if you are familiar with a point of view and can add your knowledge as an expert. This is what this method from the business world tries to do. Imagine that you can filter out other perspectives and briefly concentrate on only one.

Step 1:

When you face a political problem, **try to identify who is involved** in it. Some people are actively involved and can even cause problems. These are the so-called **players**. Other people are rather passive, even though they are also affected by the problem, law, or process. They are called the **people affected**. Make a list of the people who are involved!

Step 2:

For this step, you need to know **which dimensions** we usually work with when dealing with politics. These are:

47629EX_1 © Westermann

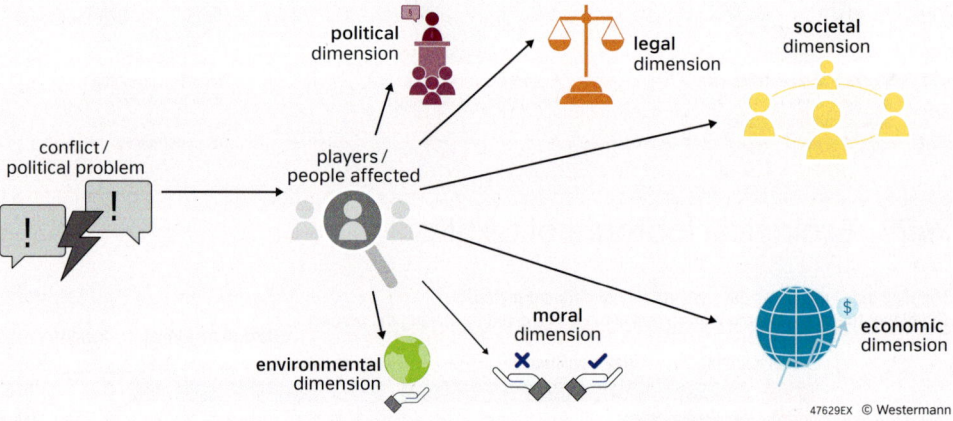

47629EX © Westermann

Look at the different players and people affected and find out **what they are interested in**. For example, an entrepreneur who wants to run his business successfully is in the economic dimension. Someone who seeks justice based on the law is in the legal dimension. People who focus on citizens' interests have a societal perspective, and so on. Of course, a person could have points of view from more than just one dimension. Sometimes, your teacher wants you to focus on just one opinion and sometimes you can consider more. If you are uncertain, ask your teacher.

Step 3:

Depending on whether you have received material, or you are doing research on a specific dimension, focus on one specific perspective (such as an entrepreneur, a citizen, a father, a child, a politician, or a judge). Examine the material or the websites **to find and make arguments that support the position** within your dimension. Make sure you use strong and vivid examples to convince others. ▸ METHOD Debate, pp. 48–49

Helpful phrases

From a political / a legal / a societal / an economic / a moral / an environmental point of view, I claim that …
As a / an [role], I'm convinced that … / … I doubt that …
One the one hand, … on the other hand, …
Consider the perspective of a / an [role], don't you see that …

Example

a) The problem

In Newtown an international entrepreneur wants to build a new shopping mall. However, to do so, the businessman must tear down a lot of small local shops. Carmen's corner shop, which is famous for the little bags of sweets students love to buy, is among them. Some people are happy because new and international shops will finally open in the city along with the mall. Others do not want to change anything. In fact, they are quite happy with how things are now and are rather afraid of the change. The entrepreneur, Mr. Baldwin, is invited to a townhall meeting to discuss his plans with the local citizens.

b) Ajla loves the corner shop

Ajla is thirteen years old and loves the corner shop. Since she was six years old, she has been buying her sweets there. She knows Carmen, who has been running the shop for about twenty years. She loves to buy a treat after school and sometimes Carmen even helps her with her maths homework. As Carmen is a business owner herself, she understands numbers. Carmen has been a huge help for Ajla, so the girl feels it is a personal duty to support her and her shop.

c) Jonas wants international flair… and the arcade and entertainment centre!

Jonas is 16 years old and loves foreign languages and cultures. When plans for the shopping mall were announced, Jonas immediately dreamt of cool shops from America he had always seen on TV. But when he heard of the arcade and entertainment centre, he was all for it. Spending a wonderful afternoon with his friends was one thing, but the option of having such a place around the corner made his summer plans perfect: relaxing in the sun, playing video games or bowling in the entertainment centre, shopping and eating in American stores … why travel far?

d) Carmen will lose her shop

Carmen Cruz is nearly 62. She has to work for only five more years before she can retire. When she heard that the entrepreneur was offering her a good sum for the shop, she at first wanted to take it. But when she heard that the shop would be torn down, she changed her mind. She knows a lot of students from the nearby school. A few of them do not want to spend much time at home and would rather visit her in her shop and sometimes even ask for help with their homework. Her corner shop has become a cultural icon of the city district. With the money she would receive from the entrepreneur, she could live well for the rest of her life, but her sense of responsibility for the children does not allow her to sell the shop.

e) Mr Baldwin believes his mall will be a great success

The new shopping mall "New Horizons" will be a big success for Mr. Baldwin. He is sure of that, as this is going to be the first international shopping mall in the city. People will come from all over the city to buy there. The only challenge is tearing down the old local shops. As beautiful as they are, Mr Baldwin's experts say they will not last long. In fact, he is doing the district a favour. As an entrepreneur, he knows it is hard to separate emotions from facts. Yet, he wants everyone to understand him. After all, if the shopping mall is successful, it will also benefit people with new jobs, a great selection of shops, and a thriving economy.

1 Apply the steps to the scenario and have a short discussion in class.
2 Leave your roles and make a **lineup** to present your own opinion.
3 Say how helpful the method is in forming your opinion on more complex problems.

VOCABULARY

lineup
hier: Positionslinie

6.5 The idea of a "global village" – curse or blessing?

M1   Living in a global village

Globalization

In a flash, we traverse from A to B,
Yet some rebel against this global decree.
Globalization's course, not good nor ill,
In human hands, its destiny to fulfil.
5 Oh, the sadness that lingers in our hearts,
As unity's power still remains apart.
Digital lives, like blossoms they've unfurled,
Yet lifeless they remain, in this virtual world.
Utterances believed, in realms unseen,
10 A paradoxical truth, a digital dream.

Text by the author

M2   What is a "global village"?

Marshall McLuhan was the first theorist who in 1964 spoke of the idea of the Global Village [...]. The idea of a global village was born in McLuhan after the observation of how the
5 media had been able to overcome any physical distance, bringing the inhabitants of the earth closer, making them close neighbours, turning the earth into a great global village. In this new global village, villagers can know what
10 they do, how they live, what other villagers say; a villager in New York can see what a villager in Hong Kong is doing and even observe him in real time.

This transformation of the world into one big
15 village has, according to McLuhan, also changed our behaviours into those typical of a villager.

Interestingly, McLuhan's visionary idea predates the popularization of the internet and social networks. Rumorology in networks, the
20 proliferation of reality shows, the desire to see what others are doing, are some of the aspects and consequences of these new behaviours. Radios, televisions and then computers, tablets and cell phones, become the new windows
25 from our homes to the street [...].

This world has already arrived, online dating, online classes, online concerts ... everything brings us closer and relates us to what is far away. We share the same series and movies in
30 the big, shared cinemas, the new video [...] platforms Netflix, HBO or Prime; we buy in the same stores, in the big supermarkets Amazon, Alibaba or eBay; we have the same big "text library" Google [...], etc. We can read the news
35 in real time from any newspaper in the world and know what is happening live in a war not so far away.

Daniela Musicco-Nombela, THE GLOBAL VILLAGE. Globalization, rethinking McLuhan in the 21st century, in: Comunicación y Hombre, Madrid: Universidad Francisco de Vitoria, Dec 2021, https://comunicacionyhombre.com/en/ article/the-global-village-globalization-rethinking-mcluhan-in-the-21st-century-4/ [24 Nov 2023]

M3 Tourism increases, repercussions as well!

Wonderful views, long mountain slopes, solitary peaks and snow-covered tranquillity – Europe's Alpine region is the place to be for many travellers in both summer and winter.
5 Increasingly, though, the Alps are becoming infamous for traffic jams, overcrowded villages and pleasure seekers obstructing hiking trails and skiing slopes. [...]
Tourism is the primary breadwinner for Al-
10 pine populations, and scaling back the annual influx of vacationers seems out of the question. Quite the contrary, said [Steffen] Reich [from German Alpine Club]. He expects the region to become "even more popular with
15 tourists" due to climate change because the mountainous region "will be cooler than lower-lying areas."
Skiing resorts are especially hard hit by climate change and need to adapt the most. Less
20 snowfall and higher temperatures are already taking their toll, substantially raising the bills for local communities to make up for the lack of natural snow with technical means. [...]

Apart from climate change, tourism in the Alps
25 is having a massive problem, with too many vacationers swarming the region every year. Local populations are overwhelmed by the mass influx of tourists, many of them only coming to chase the latest must-visit site
30 popular on social media platforms. [...]
The Italian region of South Tyrol, for example, has already restricted the number of holiday beds. Regional councillor Arnold Schuler told US broadcaster CNN earlier this year that the
35 popular resort had "reached the limit of our resources" as traffic problems abounded and local residents "have difficulty finding affordable housing."
[...] Steffen Reich believes such drastic meas-
40 ures aren't needed everywhere. "You have to precisely understand what the real problem is. Is it the negative effects on local populations? Is it a threat to wildlife? Or is it primarily a park management problem?" Each prob-
45 lem, he said, would need its own specific solution.

Insa Wrede, Europe: How climate change, mass tourism threaten the Alps, Bonn: Deutsche Welle, 11 June 2023, https://www.dw.com/en/alpine-tourism-threatened-by-overcrowding-and-climate-change/a-67311515 [27 Nov 2023]

M4 Can social media make a positive change?

Omar Wasow is steeped in both social media and the civil rights movement of the 1960s. And he marvels at how the two have blended in the current demonstrations against racial
5 injustice and police brutality.
Wasow, a professor at Princeton University [...], said social media was helping publicize police brutality and galvanizing public support for protesters' goals [...]. And he said he
10 believed that the internet was making it easier

to organize social movements today, for good and for ill. [...] The video of George Floyd taken by Darnella Frazier is an echo of the bearing witness of the beating of Rodney King, and be-
15 fore that the images of Bloody Sunday in Selma [in 1965]. Part of what social media does is allow us to see a reality that has been entirely visible to some people and invisible to others. As those injustices become visible,
20 meaningful change follows.

Shira Ovide, How Social Media Has Changed Civil Rights Protests, in: New York Times online, 18 June 2020, https://www.nytimes.com/2020/06/18/technology/social-media-protests.html [27 Nov 2023]

1 Describe the picture and explain the message of the poem (M1). List advantages and disadvantages of the idea of a "global village" which are mentioned.
2 Define the term "global village" with the help of M2.
3 Use your list from task 1 to add more advantages and disadvantages of the "global village" from M3 and M4.
4 Make a lineup on the main question: "The idea of a "global village" – curse or blessing?"

VOCABULARY

repercussions
Auswirkungen
infamous
berüchtigt, verrufen
to obstruct
blockieren
to scale back
etw. reduzieren
to adapt (to sth.)
sich (an etw.) anpassen
to take its toll
seinen Tribut fordern
to be steeped in
von etw. durchdrungen sein
to marvel at sth.
sich über etw. wundern, etw. bewundern
to galvanize
hier: wachrütteln

INFO

George Floyd
was a 46-year-old African American who was murdered in Minneapolis by a 44-year-old white police officer in 2020.

Rodney King
was an African American man who was a victim of police brutality in Los Angeles on 3 March 1991.

Bloody Sunday in Selma, Alabama
was a series of protest marches of the civil rights movement in 1965 which were ended by state troopers who used batons and tear gas against about 600 protesters. This event became known as "Bloody Sunday".

Jeopardy: important terms in global contexts

a) migrant
b) push factors
c) pull factors
d) refugee
e) integration
f) diversity
g) inclusion
h) globalization
i) social standards
j) global village

> **Example: asylum seeker**
> → Question: *What do you call a person who tries to get refuge in a country officially?*

Mini-presentations: what living in global contexts means to us

1 Find precise questions for the answers given in a) to j).
Alternative: You can play this as a game for two classmates. A moderator gives you the word in random order and you and your classmate have to formulate the questions. You can agree on more rules for the game.

2 Look at the pictures 1 to 4. Each represents a main topic from this unit. Assign all the pictures to yourself and a partner. Then prepare a flashcard that summarizes what you have learnt about the topic. Finally, take turns and present your findings to your partner. Use your flashcard and the picture only.

3 **Extra:** Make transitions between the topics, explaining how the topics relate to each other.

Cultural homogenization?

Cartoon: David Horsey, 5 Feb 2013

INFO

E pluribus unum
(Latin for "out of many, one" or "one from many") is a historical motto of the United States.

VOCABULARY

chain retail
Handelskette
blindfold
Augenbinde
expat
Auswanderer/-in
to crave
ersehen, begehren
prosperity
Wohlstand

Being an American abroad

Time abroad has given me a different perspective on chain retail: it can either limit you, or link you to others. I currently live abroad, [and I find] endless malls and chain stores you
5 can find anywhere in America – Starbucks, McDonalds, Domino's, Dairy Queen, Pizza Hut and the like. While small shop owners do exist, you could stand on almost any corner in Shanghai, put on a blindfold, spin around,
10 walk in whatever direction you choose and end up at what looks like the same mall as anywhere else. [...]
That, of course, is how things can get complicated during extended travel or after becoming an expat. I love eating local food and 15 cooking – but I am still an American, and sometimes crave a taste of home, which is where those repetitive chains can help, by easing homesickness or at least providing me with a quick meal with which I am already quite fa- 20 miliar.
Time abroad has given me a different perspective on these aspects of chain retail. A chain can be something that either restricts you or links you to others; it can provide cer- 25 tain comforts of home and also restricts the prosperity of unique businesses, regardless of global location.

Lettecha Johnson, Starbucks in Shanghai is both cultural homogenization and a welcome taste of home when away from it, in: THINK. Opinion, Analysis, Essays, New York, NY: NBC UNIVERSAL, 21 Apr 2019, https://www.nbcnews.com/think/ opinion/starbucks-shanghai-both-cultural-homogenization-welcome-taste-home-when-away-ncna994101 [3 Apr 2023]

1 Analyse the cartoon. ▸ METHOD Cartoons, pp. 26 –27
2 Apply the message of the cartoon to other examples.
3 State the pros and cons the author mentions in her article.
4 **a)** Exchange your own experiences – if you can, think also about experiences abroad.
  b) Discuss whether cultural globalization is beneficial for consumers as well as national culture in general.

Young consumers

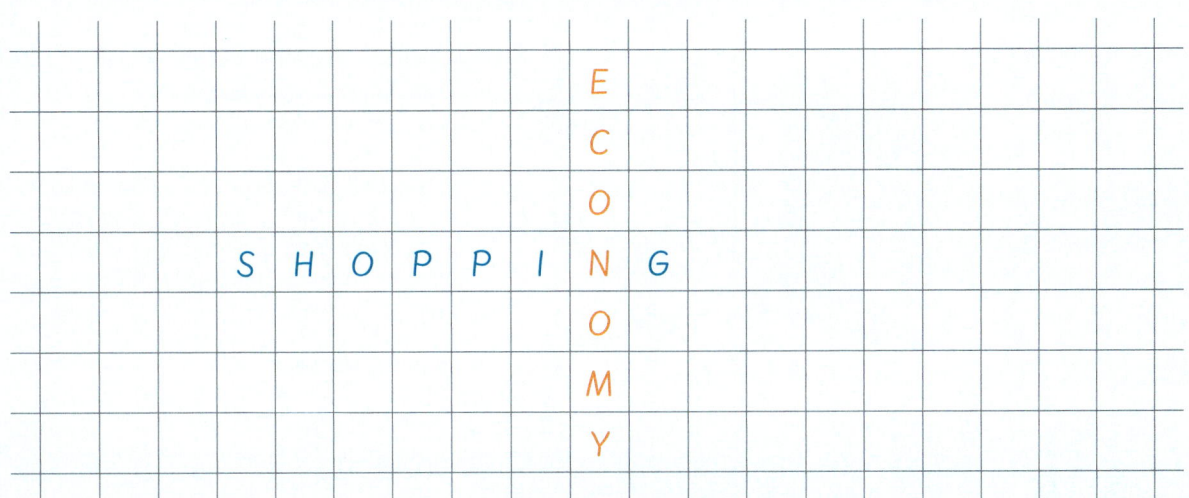

S H O P P I N G   E C O N O M Y

1 Look at the comic. Explain the economic actions it shows. **MORE HELP**

2 **a)** What comes to your mind, when you think about economy? Write the letters ECONOMY in a vertical line on a piece of heavy paper. Now find words connected to economy that contain one of the letters and write them next to it.
Tip: You can use the image above to help you.
b) In pairs, share your results and think of words to add.
c) Discuss your solutions in class.

7.1   Who decides what I buy?

M 1   An experiment

a) Someone has given you € 10 million. You have a few minutes to make a wish list of things to buy with this money and how much these things will (probably) cost.
Your goal is to spend all the money!   5

b) Unfortunately the situation has changed, and you only get € 10,000. You must cut back on your spending. Go through your list again and cross out the things you will no longer buy.   10

Text by the author

M 2   The fundamental economic problem: dealing with scarcity

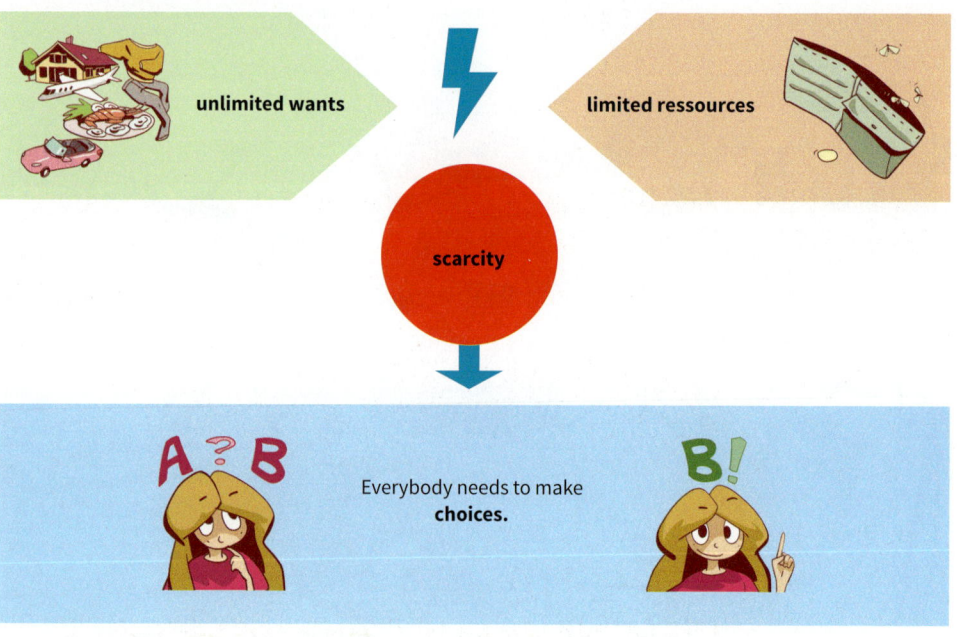

unlimited wants

limited ressources

scarcity

Everybody needs to make **choices.**

1   Explain to your partner what you would put on your wish list and why (M1 a)).
2   Give reasons why you decided to remove things from your wish list (M1 b)).
3   **Think–Pair–Share:**
    a) Define the term scarcity in your own words (M2). **MORE HELP**
    b) Find more examples of scarcity in real life.
4   **a)** Explain which option you would choose (M3).
    b) Assess whether your decision fits in Maslow's hierarchy of needs (M4).
5   **Extra:** Illustrate what your opportunity cost (M3) was in M1 b).

M3 Opportunity cost

Decisions cause opportunity cost = the lost benefit for the option not chosen

Example: What to spend the money on?

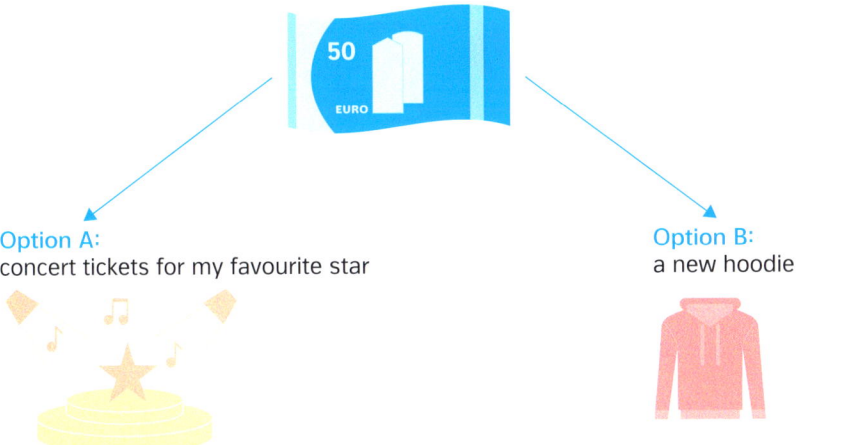

Option A:
concert tickets for my favourite star

Option B:
a new hoodie

Opportunity cost if option A
is chosen instead of B:
- no smart outfit
- not a durable product
- ...

Opportunity cost if option B
is chosen instead of A:
- missed fun
- missed unique experience
- ...

47549EX © Westermann

INTERNET
WES-116955-711
Link to film clip about
opportunity cost

VOCABULARY
benefit
Nutzen
hierarchy of needs
Bedürfnispyramide
self-actualization
Selbstverwirklichung
esteem
Wertschätzung
self-esteem
Selbtwertgefühl
recognition
Anerkennung

M4 Abraham Maslow's hierarchy of needs

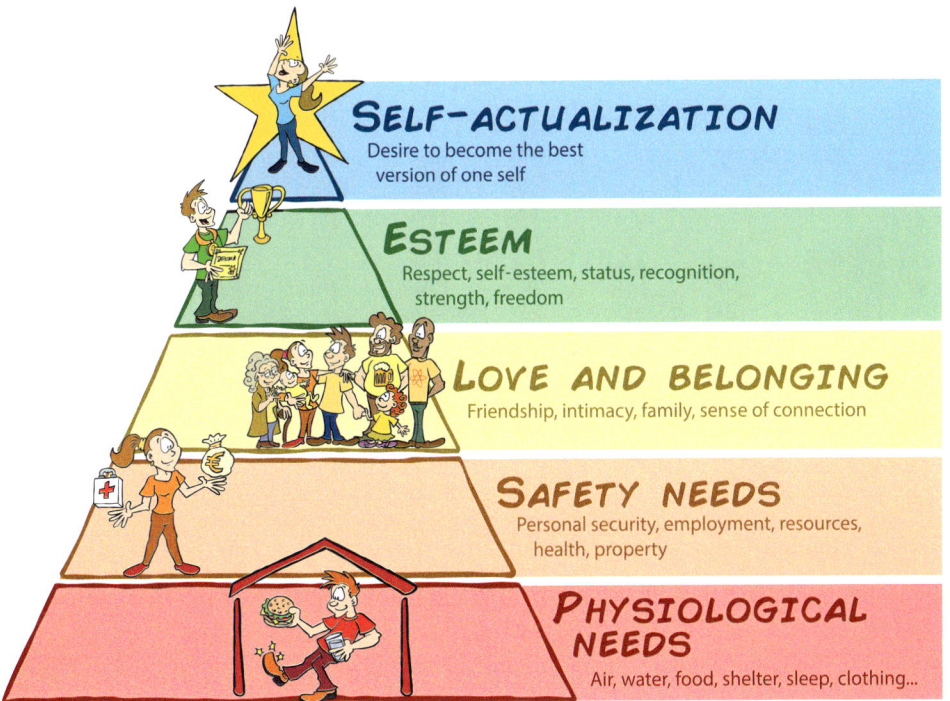

INFO
Abraham Maslow
(1908–1970) was an
American psycholo-
gist who developed
this pyramid model
to classify needs
according to their
importance.

7.2 Do brands help me decide what to buy?

M 1   World famous brands

M 2   How important are brands for teens?

Is a special brand important for you? In per cent %

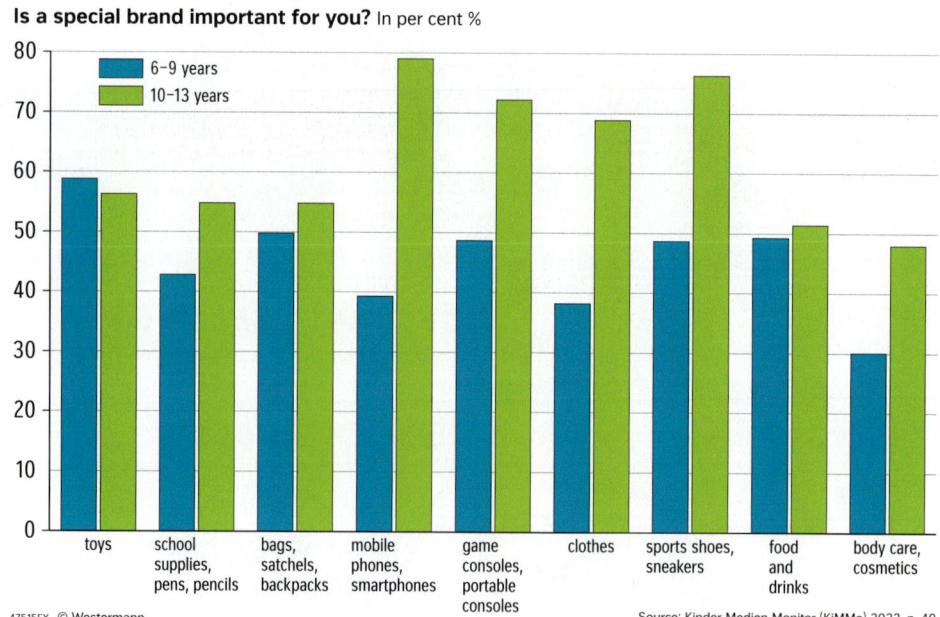

47515EX © Westermann

Source: Kinder Medien Monitor (KiMMo) 2023, p. 49

M3 Why are influencers effective?

Influencer marketing has become one of the most popular and effective marketing strategies in recent years. This phenomenon has completely transformed how businesses **promote** their products and services, as well as how consumers engage with brands. [...]
Influencer marketing is a type of social media marketing where businesses **collaborate** with individuals with a large following on social media platforms, such as Instagram, TikTok, YouTube, and Facebook. These individuals, known as influencers, use their platform to promote the products and services of the brand they are partnering with. [...]
Influencers can be anyone with a significant social media following and who has built a **reputation** for their expertise or knowledge in a particular **niche**. Influencers can be celebrities, bloggers, **vloggers**, or social media personalities. [...] They have a loyal fan base that trusts their **recommendations**. Influencers are highly **sought after** by businesses and brands due to their influence on the purchasing decisions of their followers. As a result, businesses often pay influencers to promote their products or services.
Some subject matter experts are influencers who specialize in a specific area, such as cooking, DIY [do it yourself], or fashion, and create content related to their expertise, including sponsored posts for relevant products. We also have celebrities, including actors, musicians, and reality TV stars, offer a glimpse into their personal lives and **endorse** products that fit their image, sometimes promoting their brand or merchandise. [...]

The effectiveness of influencer marketing is due to the trust and authority influencers have built with their followers. Influencers are viewed as **credible** sources of information and can influence the purchasing decisions of their followers. [...] [When they promote a product, their followers are likelier to believe it is **genuine** and **authentic**.]
Influencer marketing also allows brands to reach a highly **targeted** audience likely to be interested in their products.
[...] [T]he influencer landscape has become more **sophisticated** with the use of AI [Artificial Intelligence] and automation. This has enabled influencers to understand their audiences better and personalize their approach, leading to more meaningful connections between brands and influencers. Analytics has also allowed influencers to track their performance, optimize their strategies, and become more efficient in their campaigns.

The Power of Influencer Marketing: The Rise, Impact, and 5Ws of This Marketing Strategy, Pittsburgh (PA): AdSkate, in: LinkedIn, 5 May 2023, https://www.linkedin.com/pulse/power-influencer-marketing-rise-impact-5ws-strategy-adskate-inc [29 May 2024]

VOCABULARY

to promote
promoten, bewerben
collaborate
zusammenarbeiten
reputation
Ruf
niche
Nische
vlogger
Videoblogger
recommendation
Empfehlung
sought after
gefragt, begehrt
to endorse
empfehlen
credible
vertrauenswürdig, verlässlich
genuine
echt, genuin
authentic
echt, authentisch
targeted
gezielt, genau definiert
sophisticated
fortgeschritten, raffiniert

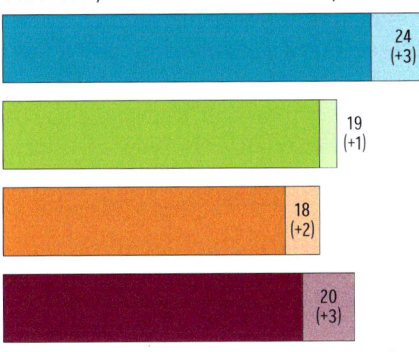

Influencers' influence on purchasing decisions
Out of every 100 internet users within a year ...

47516EX © Westermann

24 (+3)	bought something because it was advertised by a YouTuber.
19 (+1)	bought something because it was promoted by an Instagrammer.
18 (+2)	bought something because it was promoted by a blogger.
20 (+3)	bought something because it was promoted by an influencer on other social media.

Survey of 3,500 representative internet users aged 16 and over in Germany in December 2021 and January 2022
Source: Social-Media-Atlas 2022, Faktenkontor GmbH, Hamburg   +X = increase compared to previous year

---

1 **Think–Pair–Share:** Which brands do you recognize? Explain what they sell (M1).
2 Analyse the chart (M2). ▸ METHOD Statistics, pp. 20 – 21
3 Compare your experience to the chart in M3.
4 **Choose a task:**
  a) Explain why companies use influencers to promote products more and more (M3).
  b) Give reasons which influencer you would hire for your company if you had one.
5 **Milling around:** Discuss whether influencers are helpful or not when you want to buy something. ▸ METHOD Debate, pp. 48 – 49

How to conduct a survey

VOCABULARY

to sift
sichten
insights
Erkenntnisse

INTERNET

WES-116955-721
Link tips: How to
calculate your
sample size

Surveys – what are they good for?

In a democracy, we are always interested in what people think. Politicians want to know how different people react to their policies or what kind of changes they wish for. Businesses want to make sure their customers are happy with their service or their products. They also want to find new offers to sell and how to do so. Sociologists study human behaviour and draw conclusions about society from observations, interviews, and surveys.

The way a survey is conducted affects the quality of its conclusions. People are easily influenced, sometimes not even on purpose. A survey should be anonymous (without names or details that identify a person), so that people can express their opinions openly. After all, you might answer differently in a survey on how you feel about homework if you know your parents will read your answers, right?

How do I do it?

Step 1: Pick the aim.
The first step is the most important: you must decide what exactly you are trying to find out and why. What insight are you looking for? The more specific the question, the better. Think hard about how to measure your objective.

Step 2: Choose the type of questions.
1. **Multiple-choice questions** are a very common question type in surveys. You give the participants different options to choose from. It is a good idea to add "other" as an answer option because then the participant does not spoil the accuracy of the answers if he or she does not find a satisfactory option in your list. If you are interested in what this "other" is, you can allow a free answer (see open-ended question).
2. **Closed-ended questions** are typically yes/no questions or a list of answer options.
3. **Rating scale questions** are a popular variant of closed-ended questions. They let participants select the number that fits their opinion best.
4. **Open-ended questions** let your participants answer in their own words. This is more difficult to analyse in step 4, but it lets you find aspects you might not have expected.

Make your questions short and to the point. Use simple language. Be as clear as possible.

Step 3: Invite your participants.
The way you hand out or send your survey questions depends on whom you want to reach. Who do you want to target – students in your class or at your school? The British population? German managers under the age of 40? Depending on whom you want to survey, choose the location or type (in person, by telephone, online) of your survey. Decide how many responses you need to get a meaningful result (to find out more about a suitable "sample size", check out the webcode/QR code to the left). Also consider when it is best to conduct the survey.

Step 4: Gather and analyse your responses.
The hard work starts when you collect your responses. Sift through the answers to find the insights you are looking for. Visualize your data, if possible in charts or graphs. Text analysis tools or word clouds may help with open-ended questions.

Step 5: Summarize your findings in a report.
Your survey report explains your findings and shows whether you have met your research goals or not. A good survey will give you answers to the questions you set at the beginning. Ideally, this can point toward ways to improve the situation (for example, voter or customer satisfaction).

Example of a questionnaire

1. Which of the following brands have you heard of, if any?
☐ A
☐ B
☐ C
☐ D

2. How often do you purchase [brand]
☐ Never
☐ I've purchased it only once
☐ About once a year
☐ Every 7–12 months
☐ Every 2–6 months
☐ Monthly
☐ Weekly

3. How would you describe [brand] to a friend?
_____
_____
_____

4. Which of the following messages (if any) do you associate with [brand]?
☐ freedom   ☐ coolness   ☐ comfort/savour   ☐ relaxation   ☐ other: _____

5. What do you think about [brand] pricing?

| ☐ too expensive | ☐ expensive | ☐ appropriate | ☐ cheap | ☐ very cheap |

6. What do you think about [influencer X]'s advertising? (Multiple choice)
☐ [Influencer X] is the flavour of the month!
☐ I consider buying a product if [influencer X] says it's good.
☐ [Influencer X] made [brand] look interesting to me.
☐ I have bought products placed by [influencer X] before.
☐ [Influencer X] is overrated.
☐ If [influencer X] is trying to hype a product, I will not buy it for sure.

7. What words would you use to describe [brand]'s packaging?
☐ Modern
☐ Inviting
☐ Non-descriptive
☐ Old-fashioned
☐ Other: _____

8. ...

1 Choose a clothing or a food brand that is advertised by an influencer of your choice
and complete the example questionnaire above. Phrase question 8 yourself.
You can also divide your class in two groups, one to make a questionnaire on food,
the other on clothing.
2 Fill in the questionnaire, then gather all responses.
3 Analyse and visualize your results. ▸ METHOD Statistics, pp. 20–21

7.3 Does the shop layout influence the customer?

M 1 The IKEA shopping experience

Cartoon: Marco Paus, 5 Jan 2024

M 2 A path the customer should follow

If you've ever walked through an Ikea store, you know it's not a typical furniture store. You are guided along a path through various areas of the store until you see something that you
5 may want.
So if you're looking for a particular vase, you'll have to walk [through] the whole store until you get to your item. This may sound counter-productive at first, but there's an important
10 element here – customers may not know what they want so it's better to guide them in the right direction [...].

What Every Business Can Learn From Ikea and Apple, in: Helprace, Tampa, FL: Stuffix Inc., 22 Mar 2017, https://site.helprace.com/blog/what-every-business-can-learn-ikea-apple [27 Jun 2023]

M3 A supermarket layout

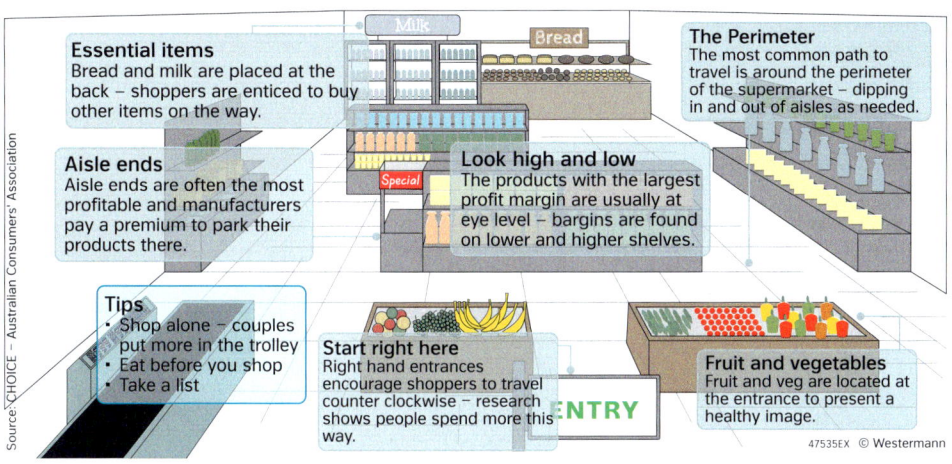

Source: CHOICE – Australian Consumers' Association

Essential items
Bread and milk are placed at the back – shoppers are enticed to buy other items on the way.

Aisle ends
Aisle ends are often the most profitable and manufacturers pay a premium to park their products there.

Tips
- Shop alone – couples put more in the trolley
- Eat before you shop
- Take a list

The Perimeter
The most common path to travel is around the perimeter of the supermarket – dipping in and out of aisles as needed.

Look high and low
The products with the largest profit margin are usually at eye level – bargins are found on lower and higher shelves.

Start right here
Right hand entrances encourage shoppers to travel counter clockwise – research shows people spend more this way.

ENTRY

Fruit and vegetables
Fruit and veg are located at the entrance to present a healthy image.

47535EX © Westermann

VOCABULARY

aisle
Gang
perimeter
Umkreis, Umfang
to dip in and out
ein- und austauchen
to monitor
hier: untersuchen
to pass through
vorbeigehen, durch-laufen
acceleration
Beschleunigung
conversion rate
Umwandlungsrate
to explore
entdecken
browsing stage
Phase des Stöberns
deceleration
Entschleunigung
determined
entschlossen
to approach
sich nähern

M4 Types of supermarket shoppers

A recent study monitored shopping behavior in more detail in a supermarket. Three shopper personas were identified in the study:
The **"passing through" shopper** – This shopper passes by a shelf on the way to another shelf. These visits are short with high acceleration and have none or minor directional changes. For these shoppers, the conversion rate to a sale is low.
The **"exploratory" shopper** – This shopper requires a browsing stage in front of the shelves before making a purchase. These are usually longer visits with a lot of direction changes, acceleration, and deceleration. For these shoppers, the conversion rate to a sale is higher.
The **"determined" shopper** – This shopper approaches a shelf, decelerates to a standstill, picks up an item, changes direction, and accelerates away from the shelf. These visits are also short, but the conversion rate to a sale is high.

Shopping behavior – what can we measure in a retail environment?, in: Behavioral Research Blog, Wageningen (NL): Noldus Information Technology BV, J8. Mar 2019, https://www.noldus.com/blog/shopping-behavior [27 Jun 2023]

"passing through" shopper

"exploratory" shopper

"determined" shopper

1 Analyse the cartoon (M1). **MORE HELP** ▸ METHOD Cartoons, pp. 26 – 27
2 Think-Pair-Share: Explain IKEA's marketing strategy (M2).
3 Describe the tricks used by supermarkets (M3).
4 Compare the different types of supermarket shoppers (M4). **MORE HELP**
5 Determine which shopping type you are (M4). You can also think about buying clothes or other products.

VOCABULARY

sales strategies
Verkaufstrategien
to lay out
anlegen, gestalten
narrow
eng
messy
durcheinander
dairy
Milchprodukte
beverages
Getränke
pantry
Vorratswaren
(= abgepackte Waren
wie Nudeln etc.)
**reverse vending
machine**
(Pfand-)Rücknah-
meautomaten
chilled convenience
gekühlte Fertig-
produkte

M5   Sales strategies in supermarkets

1.   I would lay out the corridors and aisles as wide as possible so my customers can walk through the market fast.
2.   The corridors and aisles should be rather narrow so that customers must spend more time getting around the supermarket.
3.   I would put the goods that my customers need daily up front so they can easily reach them easily.
4.   I would put the goods of daily use in a far corner because everybody needs them anyway.
5.   Some goods I would put in large containers so that they seem to be inexpensive.
6.   I would not put goods in large containers as that looks messy.
7.   I would put things that few customers want close to the check-out and registers so that there are no lines at the registers.
8.   I would put sweets close to the check-out and registers so that kids can easily reach them while waiting.
9.   I would organize the shelves so that customers must go by as many shelves as possible.

Adapted from: Verkaufsstrategien im Supermarkt, Oldenburg: wigy e. V., p. 3, http://gebonn.de/ilias/Ilias_Files_4_ Installation/Datafiles_Import/gebonn-data/ilFile/22/file_2283/001/Aufbau%20eines%20Supermarkts.pdf [27 June 2023] (translated and modified)

M6   A discounter layout

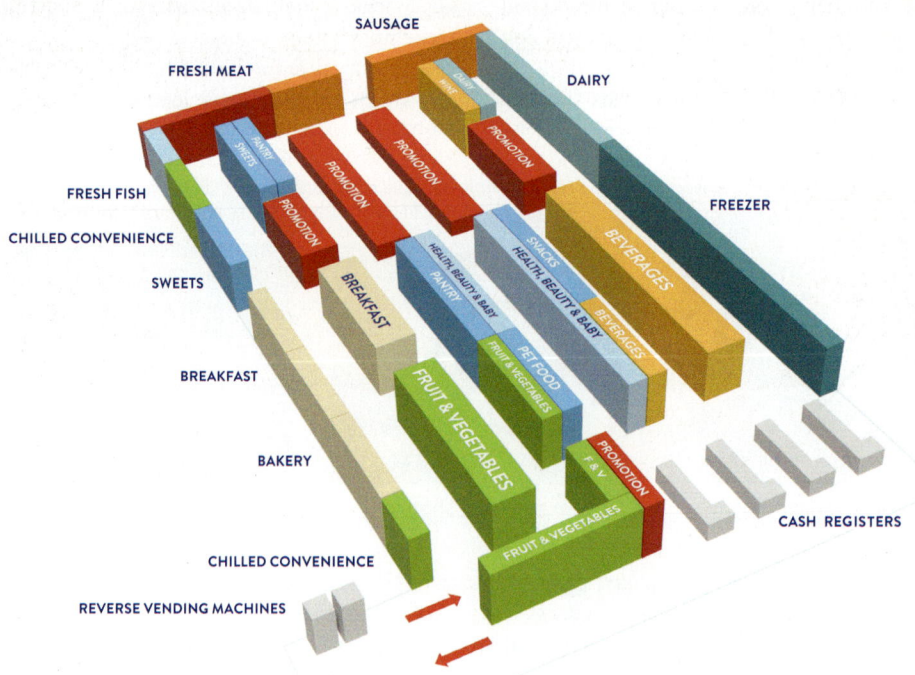

Aldi's Layout Germany 2023/2024

M 7 Supermaket shelf marketing

Super premium
smaller, gourmet and healthier brands

Premium
best sellers and leading brands with highest markup

Premium
best sellers and leading brands with highest markup

Mid priced
store brands and products with kid appeal

Value
store brands, private labels and oversize items

more expensive

less expensive

47518EX © Westermann

VOCABULARY

retailer
Einzelhändler
to measure
messen
gaze
Blick, der
to linger
verweilen

INTERNET

WES-116955-731
Links to film clips about supermarket layouts and eye-tracking

M 8 Eye tracking: important information for retailers

Eye tracking **measures** the direction of **gaze** and eye movements. It can determine where a person looks (first and last or not at all) and where the gaze **lingers** longer. Eye tracking is often used to organize shelves strategically and to improve the layout of a store. 5

Text by the author

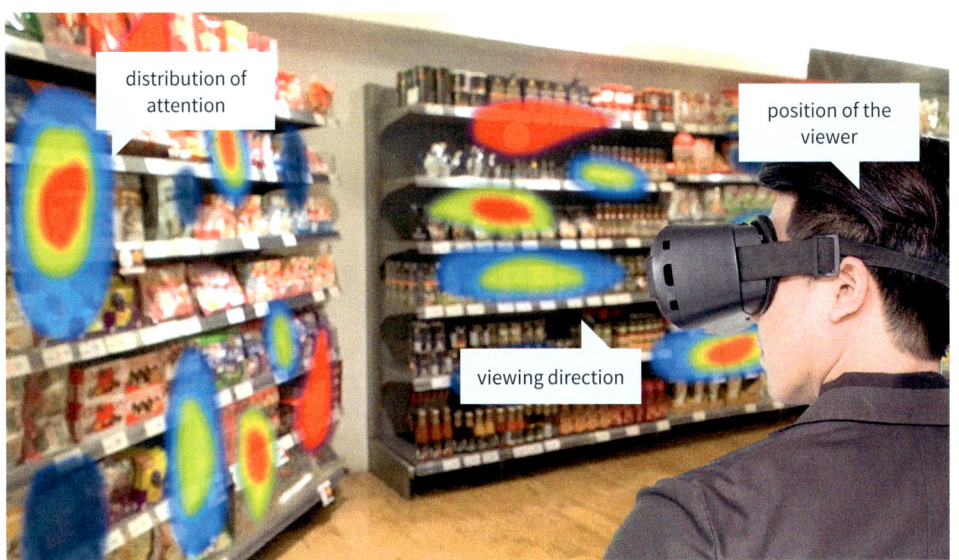

1 Imagine you manage a supermarket. Decide which statements from M5 you would agree and disagree with.
2 Compare the layouts of the supermarket and the discounter (M3 and M6).
   MORE HELP
3 **Extra:** Also compare the layout of IKEA (M2) with the other layout types (M3, M6).
4 Explain how retailers organize supermarket shelves to influence customers (M7).
5 Illustrate how supermarkets use eye tracking as a marketing strategy (M8).
6 **Inside-outside circle:** Discuss whether laws should regulate these marketing methods (M2–M8).
7 Observe next time you go shopping: How do shops try to get you to buy things?

7.4 Advertising with no limits?

M1 Competitive advertising

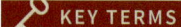

M2 Act against Unfair Competition

Section 6: Comparative advertising

(1) Comparative advertising shall mean any advertising which explicitly or by implication identifies a competitor, or goods or ser-
5 vices offered by a competitor.
(2) Unfairness is deemed to have occurred where a person conducting comparative advertising uses a comparison which
1. does not relate to goods or services which
10 meet the same needs or are intended for the same purpose;
2. does not objectively relate to one or more material, relevant, verifiable and representative features of the goods concerned or to
15 the price of those goods or services;

3. leads, in the course of trade, to a risk of confusion between the advertiser and a competitor or between the goods or services offered or the distinguishing marks used by
them;   20
4. takes unfair advantage of or impairs the reputation of a distinguishing mark used by a competitor;
5. discredits or denigrates the goods, services, activities, or personal or business circum-   25
stances of a competitor; or
6. presents goods or services as imitations or replicas of goods or services which are sold under a protected distinguishing mark.

1 **Think–Pair–Share:** Explain the ads (M1) and list more examples of comparative advertising.

2 Verify whether the ads (M1) and your examples conflict with the Act against Unfair Competition (M2). **MORE HELP**

3 **Chose a task:**
   a) Explain which emotions are used in advertising, and why (M3).
   b) Design your own advertisement for a product of your choice, taking M3 into account.

4 **Inside-outside circle:** Discuss whether the guidelines from the German Standards Advertising Council are adequate (M4).

5 Find examples of advertising within and beyond the guidelines on the German Advertising Council website (webcode/QR code).

M3 Emotional advertising – tips from an advertising agency

Emotional advertising uses emotions to connect with consumers and **encourage** them to buy a product or service. This type of advertising **appeals** to the heart rather than the head,
5 and it can be quite effective in leaving a lasting impact on customers. Informing your audience is important. You want potential buyers to understand what their problem is, and how your products or services can solve that prob-
10 lem. Unfortunately, people don't generally make purchases based on information alone. It turns out that people are more **prone** to making emotional purchases than informed purchases. [...] Targeting your audience's emo-
15 tions through your advertising efforts makes it easier for your audience to connect with your brand on a personal level. [...] One of the issues with [informational] advertising is that the audience might remember the informa-
20 tion you've **provided**, but not the brand itself. The following are just a few examples of how different emotions can be used to connect with your audience:

Happiness: Making an audience feel happy
25 is a good way to develop brand **association**. It also makes them more likely to share your content [...] with their friends and family.
Pride: Appealing to your audience's sense of pride makes them feel good about
30 themselves as well as about your brand.
Fear: You don't always have to appeal to the emotions people like. In some cases, fear can be a very effective emotion, especially if you're trying to drive audiences to take **immediate** action.
35 **Greed:** We live in a consumer society. As such, people tend to want the newest and latest of everything. Although greed tends to have a negative **connotation**, it's an emotion commonly **leveraged** by busi-
40 nesses by advertising limited editions and collectible items as well as using short-term promotions and sales. Such a strategy **incorporates** both greed and fear since people will make a purchase based
45 on both **desire** and fear of **missing out**.

Dan Gartlan, Emotional Advertising: How Brands Use Feelings to Get People to Buy, Lombard, IL: Stevens & Tate Marketing, 12 Sep 2023, https://stevens-tate.com/articles/emotional-advertising/ [6 Feb 2024]

M4 The German Standards Advertising Council

Advertising in Germany is regulated by law. The state provides guidelines for fair competition and ensures that advertising freedom is not used to the disadvantage of the public in-
5 terest – for example by banning advertisements that mislead or are harmful to children and teenagers. In addition, advertisers, the media and advertising agencies themselves actively exercise responsibility for ensuring good
10 standards in advertising. The **self-regulatory system** also has the benefit of being able to respond quickly to upcoming developments in the advertising market.
  Consumer trust must not be **abused** and
15 inexperience or lack of knowledge not **exploited**.

Children must not be **subjected** to physical or psychological harm.
Discrimination in whatever form – racial
20 discrimination, discrimination based on ethnic origin, religion, gender, age, disability or sexual preference, or by reducing an individual to a sexual object – should not be tolerated.
25 Violent, aggressive or antisocial behaviour should not be tolerated.
Fear should not be instilled nor unhappiness or suffering instrumentalized.
Behaviour that threatens consumers'
30 safety and security should not be tolerated.

Lines 1–13: English Keyfacts, https://werberat.de/content/english-keyfacts (modified)
Lines 14–31: German Advertising Standards Council – Rules on Advertising and its Appraisal, July 2014, https://werberat.de/wp-content/uploads/2023/06/dw_general_principles_en_0.pdf (modified)
both: Berlin: Zentralverband der deutschen Werbewirtschaft ZAW e. V. / Deutscher Werberat, [20 July 2023]

VOCABULARY

to encourage
ermutigen
to appeal
ansprechen
prone
empfänglich, anfällig
to provide
bereitstellen
association
Verbindung
pride
Ehre, Stolz
fear
Angst
immediate
umgehend, direkt
greed
Gier
connotation
Bedeutung
leveraged
wirksam eingesetzt
to incorporate
berücksichtigen, einbauen
desire
Wunsch, Sehnsucht
to miss out
verpassen
German Standards Advertising Council
Deutscher Werberat
self-regulatory system
sich selbst kontrollierendes System
to abuse
missbrauchen
to exploit
ausnutzen, ausbeuten
to subject
unterwerfen

INTERNET

WES-116955-741
Link to the guide to the advertising code of the German Advertising Council

7.5 Do food labels help consumers?

M 1   Temptation

Cartoon: Kim Schmidt,
29 Nov 2019

M 2   Germany next to adopt Nutri-Score

Following France and Belgium, Germany is the next country to introduce the Nutri-Score nutrition label, after an independent consumer survey commissioned by the German government found this to be the best label. [...]

5 The German Minister for Food and Agriculture [...] has announced that she intends to introduce Nutri-Score as an official food label. "In doing so, I am making a valid decision in a de-
10 bate that has been going on for more than ten years in a very emotional and sometimes polarising manner", *LebensmittelPraxis* quotes the Minister. "That is why it is all the more important that the scientific analysis and con-
15 sumer research that we have carried out should now provide us with a reliable data-

base." A survey showed that 57 % of respondents preferred Nutri-Score to other food labels, as it was best understood by consumers. In addition, the label scored very well in two 20 particularly relevant consumer groups: people who rarely or never think about the composition of food, and obese people.

Nutri-Score uses a colour (on a scale from green to red) and a corresponding letter (on a 25 scale from A to E) to indicate how healthy a product actually is. The label takes into account both ingredients that are beneficial to health (like fibres or proteins) and nutrients that are best limited in this respect (like satu- 30 rated fatty acids, sugars and salt).

*Germany next to adopt Nutri-Score, Antwerpen: RetailDetail, 1 Oct 2019, https://www.retaildetail.eu/news/food/
germany-also-chooses-nutri-score/ [20 July 2023]*

M3 The effect of food labels on consumers' food choices

A trip to the **grocery store** seems to require more reading than ever these days: Nutrition Facts panels on the back; **low-sodium**, low-fat, fat-free, **dairy-free**, no added sugar and more
5 on the front. But even as food producers adapt the "more is more" attitude toward **cluttered** packaging, little evidence exists to show if consumers improve their eating habits because of food labels.

10 **Summary:**
An analysis of studies [in the United States] looked at how labeling on food packaging, **point-of-sale materials** and restaurant menus **prompted** consumers to eat fewer calories and
15 fat, reduce their choice of other unhealthy food options, and eat more vegetables.
The study also found that labels prompted food producers to lower the amounts of trans fat and sodium in their offerings. [...]

20 **The findings:**
Because of labeling, consumers chose food with 6.6 fewer calories and 10.6 percent less total fat. They also selected 13 percent fewer other unhealthy food options such as sugar-
25 sweetened beverages, alcoholic beverages, non-alcoholic caloric beverages, french fries, potatoes, white bread, and foods high in saturated fat, trans fat, added sugars or sodium.
Labels did not seem **to alter** consumption of
30 **carbohydrates**, protein, saturated fat, fruits or **whole grains**.
Alternately, they did not **increase** consumption of healthy options such as salads, soups, low-fat dairy, lean meat, fish and seafood, and more.
35 However, consumers opted to eat 13.5 percent more vegetables because of food labels.
In addition, labeling has inspired food companies to reduce the amount of sodium by 8.9 percent and trans fat by 64.3 percent in their
40 products.

Study conclusions:
Food labels are an effective way to reduce consumers' consumption of calories and fat, as well as increase their intake of vegetables. Labeling also prompted manufacturers to re-
45 duce the amounts of sodium and trans fat in their products, but manufacturers did not significantly change the amount of calories, saturated fats, dietary fiber or the other healthy and unhealthy food options men-
50 tioned above.

Victoria A.F. Camron, Food labels have positive but limited effect on consumers' food choices, in: Supermarket News, New York, NY: Informa USA Inc., 30 Jan 2019, https://www.supermarketnews.com/health-wellness/food-labels-have-positive-limited-effect-consumers-food-choices [20 July 2023]

VOCABULARY

grocery store
Lebensmittelgeschäft
low-sodium
natriumarm (salzarm)
dairy-free
milchfrei
cluttered
überhäuft
point-of-sale materials
spezielle Werbematerialien, z. B. Flyer, Banner, Broschüren …
to prompt
auffordern
to alter
verändern
carbohydrates
Kohlenhydrate
whole grains
Vollkornprodukte
to increase
erhöhen, steigern

M4 Nutrition facts

1 Analyse the cartoon (M1). ▸ METHOD Cartoon, pp. 26 – 27
2 **Think–Pair–Share:** Explain why the government wants to introduce the Nutri-Score (M2).
3 Assess how food labels change consumer behaviour according to US studies (M3).
4 Do you use nutrition facts or food labels when buying a product (M3, M4)? Give reasons for your answer.
5 Discuss whether food labels are helpful or unnecessary. ▸ Useful phrases (A), pp. 202 – 203

7.6   Sustainability – a realistic goal?

M 1   Fast fashion

Cartoon: Gatis Sluka, 12 June 2023

M 2   What is sustainability?

There is no universally agreed definition of sustainability. In fact, there are many different viewpoints on this concept and on how it can be achieved. [...] [T]he word sustainability
5 comes from sustainable + ity. And sustainable is, for instance, a composition of sustain + able. So if we start from the beginning, to "sustain" means "give support to", "to hold up", "to bear" or "to keep up".
10 What is sustainability, then? Sustainable is an adjective for something that is able to be sustained, i.e, something that is "bearable" and "capable of being continued at a certain level". In the end, sustainability can perhaps be seen
15 as the process(es) by which something is kept at a certain level.

Nonetheless, nowadays, because of the environmental and social problems society is facing, sustainability is commonly used in a specific way. Therefore, sustainability can be 20 defined as the processes and actions through which humankind avoids the depletion of natural resources (which is influenced by the way societies are organized) to keep an ecological balance so that society's quality of life doesn't 25 decrease. In this way, we can say that resources exploitation, manufacturing operations, the direction of investments, technological developments, wealth distribution, institutional changes, among others, are being sustainable 30 if they don't hurt the ecosystem services and if they allow for society's quality of life not to decrease.

Sustainability – What Is It? Definition, Principles and Examples, Paris: Youmatter, 18 Jun 2021, https://youmatter. world/en/definition/definitions-sustainability-definition-examples-principles/ [20 July 2023]

M3 Buying sustainable clothing: How consumers can be better informed when shopping online

In the textile sector sustainability has many facets: Environmental sustainability depends, for example, on the materials and chemicals used, water consumption and the handling of
5 toxic waste. The social sustainability of clothing and other textiles depends on factors such as working conditions, workers' rights and the avoidance of child labour. However, consumers have often looked in vain for such information
10 on specific products when buying fashion online.

Since March 2022, [a] research project has been investigating why this is the case and how sustainability information could be strength-
15 ened at the online point of sale. The project is funded by the German Ministry for the Environment as an AI lighthouse project. [...] In a survey of 1,873 participants, the researchers determined which sustainability information
20 consumers find particularly important when buying clothing online.

The results show that information on the social aspects of production, such as the use of child or forced labour, is of particular interest.
25 When it comes to environmental factors, those characteristics that directly affect consumers, such as the durability of a garment or the use of chemicals in production, are especially relevant to customers. [...]
30 Whether using labels, symbols, filters or color highlighting: There are various approaches for providing information about the sustainability of products on the internet. Surveys show that there is a definite need for simplifi-
35 cation and reliable guidance in order to differentiate between credible sustainability information and advertising claims (including greenwashing).

The Nutri-Score already exists for food, indi-
40 cating the nutritional value of a product on a colored scale using the letters A to E. In the textile sector, a score indicating the degree of sustainability of an item of clothing could be used in a similar way. However, there is cur-
45 rently a lack of standardized data and methods for evaluating the sustainability of textiles. [...]

The researchers conclude that a wide variety of stakeholders need to be brought together
50 across Europe, including manufacturers, retailers, sustainability initiatives and consumer organizations. The aim should be to shift from a wide range of individual solutions to a uniform sustainability communication, for exam-
55 ple using a textile score or standardized product information.

Buying sustainable clothing: How consumers can be better informed when shopping online, Karlsruhe: Fraunhofer Institute for Systems and Innovation Research ISI, 6 Mar 2024, https://www.isi.fraunhofer.de/ en/presse/2024/presseinfo-08-zusina-nachhaltige- kleidung-online-shopping-informationen-textil-score- siegel.html [29 May 2024]

VOCABULARY

toxic
giftig
avoidance
Vermeidung
child labour
Kinderarbeit
in vain
vergeblich
lighthouse
Leuchtturm
survey
Umfrage
forced labour
Zwangsarbeit
garment
Kleidungsstück
approach
Ansatz
claim
(hier) Versprechen
stakeholder
Interessenvertreter

M4 Sustainabilty triangle

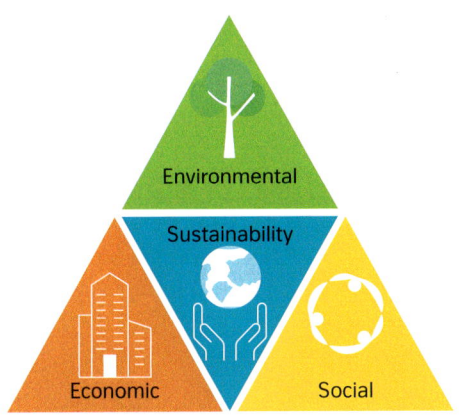

47519EX © Westermann

---

1 Analyse the cartoon (M1). ▶ METHOD Cartoon, pp. 26 – 27
2 **Placemat:** Starting from M2, name sustainable products you use daily.
3 Summarize the findings on sustainable clothing (M3). ▶ Nutri-Score, p. 166, M2
4 Discuss whether a dimension of sustainability conflicts with another (M4).
5 **Extra:** Design a flyer or a poster about fast fashion.
6 Evaluate whether the consumer is the key to saving the environment. **MORE HELP**

7.7 Investing – what is the best option?

M1   What would you do?

Imagine if you received 20 euros in pocket money every month. What would you do with it?

a) Just spend it.

c) Put it in the bank.

b) Save it in my piggy bank.

M2   The magic triangle of investing

Return
How much money can I make?
The more profit I get on the money
I invest, the greater the return.

Liquidity
How quickly can I use my invested money?
The easier I can leave my investment, the
more liquid it is.

Safety
What is my risk of losing money?
The lower the risk of the investment,
the safer it is.

47528EX © Westermann

M3 Saving and investment strategies

If you want to save or invest your money, you have different options, e.g.:

	Deposits in a bank account There are different types of bank accounts. Usually, you get rather low interest for the saved money. Depending on the type of account, you can use the money at any time (then usually you get lower interest) or lock it in for a certain time. In Germany, the state insures bank deposits for € 100,000.
	Stocks By buying a stock you invest in a company and buy a very small part of it. Stocks are bought and sold at stock markets. The stock course varies and depends on supply and demand (see chap. 8).
	Funds A fund is a pool of stocks or other valuables. Investment funds are managed by professionals. Because funds invest in various companies, the risk is spread out more than with individual stocks.
	Real estate The price of houses and land may increase over time.
	Commodities The price of gold and other commodities (like silver or oil) may increase over time.
	Collectibles The price of art and other collectibles (like watches, jewellery, stamps, coins) may increase over time.

Text by the author

M4 How to become a successful investor

1. Follow a goal-based approach
You must clearly define your various goals and invest accordingly continuously until it is achieved.

2. Don't put all your eggs in one basket
Diversification of investments minimizes risk and maximizes returns when you invest in a mix of different asset classes.

3. Opt for a dynamic plan
Your investment should have the flexibility to take advantage of changing market conditions and your financial requirements.

4. Prepare for a rainy day
To avoid financial and emotional trauma during harsh or extraordinary circumstances prepare yourself for life's contingencies.

Divya Grover, Are The Investment Lessons We Learned From Parents Still Relevant?, in: PersonalFN, Mumbai: Quantum Information Services Pvt. Ltd., 16 Sep 2019, https://www.personalfn.com/fns/are-the-investment-lessons-we-learned-from-parents-still-relevant [10 Nov 2023] (modified)

1. Explain your options and give reasons for your decision (M1). Create a mind map.
   ▸ METHOD Visualization, pp. 136–137
2. Discuss the pros and cons of investing money according to the three dimensions (M2).
3. **Bus stop:** Compare the investment options (M3) using the criteria in M2. **MORE HELP**
4. Assign the investment option (M3) to a strategy (M4).
5. The price of a good (€ 100,–) increases by 2 % every year (by inflation) while you save €100,–. Calculate the interest rates and stock profits for 3 years, if
   a) the interest rate of your bank account is 0.5 % per year
   b) your stock profits are 3 % per year.
   Now check how much of your savings remains while prices for goods rise. **MORE HELP**

VOCABULARY

deposit
Einlage
stock
Aktie
fund
Fond
asset class
Anlageklasse
contingency
Eventualität

INFO

Inflation
means that the value of money falls while prices rise. One unit of money can buy less and less.

7.8 Going into debt – a problem?

м 1   How many people are in debt?

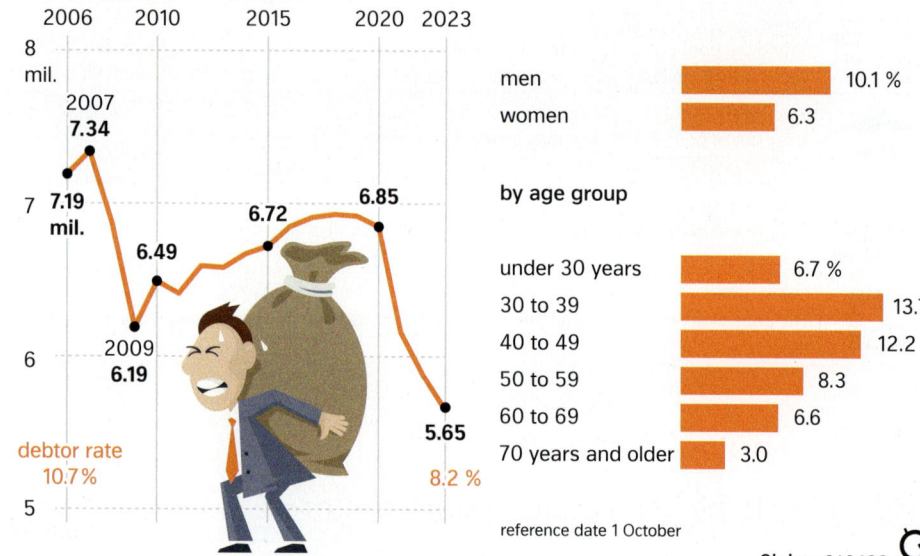

Private debt

Indebted persons aged 18 and over
in Germany in millions

Proportion of indebted people among
all adults (debtor rate) 2023 in per cent

2006   2010   2015   2020   2023

8 mil.

2007
7.34

7 **7.19
mil.**

6.49

6.72

6.85

2009
6.19

5.65

6

debtor rate
10.7 %

8.2 %

5

men	10.1 %
women	6.3

by age group

under 30 years	6.7 %
30 to 39	13.7
40 to 49	12.2
50 to 59	8.3
60 to 69	6.6
70 years and older	3.0

reference date 1 October

47531EX   Data: Creditreform; source: Globus 016490, Picture Alliance (language modified)

Globus 016490 Ⓖ

м 2   When does it make sense to borrow money?

a) Clara: "I borrowed €3 for the bus journey home. I didn't have enough money with me."

b) Jason: "My gym costs €35.00 a month. My pocket money is not enough for that. That is why I borrow from friends."

c) Luca: "I need €30.00 now to be able to repair my bike. Then can I take on my well-paid job as a bike courier during the holidays again."

d) Manou: "I borrow money from friends and relatives until I have the €500,00 I need for a new gaming console."

e) Yasmin: " The mobile phone I have been saving for for a long time is currently on sale. I'm €50.00 short. It's my birthday in a month. I'm sure I will get some money as a present."

f) Mike: "I borrowed money from a mate. He now wants it back and is putting pressure on me. So now I have to ask someone else to lend me some money."

Text by the author

M3 Reasons why people are in debt

Reasons for overindebtedness

In Germany, **5.88 million** people are overindebted in 2022, mainly due to

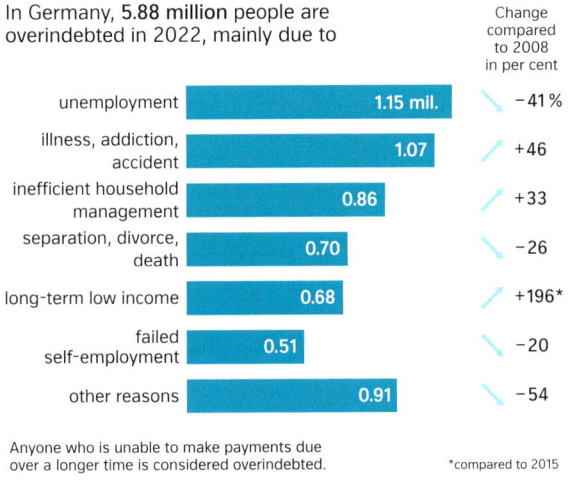

		Change compared to 2008 in per cent
unemployment	1.15 mil.	– 41 %
illness, addiction, accident	1.07	+46
inefficient household management	0.86	+33
separation, divorce, death	0.70	–26
long-term low income	0.68	+196*
failed self-employment	0.51	–20
other reasons	0.91	–54

Anyone who is unable to make payments due over a longer time is considered overindebted.

*compared to 2015

47532EX © Westermann

Data: Creditreform Schuldneratlas
Source: dpa 104936, Picture Alliance (language modified)

When young adults have debts

Creditors of 18- to 24-year-olds in Germany in per cent

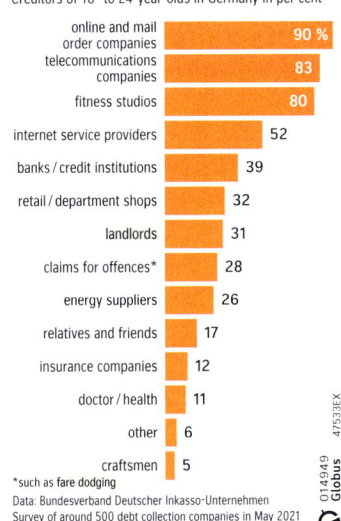

online and mail order companies	90 %
telecommunications companies	83
fitness studios	80
internet service providers	52
banks / credit institutions	39
retail / department shops	32
landlords	31
claims for offences*	28
energy suppliers	26
relatives and friends	17
insurance companies	12
doctor / health	11
other	6
craftsmen	5

*such as fare dodging

Data: Bundesverband Deutscher Inkasso-Unternehmen
Survey of around 500 debt collection companies in May 2021
Source: Globus 014949, Picture Alliance (language modified)

47533EX
014949 Globus

M4 Planning your budget in six steps

Step 1: Calculate your income
Step 2: Track your spending
Step 3: Set realistic financial goals
Step 4: Make a plan
5 **Step 5:** Adjust your spending to stay on budget
Step 6: Review your budget regularly

What is the 50/30/20 rule? 47547EX © Westermann

The 50/30/20 rule is a budgeting technique that divides your take-home income into three categories by percentages. It's a simple way to track your spending. Here's the breakdown:

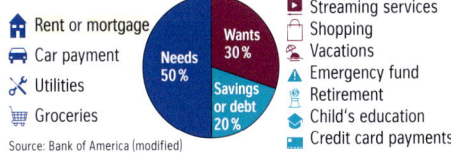

🏠 Rent or mortgage
🚗 Car payment
✂️ Utilities
🛒 Groceries

Needs 50 %
Wants 30 %
Savings or debt 20 %

▶️ Streaming services
🛍️ Shopping
⛱️ Vacations
⚠️ Emergency fund
🏛️ Retirement
💰 Child's education
💳 Credit card payments

Source: Bank of America (modified)

Creating a budget, in: Better Money Habits, Charlotte, NC: Bank of America, https://bettermoneyhabits.bank ofamerica.com/en/saving-budgeting/creating-a-budget [10 Nov 2023] (modified)

Month	Income	Spending	Total balance
January	+ €30 pocket money	–€100 new sneakers	–€70
February	+ €30 pocket money + €50 birthday money	–€50 new pullover –€50 new PC game	–€20
…	…	…	…

Table by the author

---

1 How many people are in debt? Describe the situation in Germany (M1).

2 a) Discuss in which of the situations in M2 it can make sense to borrow money.
b) Formulate general rules about borrowing money. **MORE HELP**

3 **Partner jigsaw:** Analyse the charts and compare the results (M3).
▶ METHOD Statistics, pp. 20 – 21

4 Make your own budget plan (using the provided table) (M4).

VOCABULARY

landlord
Vermieter
fare dodging
ÖPNV-Nutzung ohne gültigen Fahrschein
budget
Haushalt
to adjust
anpassen
to review
überprüfen
rent
Miete
mortgage
Hypothek, Darlehen

Multiple choice test: young consumers

1. **Opportunity cost is ...**
   - ☐ a) the cost for living expenses.
   - ☐ b) the cost for a not chosen option.
   - ☐ c) the cost for a single household.

2. **Abraham Maslow's hierarchy of needs includes ...**
   - ☐ a) needs like water, sleep and food.
   - ☐ b) needs like a big house, a nice car and a big garden.
   - ☐ c) needs like being loved by your family and friends.

3. **Influencer marketing is successful because ...**
   - ☐ a) all kids love the influencers.
   - ☐ b) influencers are superstars.
   - ☐ c) influencers are people whose opinions you tend to believe.

4. **The shop / market layout follows ...**
   - ☐ a) the idea that you must walk through the whole market before you reach the cashier.
   - ☐ b) the idea that you always see new things that attract your attention.
   - ☐ c) the idea that you can get in and out as quickly as possible.

5. **In supermarket shelf marketing you find ...**
   - ☐ a) cheap things at the top and expensive things at the bottom of the shelf.
   - ☐ b) cheap things in the middle of the shelf.
   - ☐ c) expensive things at the top and cheap things at the bottom of the shelf.

6. **The German standards for advertising do not ...**
   - ☐ a) tolerate advertising which brings physical or psychological harm to children.
   - ☐ b) forbid discrimination in advertising.
   - ☐ c) ban advertising with violent or aggressive behavior.

7. **Food labels help the consumer to ...**
   - ☐ a) identify the ingredients of a product.
   - ☐ b) find out how the product was produced.
   - ☐ c) realize if the product is healthy or not.

8. **The sustainability triangle consists of three dimensions:**
   - ☐ a) ecological, political, and social.
   - ☐ b) economic, political, and social.
   - ☐ c) environmental, economic and social.

9. **When investing money, a good strategy is ...**
   - ☐ a) not to put all eggs in one basket.
   - ☐ b) to focus on one option (e.g. stocks) alone.
   - ☐ c) to invest from time to time without a fixed plan.

10. **Planning a budget: What is the 50/30/20 rule?**
    - ☐ a) spending 50 % on shopping, vacations, etc.,
          30 % for retirement and child's education, etc., and
          20 % on groceries and mortgage, etc.
    - ☐ b) spending 30 % on shopping, vacations, etc.,
          20 % for retirement and child's education, etc., and
          50 % on groceries and mortgage, etc.
    - ☐ c) spending 20 % on shopping, vacations etc.,
          50 % for retirement and child's education, etc., and
          30 % on groceries and mortgage, etc.

1   Test yourself. Note: Sometimes several answers can be correct, sometimes only one.

What we need is consumption!

VOCABULARY

growth
Wachstum
consumption
expenditure
Konsumausgaben

Cartoon: Max Gustafson, 29 Jan 2013

US household consumption

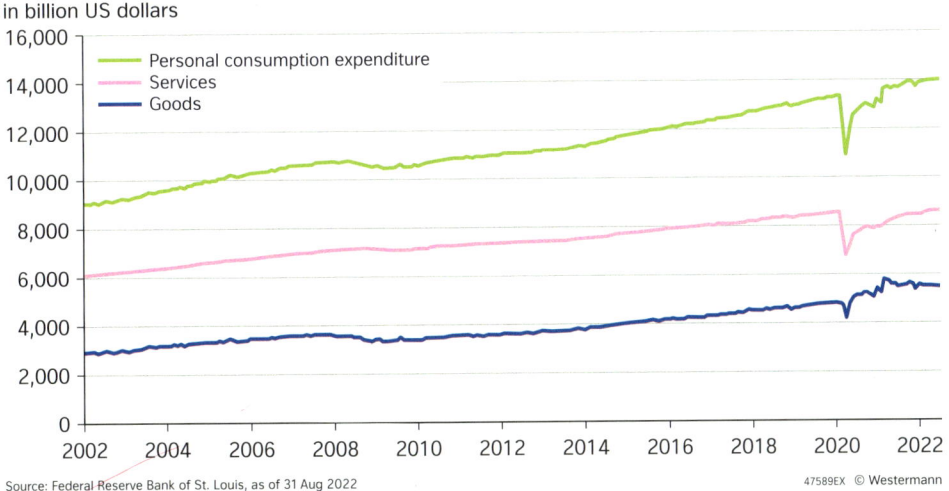

Personal consumption expenditure in the USA
in billion US dollars

Source: Federal Reserve Bank of St. Louis, as of 31 Aug 2022

47589EX © Westermann

1 Analyse the cartoon. ▸ METHOD Cartoon, pp. 26–27
2 Compare the cartoon with the chart. ▸ METHOD Statistics, pp. 20–21

8

1	**2**	
3	**4**	

Markets and prices

Yes, I understand your pricing strategy, but since I'm likely to be your only customer today, what about a big discount?

Cartoon: Hagen, 27 August 2011

1 Look at the pictures: Identify similarities and differences. **MORE HELP**

2 Focus on the picture of the farmers' market (No. 1). Imagine yourself shopping at this market. List what you would like to buy and explain your choices.

3 Analyse the cartoon. **MORE HELP** ▸ METHOD Cartoons, pp. 26 – 27

4 Imagine you are going to meet an economist who is an expert in markets and prices. Make a list of questions that you have and give reasons for asking them.

8.1 Markets – crucial for our economy?

M 1 Different markets

a) **Physical markets**	Locations where goods are bought with money and where buyers and sellers interact face-to-face, such as shopping malls or retail stores.
b) **Auction market**	A physical or virtual market where buyers bid for goods or services in public auctions.
c) **Online markets**	Markets where costumers use the internet to buy goods and services without any physical contact.
d) **Property market**	A market for buying, selling, and renting property, including residential and commercial real estate.
e) **Financial market**	A market for buying and selling financial assets, such as money, investments, currencies, and other financial tools.
f) **Informal/ illegal market**	Illegal or unofficial trade in goods or services that are prohibited or restricted. There are no taxes and no government control.

Text by the author

VOCABULARY

M2 Markets and their role in economics

Economics is the study of scarcity and how consumers manage it (see chapter 7). The resources are limited but desires are unlimited. This applies to consumers as well as to producers, workers, and governments. Markets provide firms places to sell goods and services for profit and revenue. They also provide consumers places to buy the goods and services they need.

Markets are important to the economy because they are the meeting points where what is available (supply) and what people want (demand) come together. They help producers sell their goods and services to people who want them. In a free market system, supply and demand influence prices by directing resources to those who need them most. This pricing system uses resources efficiently and motivates producers to supply the goods and services their consumers demand.

Moreover, markets support innovation and efficiency. Firms try to produce goods and services efficiently to remain competitive and maximize profits. This drive for efficiency often leads to technological advancements, increased productivity, and economic growth. In this way, markets spur economic development and progress.

Markets also keep the economy stable. Market prices can change when conditions change, which helps balance the supply and demand of goods. This flexibility reduces economic shocks and strengthens the stability of the economy.

In conclusion, markets are crucial for economic activity. They are the vital links which allocate resources, exchange goods and services, and support economic growth. It is necessary to understand market dynamics to assess how societies deal with scarcity and allocate resources to assist our social well-being.

VOCABULARY

resources
Ressourcen
limited
begrenzt
revenue
Umsatz
available
verfügbar
efficiently
effizient,
wirtschaftlich
advancement
Weiterentwicklung,
Fortschritt
allocate
verteilen, zuweisen

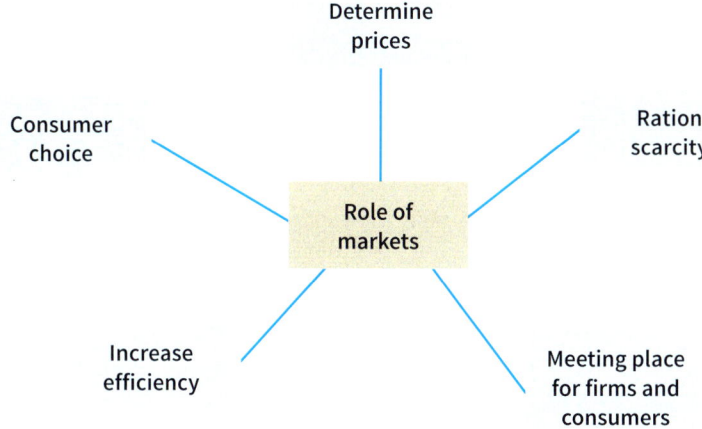

Text by the author

---

1 A market is a place where buyers and sellers come together to exchange goods and services. Name and describe what type of market is depicted in pictures 1 to 6 and what goods or services are being exchanged. Use the table below (M1).

2 **Extra:** Which other markets do you know? Make a list. **MORE HELP**

3 **Swap chairs:** Characterize the role of markets in our economy (M2).

4 Decide which market type is most important for you as a consumer and briefly explain your choice. ▸ Useful phrases (C), pp. 204 – 205

8.2 What role do prices play in our lives?

INFO

Black Friday
is a retail discount
event taking place on
the Friday of Thanks-
giving weekend.

M1   Black Friday

M2   Accommodation prices during the Munich Octoberfest 2023

Munich Oktoberfest 2023
Example accommodation prices for a 3-night weekend stay (in €)

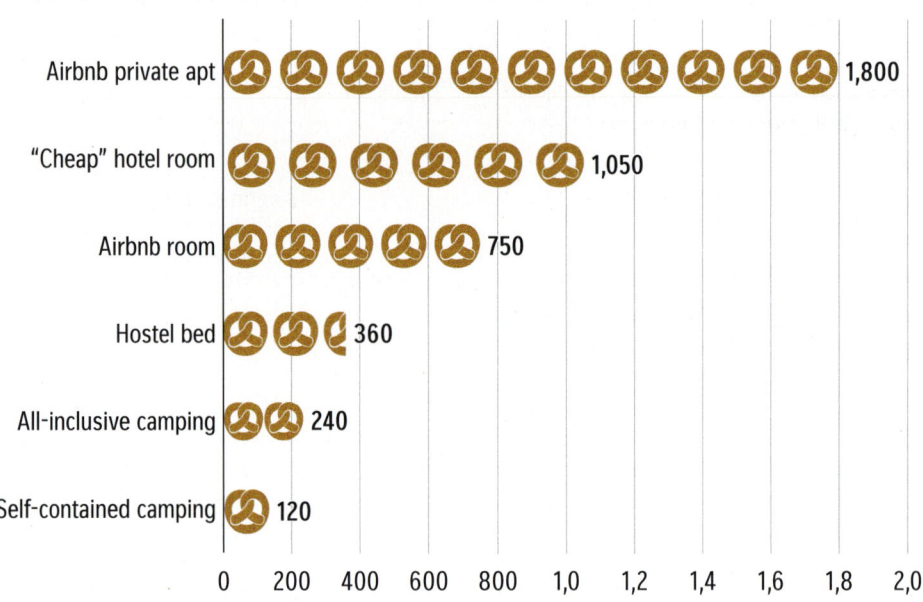

Airbnb private apt	1,800
"Cheap" hotel room	1,050
Airbnb room	750
Hostel bed	360
All-inclusive camping	240
Self-contained camping	120

0   200   400   600   800   1,0   1,2   1,4   1,6   1,8   2,0

47572EX © Westermann

Source: Roaming around the world, 2023

M 3 ## School summer fair

The school is hosting a summer fair. Most students are looking forward to it and want to get involved in making the day special. They have got loads of fun activities planned. Along with
5 music, dancing, and theatre performances, they are going to offer face painting, a **raffle**, and a second-hand market. This year, the classes from Year 7 and 8 have been chosen to sell food and drinks. They will be setting up
10 stalls with both cold and hot drinks, and there will be yummy waffles and cakes for sale. The students are quite excited and look forward to the sales because they plan to **donate** half of the money they make, but they will keep the

other half for their class funds. Now they are 15 having some serious discussions about what they are going to sell that day and especially what prices to set.

Text by the author

M 4 ## Different scenarios and their effects on prices

a) The tech revolution:
A tech giant introduces a new budget-friendly smartphone loaded with advanced features. It promises to bring **cutting-edge technology** to the masses.

b) Sneaker madness:
A **renowned** fashion brand unveils an exclusive limited-edition sneaker. With only a few pairs available, sneaker fans are eager to get their hands on this stylish rarity.

c) Release of new console:
A well-known gaming company releases a new console but the gaming community, occupied with other popular consoles and games, overlooks this new entry. Despite its advanced features, the console fails to capture the attention of gamers.

d) Decline in fashion influence:
A once-popular fashion influencer loses popularity, causing interest from followers to decline. The promoted fashion items have become **shelf warmers** that nobody wants to buy.

Text by the author

1 Think about the importance of prices in your daily life and situations where prices matter to you. Do you pay attention to prices? Why or why not? Give reasons. Speak from your experience with your peers and find out how prices influence your decisions and daily life.

2 Describe what Black Friday is and how it influences our behaviour as consumers (M1).

3 Analyse the chart M2. **MORE HELP** ▸ METHOD Statistics, pp. 20 – 21

4 Have you ever sold food and drinks at a school event? What conclusions can you draw about pricing based on your own experience? List what the students in M3 should consider in their pricing strategy.

5 **Jigsaw:** Analyse how prices are set in each scenario (M4). Do research on the actual prices for the given scenarios online. Present your findings to each other and discuss how you, as customers, would respond to these price changes.

8.3 Is there a perfect market?

M1 The delicate balance of supply and demand

THE DELICATE BALANCE of SUPPLY and DEMAND

BATTING HELMETS $25

© Wiley Ink, inc./Distributed by Universal Uclick via Cartoonstock

Cartoon: Wiley Miller, 3 Dec 2012

M2 The circular flow of economics

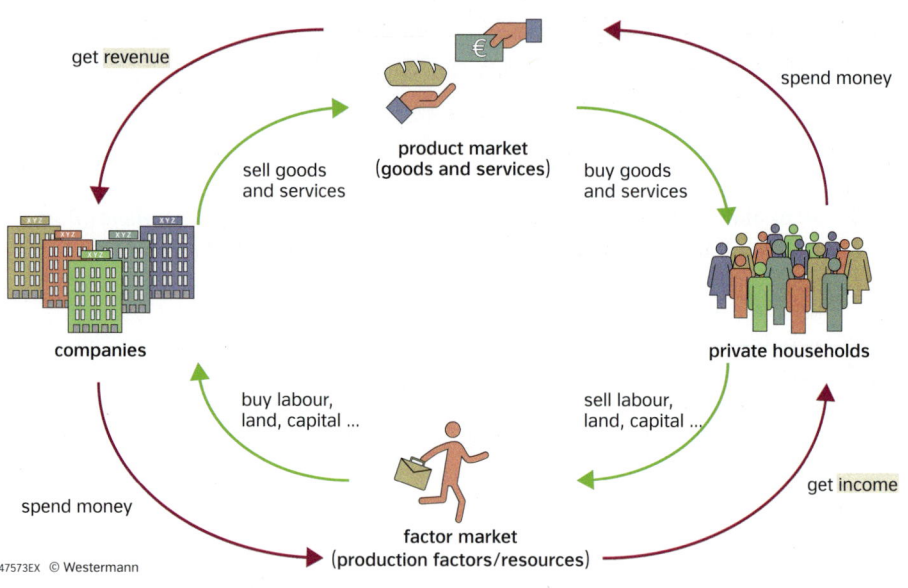

get revenue

spend money

product market
(goods and services)

sell goods
and services

buy goods
and services

companies

private households

buy labour,
land, capital ...

sell labour,
land, capital ...

spend money

get income

factor market
(production factors/resources)

47573EX © Westermann

M3 Market conditions for perfect competition

VOCABULARY

to exceed
übersteigen,
übertreffen
to increase
steigen, sich erhöhen
to decrease
sinken, fallen

Homogeneous products

All sellers produce and sell an identical product or service.

Example:
Everyone sells the same toothpaste to a village. It is the only toothpaste available.

Many buyers and sellers

There are many buyers and sellers to buy and sell the product.

Example:
A large number of businesses sell toothpaste and everyone in the village uses the same toothpaste.

Information transparency

Buyers have perfect information – all the information they need to make decisions to buy items.

Example:
The toothpaste comes with a complete breakdown of ingredients, costs, and sourcing information.

No entry oder exit barriers

Businesses can enter and exit the market freely. There are no start-up costs or legal restrictions.

Example:
Anyone in the village can start or stop selling the toothpaste.

47575EX © Westermann

Source: Semrush, 2023 (modified)

M4 The four rules of the market mechanism

1. When demand exceeds supply, the price .

2. When the price increases, supply rises, and  falls.

3. If supply exceeds , the price decreases.

4. If the  falls, supply decreases, and demand increases.

Angebot, Nachfrage und Preisbildung im Modell, Oldenburg: Institut für Ökonomische Bildung, https://de.ecedon. uni-oldenburg.de/fyls/44499/download_file [18 Mar 2024] (modified/translated)

1 Analyse the cartoon (M1). ▸ METHOD Cartoons, pp. 26 –27

2 Describe the circular flow of economics (M2). **MORE HELP**

3 Explain in your own words in German what is meant by a "perfect market" (M3).
   ▸ METHOD Mediation, pp. 72 – 73

4 Complete the diagram in your folder to state the "four rules of the market mechanism" (M4).

5 Illustrate the rules of market mechanism (M4) with real-life examples, such as sneakers, a gaming console, or a smartphone. ▸ p. 181, M4

6 a) Compare how to set prices in theory with your experience and the outcomes from this chapter.

   b) **Bus stop:** Discuss your findings within the group and cooperate to consider why your classmates may have different conclusions.
   ▸ METHOD Price-quantity diagrams, pp. 184 – 185

How to make price-quantity diagrams (supply and demand curves)

Understanding the law of supply and demand

The law of supply and demand is a fundamental principle in economics, which explains how prices are formed on markets. This theory connects how much of a product is offered (supply) with how much of it consumers want to buy (demand). Let us illustrate this with hot chocolate.

First, we need to understand the basic terms: Supply refers to the quantity of a product that producers are willing to sell at different prices. For instance, the supply of hot chocolate relies on factors like what the ingredients cost and production technology. Demand shows how much of a product consumers want to buy at different prices. In the case of hot chocolate, demand may rise during colder months or in areas with many chocolate fans. Equilibrium price shows a balance in the market where the supply equals the demand.

Imagine we are in a café that offers hot chocolate. Now let us consider what happens if the price of the hot chocolate changes. If the price is quite high, say €5.00 per cup, the café will be willing to sell more hot chocolate, so supply increases. However, fewer people will be willing to buy it at a higher price, so demand decreases. This creates a supply surplus, because there is more hot chocolate on hand than people want to buy. They will probably look elsewhere to see if there is cheaper chocolate, so the café will adjust the price to keep selling. However, if the price is rather low, say €2 per cup, more people will be willing to buy hot chocolate because it is cheap. So demand increases, but supply decreases because it is not profitable for the café to sell the hot chocolate at the lower price. Now there is a supply shortage, as more people want hot chocolate than the café offers.

The interaction between supply and demand determines the equilibrium price: in our example, it turns out that the café offers exactly 200 cups of hot chocolate at a price of €3.50 per cup and that there is demand for exactly 200 cups at this price (see also tables on p. 185). So in this case €3.50 is the equilibrium price at which supply equals demand. At the equilibrium price, the equilibrium quantity is also reached, here 200 cups.

In conclusion, the law of supply and demand helps us understand that the market determines the price. An analysis of supply, demand, and equilibrium price reveals how markets reach a balance between sellers' offers and buyers' choices.

Equilibrium price for hot chocolate

47576EX © Westermann

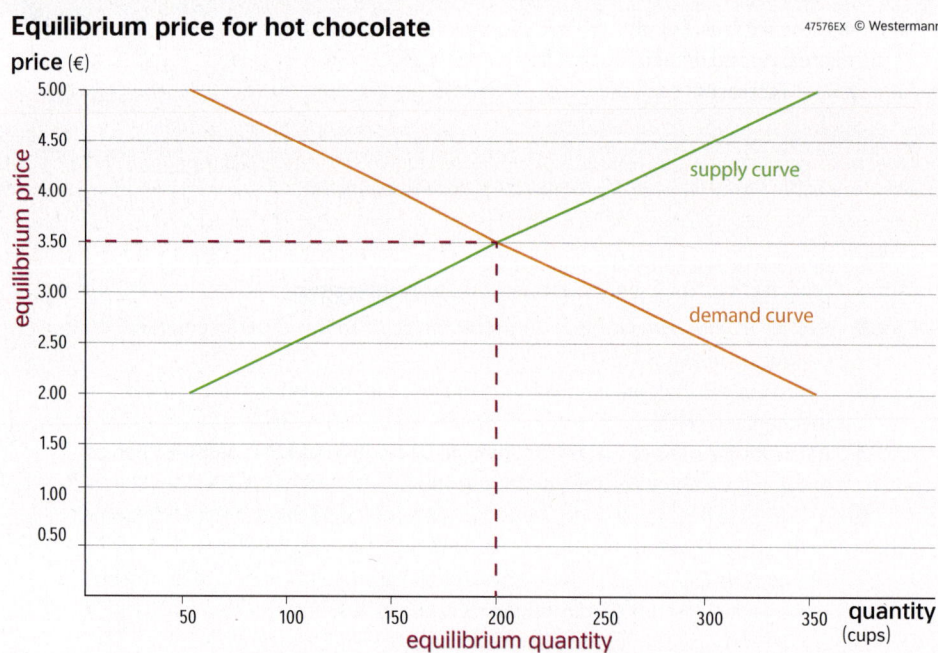

Making a price-quantity diagram – how do I do it?

Step 1: Setting title and axes
- Tip: Chequered paper works well for this.
- Give your diagram a clear title.
- Draw two axes: one for price (vertical = y-axis) and one for quantity (horizontal = x-axis).
- Label the vertical axis as "price (€)" and the horizontal axis as "quantity" (units, such as cups).
- Divide both axes into steps. Pay attention to the values you have for price and quantity so that you can enter all off them in the axes. ▸ Use the diagram on page 184 as a model.

Step 2: Drawing the supply curve
- Mark the points for the values you have for the supply in the diagram.
- Connect the points to form the supply curve.
- Label the curve.

Price per cup (€)	Quantity supplied (units)
2.00	50
2.50	100
3.00	150
3.50	200
4.00	250
4.50	300
5.00	350

Step 3: Drawing the demand curve
- Mark the points for the values you have for the demand in the diagram.
- Connect the points to form the demand curve.
- Label the curve.

Price per cup (€)	Quantity demanded (units)
2.00	350
2.50	300
3.00	250
3.50	200
4.00	150
4.50	100
5.00	50

Step 4: Finding equilibrium price and quantity
- Identify the point of intersection where the supply curve meets the demand curve.
- From the intersection, draw a horizontal line on the y-axis and a vertical line on the x-axis.
- Read off the values for the equilibrium price and the equilibrium quantity and note them.

Understanding the limitations of economic models
In conclusion, it is important to see that the price-quantity diagram is a fundamental model in economics. Like all models, it simplifies complex facts to provide insights and predictions. However, remember that models are abstract and may not be able to show how complex the actual economy really is. In the case of Germany, factors such as government regulations, cultural norms, and historical contexts can have strong effects on market dynamics. While models are valuable tools for analysis, they also have limits because they only focus on certain aspects while leaving out others. Therefore, while the price-quantity diagram helps us understand market dynamics, we must interpret its results with caution and consider other factors that may influence economic outcomes.

1 Freshly baked waffles are for sale at the school summer fair.
The values for the supply and demand of waffles are as follows:

Supply	10	20	30	40	50	60	70	80
Demand	40	35	30	25	20	15	10	5
Price	€0.50	€1.00	€1.50	€2.00	€2.50	€3.00	€3.50	€4.00

a) Use the values in the table to make a price-quantity diagram.
b) Determine the equilibrium price and the equilibrium quantity.

8.4 Market structures – who is in charge?

M1 Market structures in our everyday lives

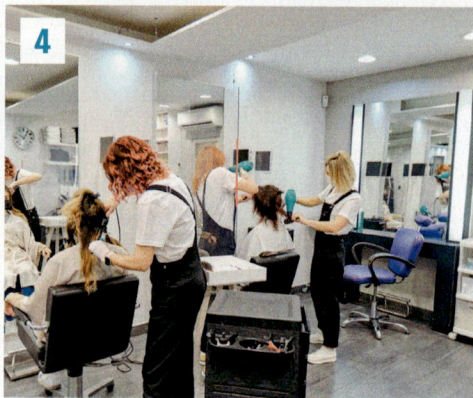

M2 Understanding market dynamics

What if there was only one provider for a product in the market? In the marketplace, firms compete for customers, sales, and market share. This competition can take various forms. There is the form of price competition, where firms compete by offering lower prices. There is also the form of non-price competition, where firms compete by making changes to the product, using different marketing strategies, or improving customer service. Competition drives innovation, efficiency, and consumer welfare within markets.

Different types of market structures are classified to understand how economic activity develops and who has the power in these markets. They help us analyse how prices are determined, how resources are allocated, and who is in charge of shaping market outcomes. By examining various market structures, such as perfect competition, monopolistic competition, oligopoly, and monopoly, we gain insight into the behaviour of firms, the impact on consumers, and the effectiveness of government intervention. However, it is important to recognize that these models have limits and may not show completely how complex the markets are. Nonetheless, they are invaluable tools for understanding market dynamics.

Text by the author

M3 Market structures

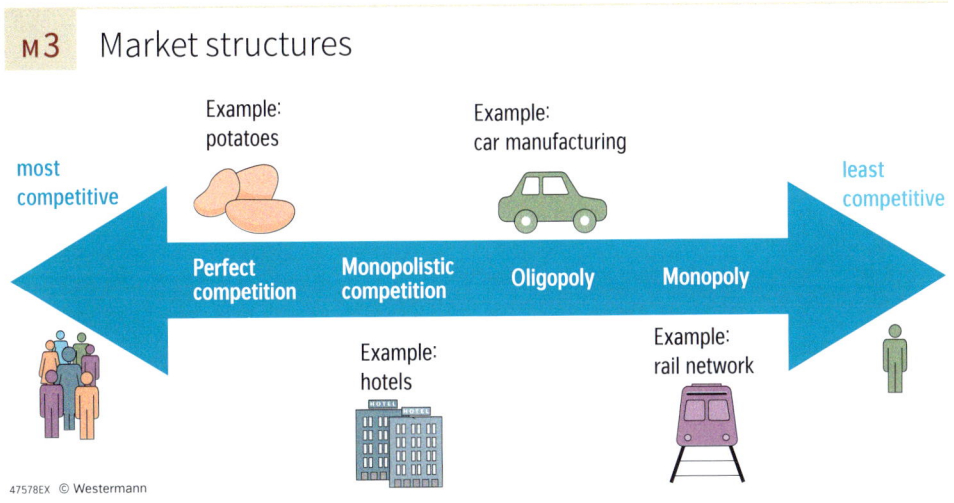

47578EX © Westermann

Perfect competition – many competitors with identical products

Perfect competition is a market structure characterized by many small firms selling
5 identical products, with no barriers to entry or exit. In this market, firms cannot set prices and must accept the market price determined by supply and demand forces. For instance, in the agricultural sector, many farmers sell
10 identical products. Each farmer has no influence over the market price, which is determined only by supply and demand.

Monopolistic competition – many competitors with slightly different products

15 In monopolistic competition, many competitors offer slightly different products or services. Unlike perfect competition, firms in this market can set some prices because the products are slightly different. For instance, in the
20 smartphone market, brands offer similar devices with varied features and designs, aiming to attract customers with unique aspects like camera quality or design aesthetics.

Text by the author

Oligopoly – only a few decide

In some markets, only a few sellers exist, aim- 25 ing to maximize profits. In an oligopoly, these sellers can coordinate with each other to control the quantity and prices of their products. This coordination can lead to less competition and higher prices. Take the German auto- 30 mobile industry, for example, where several major car manufacturers dominate the market. Together, these companies have strong control over pricing and production decisions, thus influencing market outcomes. 35

Monopoly – when only one wins

In some markets, there is only one company selling a specific product or service and many people want to buy it. This situation is known as a monopoly. For example, the postal service 40 and the railway in Germany used to be state monopolies until the mid-1990s. While genuine monopolies are rare in Germany due to strict competition laws and the oversight of the Federal Cartel Office, they may exist in 45 other countries where competition regulations are less strict.

HOT SPOT

In English-speaking contexts, the German term **"Polypol"** is not used. Instead, **"perfect competition"** refers to a market with many small firms producing identical goods, where entry and exit are possible, and firms accept the market price.

INFO

Federal Cartel Office (Bundeskartellamt) is an independent federal competition authority based in Bonn and assigned to the Federal Ministry for Economic Affairs and Climate Action. Its task is to protect competition in Germany.

1 Describe the market situations depicted in M1 and assign them to the market structures presented in M3.

2 Explain what competition is and why it is important (M2).

3 Compare the market structures (M3). Use a table for your comparison. **MORE HELP**

4 Gallery Walk: Choose a sector or product with various options available, such as cars, smartphones, clothing, groceries, or electronics. Verify how market conditions influence your decisions as a consumer and present your considerations.

8.5 How do markets respond to digitalization and changes in society?

HOT SPOT

Digitalization
means integrating and applying digital technologies into business or society to improve efficiency, productivity, and innovation.

Digitization
is the process of converting data into a digital format, usually by scanning or digitizing physical documents or media.

The difference between the two lies in what they are mainly about: digitization is mostly about changing things from non-digital to digital, while digitalization involves using digital technologies to improve various aspects of life.

M1   Shopping now and then

M2   What people buy online

Most popular online purchases of goods and services, EU, 2022*
(% of people who bought or ordered goods or services over the internet for private use in the previous 3 months)

47579EX © Westermann

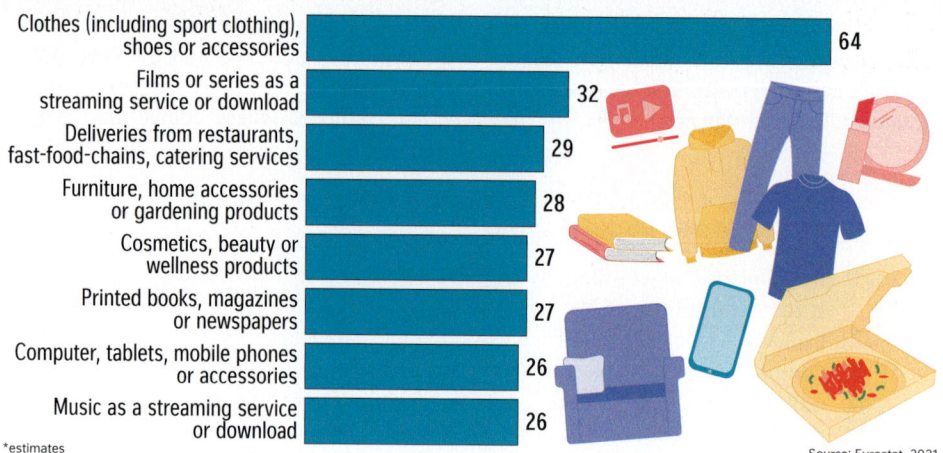

Category	%
Clothes (including sport clothing), shoes or accessories	64
Films or series as a streaming service or download	32
Deliveries from restaurants, fast-food-chains, catering services	29
Furniture, home accessories or gardening products	28
Cosmetics, beauty or wellness products	27
Printed books, magazines or newspapers	27
Computer, tablets, mobile phones or accessories	26
Music as a streaming service or download	26

*estimates

Source: Eurostat, 2021

M3 Online commerce on the rise

TOP 10 online shops in Germany
E-commerce net sales 2022 in billion €*

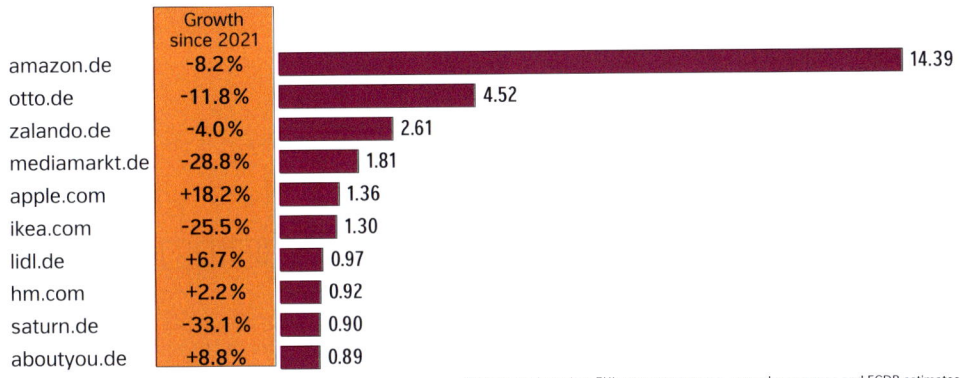

	Growth since 2021	E-commerce net sales 2022 in billion €
amazon.de	-8.2%	14.39
otto.de	-11.8%	4.52
zalando.de	-4.0%	2.61
mediamarkt.de	-28.8%	1.81
apple.com	+18.2%	1.36
ikea.com	-25.5%	1.30
lidl.de	+6.7%	0.97
hm.com	+2.2%	0.92
saturn.de	-33.1%	0.90
aboutyou.de	+8.8%	0.89

*Figures are based on EHI company surveys, secondary sources and ECDB estimates
Source: ECDB (eCommerceDB GmbH)/EHI-Commerce Market Germany, 2023

47581EX © Westermann

M4 Does online shopping kill our high streets?

The number of shops in Germany has been declining for quite some time. The decline was particularly strong in the years 2020 to 2022, influenced by the COVID-19 pandemic, with
5 the number of stores decreasing by 11,000 per year. However, even in the pre-crisis years from 2015 to 2019, an average of 5,000 stores closed annually.
Public attention focuses mainly on the clo-
10 sures of well-known chain stores: the planned closure of 47 Galeria Karstadt Kaufhof department stores, the liquidation of numerous branches of the shoe retailer Görtz, or the announced reduction in the stores of the fashion
15 chain Gerry Weber. However, according to the HDE (German Retail Association), most clos-

ures affect smaller specialty retailers – such as fashion boutiques, shoe stores, and bakeries. Finally, online commerce has transformed the business landscape in recent years. During the
20 COVID-19 crisis, even more customers became accustomed to shopping online.

BR24 Redaktion/Felix Lincke, Einkaufsstraßen in der Krise: Das Ladensterben geht weiter, München: Bayerischer Rundfunk, 24 Apr 2023, https://www.br.de/nachrichten/wirtschaft/einkaufsstrassen-in-der-krise-das-ladensterben-geht-weiter,TcKyPGC [11 Mar 2024] (translated and modified)

1 Interview an older relative, such as parents or grandparents, about their childhood shopping experience. Compare these accounts with the images (M1). What has changed for the consumer?
2 **Milling around:** Discuss with classmates what you typically purchase online and how it relates to the information in M2.
3 Analyse the chart (M3). ▸ METHOD Statistics, pp. 20 – 21
4 Describe the reasons for shops closing in German city centres (M4).
5 **Fishbowl:** Discuss the pros and cons of opening retail stores on Sundays in Germany and whether this would be an effective measure to stop the decline of city centres.
MORE HELP

Word scramble: markets and prices

1) CRAURILC WOLF FO MONISECCO
2) MADDEN
3) ZIDOTAGIANITLI
4) NOCCEMOIS
5) MEYCOON
6) QUEMILIBURI CRIEP
7) KARTEM
8) TRAMKE MAINSCHEM
9) POLSTONOMICI NOCTOMEIPIT
10) MERAKT TRETCURUS
11) YOMONLOP
12) LINNEO GISHNOPP
13) PFERTEC TREKAM
14) RECPI
15) YPSULP

Matching exercise: market structures

A) Perfect competition

a) A market structure with many firms selling similar but differentiated products.

B) Monopolistic competition

b) A market structure with one dominant seller controlling the market.

C) Oligopoly

c) A market structure with a small number of large firms dominating the market.

D) Monopoly

d) A theoretical market with many small firms producing identical goods, where entry and exit are easy, and firms take the price they can get.

1 **a)** Rearrange the letters in the word scramble to find the correct words.
  b) Partner or group activity: Choose four words from the word scramble.
   Your task is to describe each word to your group members without using the word itself or any parts of it. Your group members will then try to guess each word.
2 Match the descriptions a) to d) on the right with the corresponding market structures A) to D) on the left.

School uniforms and prices

School uniform rankings by price

Brand	Polo	Jumper	Trousers	Socks	Total 2022	Total 2021	Change
M&S	£3.20	£6.50	£6.50	£1	£17.20	£20.60	-£3.40
Nutmeg at Morrisons	£1.60	£3.50	£4.50	50p	£10.10	£8.56	+£1.54
Next	£3.80	£9	£10	£1.20	£24	£22.40	+£1.60
Tu at Sainsburys	£2	£4.50	£4.50	90p	£11.90	£10.70	+£1.20
George at Asda	£1.70	£4	£4	70p	£10.40	£9.30	+£1.10
Aldi	88p	£1.50	£1.75	50p	£4.63	£4.13	+50p
John Lewis ANYDAY	£3	£6.50	£6.50	£1.14	£17.14	£21.64	-£4.50
Matalan	£2	£5	£6.80	80p	£13.80	£12.70	+£1.10
F+F at Tesco	£1.30	£6	£3.50	50p	£11.30	£9.45	+£1.85
John Lewis (Standard)	£4.50	£10	£11	£2	£27.50	£27.50	no change
Gap	£14.95	£19.95	£24.95	£3.32	£63.17	N/A*	N/A*

47583EX © Westermann

*not available   Source: MadeForMums, 2022

INFO

Each year, MadeFor-Mums, a parenting website, reviews school uniforms to help parents find the best options for the new school year. They survey hundreds of UK families to identify preferred brands and shopping plans. Home testers evaluate uniform quality, fit, and value for money from various retailers. The chart on the left shows the uniform rankings by price.

1 Brainstorm ideas on the topic of school uniforms and their relevance to "markets and prices."
2 Describe the chart concerning "school uniform rankings by price."
3 Characterize the market situation evident in the UK for school uniforms based on the available statistics.
4 Imagine you live in the UK for some time and attend school there. Where would you buy your school uniform? Give reasons for your choice.
5 **Extra:** Compare the market for school uniforms in the UK with the situation in Germany. Present the advantages and disadvantages for parents and students as well as for producers. ▸ chap. 4.2, pp. 94–95

1. Living together

Page 15, task 1 a)
Here are some ideas:
1. Family
2. School
3. Friends / peer group
4. Clubs and teams (e.g. football team, orchestra)
5. Social media (e.g. chatgroups)
6. Political groups (e.g. parties)
7. Religious groups (including youth organizations such as CVJM, Scout Movement)
8. Gender
9. Ethnic or cultural background

Page 29, task 1
If you have difficulties finding something the headlines have in common, first describe the respective problems they refer to, then find a heading for the different problems.

Page 29, task 2
The original German text of the Basic Law (Grundgesetz):

Artikel 6 Grundgesetz
(2) Pflege und Erziehung der Kinder sind das natürliche Recht der Eltern und die zuvörderst ihnen obliegende Pflicht. Über ihre Betätigung wacht die staatliche Gemeinschaft.

Page 29, task 3
Some of the statements might not be clearly pro or con but can be used for both sides of the debate.

Page 31, task 4
Some ideas for measures:
state
- expand and subsidize childcare
- recognize the value of care work – both financially and culturally (e.g. through education and awareness campaigns)
- tackle the gender pay gap
- …

employers
- offer flexible work arrangements (part-time, working from home, …)
- offer on-site childcare
- develop a family-friendly working culture (e.g. encouraging moms and dads to take parental leave, managerial staff leading by example)
- …

families
- discuss the division of labour seriously and openly – rather than just follow the model of your parents or friends
- make sure everybody's needs are taken into account
- be prepared to revise earlier decisions if they do not work out
- …

Page 37, task 4 b)
You can take the following aspects into account:
- Did Tom's role conflict become clear?
- Were the arguments used good?
- Was the acting convincing?

Page 39, task 2
First decide which pieces of information you want to choose.
Then find suitable headings for the different sub-topics.

2. Media and its role in our lives

Page 43, task 1

You can follow these steps:
- **Brainstorming:** Think about media for yourself and note important terms and phrases.
- **Comparison:** Share your thoughts with a partner. Identify similarities and differences.
- **Image analysis:** Examine how the symbols on p. 42 represent different aspects of media. The symbols stand for the following media (from left to right, top to bottom):
  video game, book, e-mail, telephone, DVD/Blue-Ray,
  newspaper, tablet, vinyl record, internet/world wide web,
  smartphone, radio, (chat in a) messenger, photo (camera), (music/video) streaming,
  television, social media (profile), (cinema) film.
- **Discussion:** Formulate topics to discuss based on your brainstorming and the images. Focus on social media, traditional media, digitalization, etc. Practice active listening and respectful communication. Use phrases such as "I see your point, but …" to engage.
- **Reflection:** After discussion, reflect on new insights gained. Consider how the conversation added to your understanding of media.

Page 43, task 2

The following terms are included in the crossword (here in alphabetical order): BLOG, CARTOON, LIVESTREAM, NEWSPAPER, PODCAST, RADIO, STREAMING, TELEVISION, TIKTOK.

Page 43, task 3 a)

Tips for your media diary:
- **List media types** you regularly engage with. Think of both traditional and digital media formats, such as book, TV, radio, newspaper, social media, podcast, etc.
- **Estimate the time** you typically spend on each medium daily or weekly. Be as accurate as possible, considering both active and passive consumption.
- **Identify the main platforms in your media consumption**, e.g. social media platforms, TV channels, streaming services, websites, newspapers, radio stations, etc.

You can also add notes such as what you used the medium for, whether you felt well while using it or not, etc.
Create a table, for example like this:

Day/Time	Media type	Time spent	Platform	Notes
…	…	…	…	…

Page 47, task 2

For positive impacts, think for example of: maintaining connections with friends and family, access to news and information, networking and job opportunities, expression of thoughts and interests …
For negative impacts, think for example of: data protection, fake news, effects on self-esteem, cyberbullying or harassment …

To reflect your personal experience, you can think about these questions, for example:
- What positive experiences have you personally had with social media?
- Have there been times when social media negatively affected you?
- How do you maintain a healthy relationship with social media?
- If social media causes significant distress, who can you turn to for support?

Page 51, task 4 b)

You can adress the following aspects, for example:
- On which kind of media are manipulated images and fake news mainly spread? Use M2 and also think about your own experience.
- Why can false information be easily spread on this kind of media platforms? For example, think about who produces the content and whether there is quality control.
- What could be done about it? Think about both the behavior of the users and the owners of the platforms.

Page 55, task 2	Some useful vocabulary:
	■ indications: Hinweise,
	■ to merge/to blend: verschmelzen,
	■ crucifix: Kruzifix.

Page 57, task 5	You can prepare the discussion with these steps:
	■ Analyse M3: What is the General Data Protection Regulation and what is its purpose?
	■ Remember: What risks did you identify in task 3 from the text M2 about digital footprints?
	■ Connect: Does the GDPR cover the risks of the digital footprint in your eyes?
	■ Discuss: Do you think that the GDPR can improve the situation for digital footprints? Are there still things to worry about and to be aware of?

Page 58, task 1	The terms are hidden forwards and backwards, horizontally and vertically. The following terms are missing (here in alphabetical order without blanks):
	BROADCAST, CONTENT, CYBERBULLYING, DATAPROTECTION, FAKENEWS, INTERNET, IPADDRESS, JOURNALISM, MISINFORMATION, ONLINE, PHISHING, PRINTMEDIA, PROPAGANDA, REACH.

3. Young people and the law

Page 63, task 4 a)   Easier language in the explanations:

Explanation	Function	Example
I) The function is to get control over the country and make people's behaviour more predictable. If people violate the law, they can be brought to court.	1) peace	a) Rule of law and Basic Law, separation of powers
II) If the law is widely accepted by citizens and the state, the law offers freedom, equality, and protection against random state action.	2) obligation	b) Representatives in parliament make laws; everybody accepts the way the laws are made; Basic Law and rule of law, separation of powers.
III) Everyone has to respect and follow the laws. The power to carry out the legal order lies only in the hands of the state.	3) order	c) Everyone can read the laws (they are also online), commentary helps to clarify them, forums help out, laws cannot be made to punish someone after the fact.
IV) Laws have to be accessible and available for everyone. They must be precise so that citizens know how and under what circumstances they work so that e.g. no unexpected punishments occur.	4) legal security	d) Traffic regulations, compulsory school attendance, legal age for drinking alcohol and smoking, etc.
V) The main aim is to reach an agreement between opposing parties. It calms conflicts and should prevent future conflicts.		e) Everyone can file a (justified) complaint, sentences (as in prison sentences) deter crimes.

Based on: Mathias Hütwohl, Einführung in das Recht. Grundzüge des Rechtssystems und der Rechtsmethodik, München: C.H. Beck, 2022, pp. 4 ff. (translated and modified)

Page 63, task 5	Things to consider: ■ What do laws regulate in general? ■ What effects do laws have on us? ■ Can laws be dangerous, or can they be used for vicious means?
Page 65, task 4 a)	The German translation of Article 6 (2) can be found on p. 192 (more help for page 29, task 2).
Page 67, tasks 3 a)	**Focus on the questions:** What are the conditions which can cause a criminal offence when tattooing or piercing someone? How can the criminal offence be revealed and punished?
Page 67, task 3 b)	**Focus on the question:** Are there exceptions that would make the intervention legal?
Page 69, task 1	It might be helpful to use these phrases: ■ If you are under 18 … ■ Your parents have to agree if … ■ If someone offers you money but you do not have to do anything for it … ■ If you buy something and your parents do not know about it … ■ If the salesperson wants to know … then your parents have to … even if …

Page 71, task 2 — The original German text of the German Civil Code (Bürgerliches Gesetzbuch, BGB):

§ 110 Bewirken der Leistung mit eigenen Mitteln
Ein von dem Minderjährigen ohne Zustimmung des gesetzlichen Vertreters geschlossener Vertrag gilt als von Anfang an wirksam, wenn der Minderjährige die vertragsmäßige Leistung mit Mitteln bewirkt, die ihm zu diesem Zweck oder zu freier Verfügung von dem Vertreter oder mit dessen Zustimmung von einem Dritten überlassen worden sind.

Page 83, task 2 b)	Focus on the following questions and use the material only: ■ What is intended? ■ What means are used? ■ Is it effective? Why / Why not?
Page 83, task 3	Questions for examining efficiency: ■ Does the type of punishment achieve a desirable result either for society or for the punished individual's development? Consider the aims for society: to protect people and property, to prevent crimes … Consider also the aims for the individual: to learn to live a satisfied life, to be part of society, to find a job that finances one's life … ■ Does the type of punishment lead to an efficient use of resources (e.g. money paid in taxes, workforce,) or could there be a better solution which requires fewer resources? ■ Does the type of punishment have undesired side-effects? If so, are they justifiable?
Page 85, task 1	Check the following articles of the Basic Law: Art. 5 (1) and (3), Art. 1 (1) and 2 (2), Art. 104 (1), Art. 2 (1).
Page 89, task 3	**Questions for efficiency:** ■ Is it effective to make decisions with the help of a jury? ■ Does the state save resources when using lay judges or jurors (what would be the alternative)? ■ Does a jury or do the lay judges lead to decisions in the interest of the people? ■ Are there any (undesired) side effects? **Questions for legitimacy:** ■ Does the jury or do the lay judges respect the law and the basic rights / human rights (how is this ensured)? ■ Is a jury or are lay judges in the interest of the people? ■ Is the employment of a jury or lay judges proportionate?

4. Democracy in school

Page 91, task 4 For example, think of:
- the seating order in your classroom,
- the destination of your class trip,
- the amount of homework you get,
- …

Page 93, task 2 You can ask yourself the following questions:
- Should every vote count the same?
- Do you have to vote?
- Can you delegate your vote to someone else?
- Is it a direct vote?
- …

Page 95, task 1 Useful vocabulary to describe the cartoon:
sweatsuit, hoodie, gate, schoolyard, brick wall, ancient building, sign

Page 97, task 3 What "effectivity" could mean:
- Did the students get public attention for their concerns?
- Did something change politically?
- Were they successful with their demand?

Page 99, task 5 Consider these questions, for example:
- What is better/worse if only one person makes all decisions? (efficiency vs. acceptance)
- What is better/worse if a group of people make a decision? (maybe a compromise)
- The headteacher is also a teacher – does that have an influence on the decision-making?

Page 103, task 3 You can address these aspects, for example: social interaction and co-operation, diverse content/different subjects, (self) responsibility, social pressure, bullying …

Page 104, task 2 You can proceed as follows:
- First describe the basic structure of the model. Pay special attention to what the areas "above the surface" and "below the surface" mean and what proportions they have.
- Then apply the model to the conflict in M1. First answer the questions "above the surface".
- Then look for clues in the text as to which aspects "below the surface" play a role here. Are there hurt feelings, etc.?

Page 109, task 5 The following aspects could play a role in your discussion: (self) responsibility, active participation, stress/overload, lack of orientation/rules, different types of students …

Page 110, task 2 The following terms are missing (here in alphabetical order): class representative(s), school conference, state student council, student council, student representation, student school representative(s).

5. Local politics

Page 113, task 1 In the pictures you can see:
1. Public outdoor pool / swimming pool
2. Elections
3. Sewage disposal (to remove dirty water)
4. Public library
5. Passport
6. Road construction / maintenance (to build / repair roads)
7. Sports ground / field
8. Marriage (at a registry office)
9. Public transport
10. Public school
11. Fire brigade
12. Waste disposal

Page 115, task 4	Consider these questions: ■ What decisions can municipalities make on their own? ■ How dependent are they on the state / the federation? (See also p.114, M1 and M2.)
Page 119, task 4	The municipality could either try to reduce its expenses or to earn more income: ■ Consider which kind of expenses a municipality is likely to reduce first, taking into account the different types of municipal tasks (p. 114, M1). ■ Also differentiate between the different types of income (p. 119, M7). Of course, every decision will influence the life in the municipality. So you should think of what might happen, if it e.g. raises taxes for companies or reduces expenses for public attractions. Another way for the municipality to improve its financial situation is to try to fulfil its tasks more efficiently, for example to reduce operating costs for buildings through better insulation or by setting incentives for sustainable behaviour among users of public buildings. The municipality could also think about becoming more attractive for new inhabitants, tourists, visitors, and companies, to earn more income in the long term.
Page 121, task 4	■ Who can get involved in local politics? ■ How can people get involved in local politics? ■ What is the idea of representation in our democracy? ■ What problems might be there if a large number of people directly get involved? Possible aspects for your discussion: time and effort to prepare decisions, complexity of decisions, possibility of compromises, danger of manipulation and populism, acceptance of decisions, responsibility for decisions, …
Page 127, task 5	Think about the following questions. You can also include your own research (task 4). ■ Were the members of the youth parliament able to change something for the better? ■ Did the municipal council act according to their demands? ■ Were they able to maintain their work over a long period of time? ■ Was it easy to find new candidates for the youth council? Why (not)?

6. Living in global contexts

Page 133, task 2	Think about these issues: ■ working conditions, ■ cultural problems, ■ the digital world, ■ climate, ■ conflicts among people, ■ goods and services from all across the globe ■ …
Page 135, task 3	Watch out: Look for the reason why they left their home country.
Page 141, task 2 b)	Think about what you would wish for when working for a company and when would you believe a company which makes you promises. Include those ideas in the answer. Start like that: *It is a successful diversity concept, …* ■ *… if the company …* ■ …
Page 141, task 3	■ When doing research online, use the name of a brand or company and add "diversity" and "concept" to your search. ■ Use your criteria as a check list. If something cannot be answered, this might be an answer, too!

Page 145, task 3   Focus on the key terms of each pie chart and combine the results if they are about the same topic.

Living wages

47627EX_1 © Westermann

Each year, the Fashion Transparency Index explores some key issues in more detail.
In 2023, the index examined decent work and purchasing practices. The main question was what major brands and retailers are doing to improve conditions for workers within the companies and their supply chains. One important issue was living wages and wage data in the supply chain. The following statistics focus on a few details of that category.

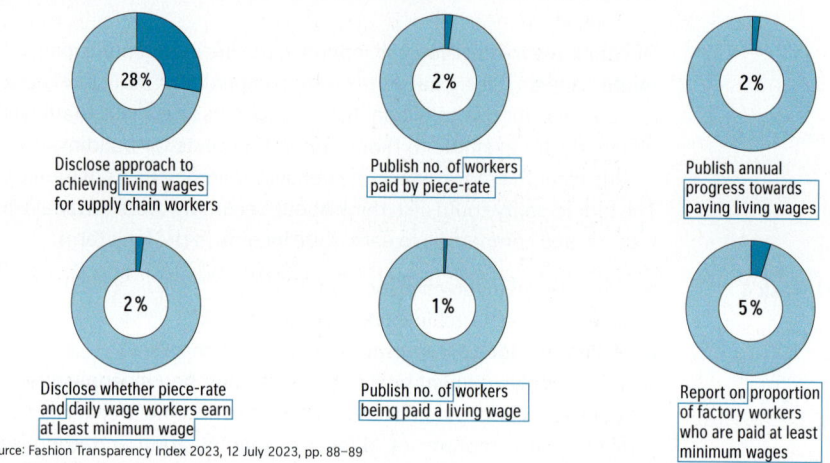

28% — Disclose approach to achieving living wages for supply chain workers

2% — Publish no. of workers paid by piece-rate

2% — Publish annual progress towards paying living wages

2% — Disclose whether piece-rate and daily wage workers earn at least minimum wage

1% — Publish no. of workers being paid a living wage

5% — Report on proportion of factory workers who are paid at least minimum wages

Source: Fashion Transparency Index 2023, 12 July 2023, pp. 88–89

Page 145, task 5   Consider the following aspects:

For the consumer	For the company	For politics
Think about what the consumer does for the company.	Think about what the company could do to improve the situation for the workers / for the environment.	Think about what politicians do in the parliament and how they could use that tool to improve the situation.

7. Young consumers

Page 153, task 1
- Pay special attention to actions you have to pay for.
- Vocabulary you might use: pretzel, petrol / fuel, petrol station, electronics store / electronics retailer, supper, download / streaming.

Page 154, task 3 a)   This illustration may help you:

"What is the opposite of scarcity?"

"Abundance, excess, surplus, plenty, sufficiency, copiousness, enough, commonness, opulence, surfeit …"

Page 161, task 1   Useful words and phrases for the description of the cartoon:
- security staff carries shopper
- to buy tea light
- at the exit
- speaks via headset with his boss

Page 161, task 4   Possible criteria for your comparison:
- planned shopping
- time spent at the shop
- shopping behaviour
- conversion rate to sale.

Page 163, task 2   Possible criteria for your comparison:
- What is located where?
- Why is it located there?
- Where are the registers located?

Page 164, task 2   The original German text of the Act against Unfair Competition (M2):

Gesetz gegen den unlauteren Wettbewerb
§ 6 Vergleichende Werbung
(1) Vergleichende Werbung ist jede Werbung, die unmittelbar oder mittelbar einen Mitbewerber oder die von einem Mitbewerber angebotenen Waren oder Dienstleistungen erkennbar macht.
(2) Unlauter handelt, wer vergleichend wirbt, wenn der Vergleich
1. sich nicht auf Waren oder Dienstleistungen für den gleichen Bedarf oder dieselbe Zweckbestimmung bezieht,
2. nicht objektiv auf eine oder mehrere wesentliche, relevante, nachprüfbare und typische Eigenschaften oder den Preis dieser Waren oder Dienstleistungen bezogen ist,
3. im geschäftlichen Verkehr zu einer Gefahr von Verwechslungen zwischen dem Werbenden und einem Mitbewerber oder zwischen den von diesen angebotenen Waren oder Dienstleistungen oder den von ihnen verwendeten Kennzeichen führt,
4. den Ruf des von einem Mitbewerber verwendeten Kennzeichens in unlauterer Weise ausnutzt oder beeinträchtigt,
5. die Waren, Dienstleistungen, Tätigkeiten oder persönlichen oder geschäftlichen Verhältnisse eines Mitbewerbers herabsetzt oder verunglimpft oder
6. eine Ware oder Dienstleistung als Imitation oder Nachahmung einer unter einem geschützten Kennzeichen vertriebenen Ware oder Dienstleistung darstellt.

Page 169, task 6   For example, think about these questions:
- What other groups play a role (companies, the state, …)?
- In what other ways can consumers do something for the environment?

Page 171, task 3   You can use this example as a guide:
- **Liquidity:** If you save your money in a bank account, you have high accessibility to medium-term accessibility depending on the type of account / the duration of a fixed investment.
- **Return:** The interest rates are rather low.
- **Safety:** Your money is very safe as banks have insurance on all the deposited money (most of it is only cheque money anyway). In the event of a crisis, savings of up to 100,000 euros are protected by the state.

Page 171, task 5   Start with
$€100 × 0.5\% = €0.50 → €100 + €0.50 = €100.50$ (year 1)
(side note: $0.5\% = 0.005$)
$€100 + €100.50 = €200.50 × 0.5\% = …$ (year 2)
$€100 + €201.50 = €301.50 × 0.5\% = …$ (year 3)

Page 173, task 2 b)   This illustration may help you:

Good debt vs. bad debt

Some examples – of course it always depends on the specific case.

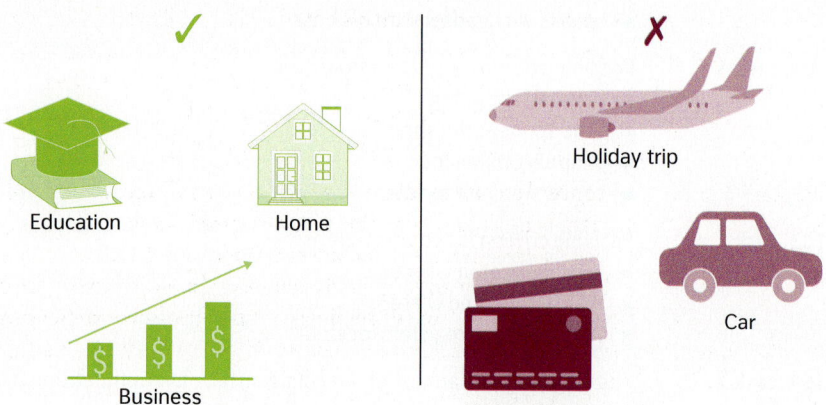

Education

Home

Business

Holiday trip

Car

High credit card debt

8. Markets and prices

Page 177, task 1

The images show the following types of markets:

1. farmers' market / weekly market,
2. stock market / stock exchange,
3. online shopping / virtual market,
4. department stores / physical market.

Ask yourself, for example: What is being traded here? How is it traded (e.g. direct contact or not)? Who are the market participants? What are possible characteristics of each market?

Page 177, task 3

- Name the formal aspects and describe the scene: *"The cartoon published by Hagen on 27 August 2011 shows a desert scene with a desert fox standing at a stand and a camel ..."*
- Think about the topic the cartoon is dealing with: *"The cartoon is about ... / The subject of the cartoon is pricing strategies and price negotiations. ..."*
- Pay attention to all texts and the caption: *"The caption reads ... / Under the cartoon is written ... The stand is labelled with signs that say ..."*
- Compare and contrast the characters or objects in the cartoon: *"Both the fox and the camel are in the desert, but the fox ... while the camel ..."*
- Try to understand why the situation depicted in the cartoon is funny or satirical: *"The cartoon plays with irritation by "twisting" the situation: the fox thinks ... But the camel holds against it ..."*
- Based on your analysis, draw conclusions about the cartoon's meaning or the artist's intent: *"The cartoonist wants to point out with his cartoon ... / The message of the cartoon is ..."*
- Explain whether you agree / disagree with the cartoonist. *"In my opinion, the cartoon is accurate / inaccurate / exaggerated / unconvincing / ... because ..."*

Page 179, task 2

Think, for example, of

- someone who needs a haircut,
- a person who would like to sell clothes they no longer need,
- companies that need materials to manufacture their products,
- people who are looking for a job,
- people who have useful knowledge about a particular technique.

Page 181, task 3

- Describe the data/chart: *"The chart displays accommodation prices for a 3-night weekend stay during the Munich Oktoberfest 2023. It is a bar chart but shown with pretzels. It was published by … in … The chart shows / lists … on the y-axis and … on the x-axis …"*
- Analyse the chart (peak and minimum, striking trends, patterns or correlations): *"The most expensive accommodation by far is … for … euros, followed by … for … euros. The cheapest is … for … euros. This makes … 1,500 per cent more expensive than …"*
- Based on your analysis, draw conclusions: *"It can therefore be said that the more comfortable and convenient the accommodation, the … For visitors to the Oktoberfest, this means … There is also the aspect of availability, as presumably …"*

Page 183, task 2

- Begin by explaining the concept: *"The circular flow of economics shows …"*
- Identify the main elements: *"In the diagram, you'll see …"*
- Describe the movement of money: *"Money flows …"*
- Explain the exchange of goods and services: *"Goods and services flow …"*
- Highlight the mutual dependence: *"The circular flow demonstrates …"*
- End your description with a concluding statement: *"So, the circular flow …"*

Page 187, task 3

- **Understand the market structures:** Begin by reviewing the characteristics of each market structure (perfect competition, monopolistic competition, oligopoly, monopoly). Pay attention to key features such as the number of firms, product differentiation, pricing power, and barriers to entry.
- **Identify effects on consumers and producers:** Consider how each market structure affects consumers and producers. Look for advantages and disadvantages associated with each structure, such as lower prices, product variety, pricing power, and barriers to entry.
- **Create a table:** Use the information gathered to create a table. Be sure to include specific examples and explanations to support your comparisons.
- **Review and analyse:** Once the table is complete, review and analyse the information to identify patterns and differences in the market structures. Consider how each structure impacts consumers and producers differently and reflect on the overall implications for market dynamics.

Market structure	Characteristics	Effects on consumers	Effects on producers
Perfect competition	▪ *many small firms* ▪ *identical products* ▪ *no barriers to entry or exit*	▪ *lower prices due to intense competition* ▪ *wide variety of products to choose from* ▪ *higher quality products due to innovation*	▪ *limited pricing power due to competition* ▪ *limited ability to differentiate products*
Monopolistic competition	…	…	…
Oligopoly	…	…	…
Monopoly	…	…	…

Page 189, task 5

When developing arguments, consider, for example, the perspectives of:

- people who work in retail
- other professionals
- business owners
- families
- young people
- clubs and churches
- …

A) Useful phrases for discussion

introducing a point
first of all, I'd like to point out
have you ever thought about
I was really surprised to find out that
what we have to decide is
the main problem is
the question of
speaking of

listing points
first of all, I'd like to say
to begin/start with
first, second, third
in addition to that
another example of this is
moreover
furthermore
finally
last but not least
to conclude

stating something as a fact
as everyone knows
everyone knows that
it is generally accepted that
there can be no doubt that
it is a fact that
nobody will deny that

emphasizing arguments
extremely
clearly
completely
seriously
entirely
as a matter of fact
evidently
undoubtedly
thoroughly
utterly
not in the least

expressing a personal opinion
in my opinion/view
as I see it
the way I see it
it seems to me that
from my point of view
if you ask me
personally, I believe/suppose/ feel (that)

I have the feeling that
I'm absolutely convinced that
to my mind

referring to someone or something
according to
with reference to
regarding
concerning
as for

including your conversation partner
So what do you think, [name]?
what is your opinion on/of/about
what is your view on
do you agree with me on the matter of

expressing pros and cons
There are two sides to the question.
some people think that ..., others say that
on the one hand ..., on the other hand
an argument for/in favour of/against is
while admitting that ... we should not forget
    that

bringing in further aspects
while I think of it
in addition to that
before I forget
besides
what's more
in any case
by the way
there is something else I want to say/mention/
    ask you
let's also consider

expressing doubt or disagreement
I'm not sure if
I doubt that
I'm not convinced that
I wonder if you realize that
I take your point, but
I see what you mean, but I don't believe that
I don't agree with you about
Do you really mean to say that
I can't accept your view that
I'm of a different opinion
I can't see why
except for

even so
on the contrary/in contrast
however
compared to
alternatively
in spite of
nonetheless

expressing support
You're quite right.
That's a very important point.
You've got a good point there.
I couldn't agree with you more.
You took the words right out of my mouth.

giving reasons
for example
for instance
that is to say
the reason for this is (that)
I base my argument on
I tell you all this because

holding the floor
Please let me finish my sentence and then it's
    your turn/it's over to you.
if I might just say this.
Let me just add one more thing.
This is my final point.
Do you mind if I just finish what I was saying?

politely interrupting (if really necessary)
excuse me, I would like to add to that
yes, you're right there, but

sorry, but did you say
that illustrates perfectly what I would like to say
wait a minute
Can I jump in here?
Sorry, can/may I interrupt you here?
Perhaps I can interrupt you here.
(I'm) sorry to interrupt, but

keeping to the point
to get back to what we were talking about
let's get back to the point
I'm afraid that's not relevant.
… has nothing to do with my argument.
it would be more to the point if
I think we stray from the actual problem.
That's not actually the problem. What we are
    discussing is

drawing conclusions and summing up
all in all
as a result
in conclusion we can say that
summing up, I'd like to say that
the only alternative (left) is
the majority thinks that
some are in favour of …, others against …
the only possible solution/conclusion is
taking everything into account
the obvious conclusion is
consequently
accordingly
hence
therefore
last but not least

B) Useful phrases for describing a picture

general information and your first impression
this is a photograph/an illustration/a portrait/
    a painting/a cartoon/a caricature of
This painting was drawn by [name] and is
    called [title]. It shows
The given picture was taken by … on [date].
It was published on [date].
the picture gives the impression that/reminds
    me of/illustrates/shows
the first impression of the picture is that
the picture was arranged/is a snapshot/
    was photoshopped

describing the picture
This is a colour picture/a black and white
    picture.
the picture depicts/shows/displays/reveals
the photographer shows the
the image is taken from a film/the internet/an
    advert/…
the viewer's eye is drawn to
the artist mainly uses [form, colour, …] to
    express
the central focus of the picture is
the pictures focuses on
the main subject of this picture is

in the top left-hand corner   at the top

on the left

in the background

in the centre

in the foreground

at the bottom   in the bottom right corner

there is/there are … next to/in front of/
    behind/near/on top of/under…
it looks like/it might be
the landscape/object/person implies that
the people look as if they
it appears as if
on the left/right side/in the middle/in the
    corners, there is/there are …
also/additionally/furthermore/moreover,
    there is/there are

interpreting the picture
the atmosphere in the picture is calm/
    depressing/exuberant
from the arrangement of the items, we can
    assume that
the image addresses

the image appeals to … [emotion, e.g.
    sadness, joy]
there are several cultural/political/social
    implications in this picture
… [e.g. symbol] references the historical/
    religious/political background of this
    picture.
the facial expressions of the people show that
the elements in the picture are arranged in a
    … way
… [e.g. colour] is used to show
… is used as a visual symbol and it functions
    as
the problem illustrated here is
the picture inspires the viewer to think about
the picture is (not) convincing in its message
    because

C) Useful phrases for connecting your sentences

adding points
at the same time,
however,

although
despite
nevertheless,

nonetheless
another point is
instead
in any case
in contrast to
whereas,
even though

cause and effect
on the one hand … on the other hand
consequently
owing to
as a result of/because of
thus
not only … but also
provided
once

comparison
likewise
similarly
correspondingly
compared to

stringing arguments
next
in addition

since
further/furthermore
finally

prioritizing
specifically
especially
above all
in fact
clearly
indeed
obviously
in particular
notably

illustrating
for example
one example is
as shown by
such as
for instance

summary
overall
generally/in general
in short
on the whole

D) Useful phrases for answering tasks

general information
The text ["title"] written by [name] was
  published in [medium] on [date]. It is
  about
the caricature [title] drawn by [name] shows/
  depicts
[Name] has published the graph/chart [title] in
  [date]. It shows
when [name] was interviewed by [name] in
  [date], he/she

introducing the structure of your answer
the following text describes/defines/outlines
In the following, the text [title] by [name] will
  be summarized.
The text [title] will be interpreted by first
  looking at … A second/another aspect of
  interpretation is
There are [economic] and [legal] points
  speaking in favour of the author's proposi-

tion. They will be looked at first. The
second part of this text covers counter-
arguments focussing on [sustainability]
and [fairness].

the author's point of view
[author]'s view on … is
the main/central idea of the text is
according to the author,
the author illustrates his/her point of with
the author's theses are

expressing your own opinion
after considering both sides, I conclude that
personally, I (do not) agree with the author
  because
Based on the following arguments, I cannot
  agree with the author. First, …
There are three reasons why I (cannot) come
  to the same conclusion as the author.

1. Living together

English word	Description	German translation
absolute poverty	Absolute poverty means lacking the basic necessities of life. Health and even life itself are threatened. The World Bank defines poverty as income of less than US $2.15 per day.	absolute Armut
at-risk-of-poverty threshold	The at-risk-of-poverty rate measures the proportion of people with an income below the at-risk-of-poverty threshold. In Germany that means an income of less than 60 per cent of the median income (see also median and relative poverty).	Armutsgefährdungs-schwelle
childcare	Childcare refers to the professional care of children (such as in a nursery or kindergarten) while their parents are at work or absent for another reason.	Kinderbetreuung
divorce	When a married couple decides to separate legally, they get a divorce. This is the official process to end the marriage.	Scheidung
extended family	In contrast to the nuclear family (parents and children), the extended family includes other relatives of different generations such as grandparents, aunts, uncles, or cousins who live together or nearby.	Großfamilie
gender role	A gender role is a set of behaviours, attitudes and personality traits that are stereotypically thought of as masculine or feminine within a culture.	Geschlechterrolle
joint living	Some people live together although they are not in a romantic relationship with each other. Their relationship can vary from functional communities to friendships. This form of living together is called joint living.	Wohngemeinschaft
marriage	When two people get married, their union is legally recognized. They are then called spouses. Their marriage creates rights and responsibilities.	Eheschließung
median	The median divides a data sample into two halves: 50 per cent of the sample is above the median and 50 per cent is below the median.	Median
nuclear family	A nuclear family consists of two generations: a married or cohabiting couple and their child or children, typically living together in one household.	Kernfamilie
paid work	Paid work is employment for which individuals receive money (such as wages) in exchange for their work.	bezahlte Arbeit, Erwerbsarbeit
parental leave	Parental leave is unpaid time off work for parents who are raising their children. In Germany, employees can request up to three years' leave from their employer and apply for a maximum of 14 months of parental benefits.	Elternzeit
parenting style	Parenting style refers to the different ways parents raise their children, including their approaches to discipline, guidance, and emotional support.	Erziehungsstil
peer group	A peer group is a social group of about the same age, status, and interests. The peer group usually plays an important role for young people in their learning, education, and socialization.	Gleichaltrigengruppe
peer pressure	Sometimes members of a peer group use peer pressure to influence other members to do things that they might not otherwise choose to do.	Gruppendruck
poverty line	The poverty line represents how much income a person or family needs to maintain an acceptable standard of living, below which they are considered poor (see also relative poverty).	Armutsgrenze
reconstituted family	Reconstituted families are also called blended families or stepfamilies. In these families, one or both partners have a child or children from a previous relationship living with them.	Patchworkfamilie, Stieffamilie
relative poverty	Relative poverty exists when people earn so much less than average pay that they cannot participate in the ordinary standard of living. For European countries, usually a relative poverty line is set at 60 per cent of the national median income.	relative Armut
role conflict	A role conflict arises when a person faces conflicting demands from different social roles. For example, your parents and your friends may expect very different things of you.	Interrollenkonflikt
role strain	Role strain results from the different demands and expectations within a particular social role (such as being a student).	Intrarollenkonflikt
single parent	A single parent is a woman or man with a child or children who does not live with a partner or spouse.	Alleinerziehende/-r
socialization	Socialization is the process by which people learn the culture, values, and norms of society.	Sozialisation
unpaid work	There is no direct payment for unpaid work, such as housework and caregiving.	unbezahlte Arbeit

2. Media and its role in our lives

English word	Description	German translation
artifact	Artifacts are unwanted distortions or imperfections in digital images. It is sometimes possible to detect image manipulation through artifacts.	Verzerrung oder Fehler in digitalen Bildern
Artificial Intelligence (AI)	Artificial intelligence (AI) is when a computer imitates human thinking and can learn.	Künstliche Intelligenz (KI)
broadcast media	Broadcast media are distributed via use of the airwaves, including television and radio.	Rundfunkmedien
cyberbullying	Bullying is an unwanted, aggressive behaviour with a real or felt power imbalance. Cyberbullying is bullying on the internet, via social media, etc.	Cybermobbing
cybersecurity	Cybersecurity includes all measures taken to protect computer systems, networks, and data from cyber threats.	Cybersicherheit
cyber threats	Cyber threats are wrongful activities or attacks aimed at disrupting, damaging, or gaining unauthorized access to computer systems, networks, or data.	Cyberbedrohungen
data protection	Data protection means safeguarding sensitive information from unauthorized access, use, or disclosure.	Datenschutz
data trail	A data trail is the digital path or history of information used during online interactions.	Datenspur, Datenpfad
digital footprint	Because the data trail that each person leaves behind with their online activities is individual, it is also referred to as a digital footprint.	digitaler Fußabdruck
disinformation	Disinformation means spreading false or misleading information intended to deceive.	Verbreitung von gefälschten Informationen, Desinformation
fake news	Fake news is false or misleading news that is deliberately spread, e. g. to anger and manipulate people.	gefälschte Nachrichten
freedom of the press	Freedom of the press is the right to publish without censorship or government interference. It is an important indicator of democracy. The Basic Law guarantees freedom of the press in Article 5 (1).	Pressefreiheit
image manipulation	Image manipulation alters or modifies visual content. As with fake news, manipulation is usually carried out to deceive people.	Bildmanipulation
journalism	Journalism is the professional research, preparation, and publication of information in various media.	Journalismus
mass media	Mass media are means of communication that reach many people at the same time, for example, traditional media such as newspapers or radio, but also the new online media.	Massenmedien
online media	Online media distribute content via the internet, including online newspapers as well as social media and blogs.	Onlinemedien
print media	Print media include traditional publications such as books, magazines, and daily newspapers.	Printmedien
propaganda	Propaganda aims to manipulate public opinion – and ultimately entire ways of thinking, feeling, and acting – through various techniques, such as "mood-making", disinformation, censorship, etc. The term is usually refers to authoritarian states.	Propaganda
reach	The reach of a medium refers to how many people use it and therefore how much influence it has. It is measured in sales figures (newspapers), viewing figures (television), or access figures (online media).	Reichweite
social media	Social media are online platforms for users to create, share, and interact with content, often in real time.	soziale Medien
traditional media	Traditional media include mass media like newspapers, television, and radio that share news and information professionally (and also use the internet and social media as platforms today).	traditionelle Medien

3. Young people and the law

English word	Description	German translation
capacity for tortious liability	The capacity of tortious liability means that someone can be held liable for damage that they have caused (in Germany: limited from the age of 7, fully from the age of 18).	Deliktsfähigkeit
child protection	Child protection is an umbrella term for regulations and actions by the state and non-governmental institutions to protect children and young persons.	Kinderschutz
children's rights	Children's rights aim to protect all children and young people from harm.	Kinderrechte
civil law / private law	The civil law (or private law) is the collection of laws that focuses on two equal parties (citizens). Its main legal framework is the German Civil Code.	Zivilrecht / Privatrecht
constitution	The constitution is the collection of fundamental principles of a state that found and shape the legal basis of a country. It prescribes how a state should be governed. The German constitution is the Basic Law.	Verfassung
constitutional state / state under the rule of law	In a constitutional state or state under the rule of law the governmental power is bound to the law. It limits the power of the state to protect citizens from arbitrary use of authority.	Rechtsstaat
contractual capacity	Contractual capacity is the legal competence of a person or organization to make a contract (in Germany: limited from the age of 7, fully from the age of 18).	Geschäftsfähigkeit
criminal capacity	Criminal capacity describes the age from which someone can be charged with criminal offences (in Germany: limited from the age of 14, fully from the age of 18).	Strafmündigkeit
criminal law	The criminal law is a collection of laws which defines what is illegal and therefore requires punishment. It is defined in the German Criminal Code.	Strafrecht
detention centre	A detention centre is a place where especially young persons serve their sentences.	Jugendstrafanstalt
fundamental rights	Fundamental rights are guaranteed by the state. Usually, they focus on defence against arbitrary state power, but can also focus on the relationships among citizens. They are usually found in a constitution.	Grundrechte
human rights	Human rights protect human beings as such. They are universal (apply to everyone), inalienable (cannot be taken or given away), and indivisible (cannot be separated).	Menschenrechte
incarceration	Incarceration is the punishment of putting someone in prison.	Freiheits-/Haftstrafe
juvenile criminal law	The juvenile criminal law is the collection of laws on crimes committed by young people.	Jugendstrafrecht
juvenile delinquency	Juvenile delinquency is an umbrella term for the illegal behaviour of young persons. A young person who commits a crime is called a juvenile delinquent.	Jugendkriminalität
law	A law is a binding state rule that prescribes or forbids certain actions.	Gesetz
legal capacity	Legal capacity means having rights and obligations.	Rechtsfähigkeit
legal order	All rights shaping a legal and state system is the legal order.	Rechtsordnung
majority	Majority is the age at which a person is deemed mature by law (in Germany: 18 years).	hier: Volljährigkeit
minor	Minors are those who have not yet reached the age of majority.	Minderjährige/-r
parental permission	Parental permission is approval expressed by parents and can be written or verbal, depending on the specific case.	elterliche Zustimmung
public law	Public law is a collection of laws on the relationship between the state and citizens as well as the relationship among members of the state administration, and the organization of the state itself.	Öffentliches Recht
rehabilitation	Rehabilitation in a legal context includes all the measures to reintegrate a person into society, usually after incarceration.	hier: Wiederein-gliederung
separation of powers	The separation of powers is a concept of the rule of law. According to this concept the state powers (legislature, executive and judiciary) are separated to avoid abuse of power.	Gewaltenteilung
suspect	A person who is thought to have committed an offence is called a suspect.	Verdächtige/-r
Youth Protection Act	The German Youth Protection Act is a federal law which protects children and young persons under 18 in public and in their use and consumption of media.	Jugendschutzgesetz (JuSchG)

4. Democracy in school

English word	Description	German translation
class council	You can set up a class council to discuss important issues and problems in your class and decide them together.	Klassenrat
class representative	Every year you elect one (or sometimes two) class representatives who presents the interests of your class to teachers and the headteacher as well as the student council.	Klassensprecher/-in
compromise	Resolving a conflict often requires finding a compromise. This means that both sides move towards each other and try to find an agreement that everyone can live with.	Kompromiss
compulsory schooling	In Germany there is compulsory schooling from ages 6 to 18. During this time, you must attend school, (permanent) homeschooling is not permitted. (However, after the 9th or 10th grade, it is possible to begin training at a professional school.)	Schulpflicht
conflict	Wherever people come together, there can be conflicts. These are not always open disputes, there can also be underlying conflicts. To resolve conflicts, it is important to address the causes openly and try to find compromises, for example, with the help of mediation.	Konflikt
democracy	Democracy means "rule by the people". In representative democracies like Germany, this means that citizens elect their political representatives in democratic elections. There are many features of democracy, such as freedom of expression and the press, the separation of powers, and the rule of law, among others.	Demokratie
election	In democracies, candidates for political office are elected freely by the people. You cannot vote for politicians yet, but you already have elections at school, for example, you can elect your class representative.	Wahl
electoral principles	The electoral principles are the rules that democratic elections in Germany must follow. They state that elections must be general, direct, free, equal, and secret.	Wahlprinzipien
freedom of choice	Freedom of choice means that there are different options to choose from and that you can choose between them independently.	Wahlfreiheit
headteacher	The headteacher leads the school. She or he has many organizational tasks and is responsible for the further development of the school.	Schulleiter/-in
(social) interaction	As soon as people meet other people, they influence each other – they interact. This happens not only through what is said openly, but also through facial expressions, gestures, etc. To ensure that interaction in a group, such as at school, is good for everyone, certain rules can be agreed upon.	(soziales) Miteinander
(dispute) mediation	Mediation is a process to resolve conflicts. People who are not involved in the conflict – the mediators – talk to those involved and try to find solutions together. In this process it is particularly important to get to know the other person's perspective.	(Streit-)Schlichtung
school conference	In the school conference all relevant groups of the school (especially teachers, students, and parents) are represented. It advises on and decides important issues affecting the school.	Schulkonferenz
school law / school regulations	Certain rules apply in schools. On the one hand, the federal state determines some of these (school law and school regulations). On the other hand, many schools also have house rules.	Schulgesetz / Schulordnung
student council	All the elected class representatives together form the student council. It represents the interests of the entire student body and meets regularly to discuss current questions and issues.	Schülerrat
student representation / student co-responsibility	Students shape school life through the student representation (usually called the SV). The SV represents the interests of the students, advises on problems, and starts projects. It includes everyone who has been elected to an SV office, such as the class representatives and student council. Beyond the individual school, the SVs work together in the state student council.	Schülervertretung (SV) / Schülermitverantwortung (SMW)

5. Local politics

English word	Description	German translation
administration	All offices of a municipality form the administration. You can probably find some of these offices in your town hall. The administration is led by the mayor (or Lord Mayor) of the municipality and puts the decisions of the city council / municipal council into effect.	Verwaltung
citizen	A citizen has the rights which a state gives to its people, such as the right to vote and to live in the country permanently. At the municipal level, however, all EU citizens who have lived in a German municipality for a certain period of time can also vote.	Bürger/-in
citizens' initiative	A citizens' initiative is a group of people with a specific goal to influence politics, especially through information campaigns. Citizens' initiatives are usually locally limited and only active until they have achieved their goal.	Bürgerinitiative
citizens' petition	Citizens can formally request a political decision. If they collect a certain number of signatures in a set time, a citizens' referendum is held on the issue.	Bürgerbegehren
citizens' referendum	In a referendum, citizens can vote directly on an issue. The prerequisite for this is a successful citizens' initiative. The question in the referendum can only be answered with "yes" or "no".	Bürgerentscheid
city council / municipal council	The municipal council or city council (in bigger cities) represents the citizens in the municipality. Its members are elected and called councillors. The council makes the decisions in the municipality. The decisions are prepared in the committees made up of the political groups – called factions – in the council.	Stadtrat / Gemeinderat
faction	Factions are associations of councillors in the council. Faction members usually belong to the same party or voters' group. The factions discuss the council's topics in advance and usually vote together on decisions. However, there are also councillors who do not belong to a faction.	Fraktion
(Lord) Mayor	The mayor is elected by the citizens of the municipality. She or he heads the administration and represents the municipality in public. In bigger cities the mayor is called Lord Mayor.	(Ober-) Bürgermeister/-in
municipal autonomy	Municipal autonomy means that municipalities have the right to decide local issues on their own. This corresponds with the principle of subsidiarity. In addition, the municipalities fulfil tasks assigned to them by the federal and state levels.	kommunale Selbstverwaltung
municipal elections	These are elections held at the municipal level, for example, for mayor or city council. The same principles apply here as for all German elections: they must be general, direct, free, equal, and secret (see also glossary for chap. 4: election, electoral principles).	Kommunalwahlen
municipality	A municipality can be a village, town, or city. It is the local level of administration in Germany and is responsible for the well-being of its inhabitants.	Kommune, Gemeinde
policy cycle	The policy cycle is a model of the process of political decision-making. The complex process is divided into different stages. The cycle often restarts when the situation has changed, or the decision taken has not produced satisfactory results.	Politikzyklus
political interest	People show political interest when they are informed and care about politics. It is an important factor for political participation.	politisches Interesse
political participation	Political participation means getting involved in politics, for example, by voting, becoming active in a citizens' initiative or party, or standing as a candidate in an election.	politische Teilhabe, Partizipation
subsidiarity	The German state (and the European Union) is organized according to the principle of subsidiarity, which states that a public task should always be fulfilled by the authority that is closest to it. If a lower level cannot fulfil the task, the next higher level takes over.	Subsidiarität
youth parliament / youth city council	Many municipalities have a council elected by the young people to represent their interests in the municipality.	Jugendparlament / Jugendgemeinderat

6. Living in global contexts

English word	Description	German translation
acceptance	Acceptance is an umbrella term for recognition, confirmation, tolerance, or approval. It is often used in the context of different people in a group or society living together respectfully.	Akzeptanz
asylum seeker	An asylum seeker is a person who flees to another country and asks for permission to stay there as protection from political, religious, or other types of persecution.	Asylsuchende/-r, Asylbewerber/-in
disparity	Disparity describes the existence of unequal conditions, for example, in a country or between different countries.	Ungleichheit, Disparität
diversity	Diversity is an umbrella term for people of sometimes different ages, ethnic backgrounds, religions, sexual orientations, identities, and social backgrounds in a society.	Vielfalt, Diversität
global village	The term "global village" was coined by Marshal McLuhan in 1962. It describes our modern world as a "village" which is digitally connected. Today, it is often used as a metaphor for the internet.	Globales Dorf
globalization	Globalization refers to the increasing global interconnection in economics, politics, culture, the environment, and communication among individuals, societies, institutions, and states.	Globalisierung
inclusion	Inclusion means that everyone in a society can take part equally in every aspect of social, cultural, and political life. inclusion goes beyond integration because it changes the society itself.	gleichberechtigte Teilhabe, Inklusion
integration	Integration is the social incorporation of different people in a society, for example, the integration of migrants and their offspring in the society they live in. Central aspects of integration include language, education, the labour market, participation, norms, values, and identity.	Integration
migrant	A migrant is someone who moves from one place to another for a longer time.	Migrant/-in
push and pull factors	Push factors are harmful or undesirable conditions which drive a person to leave a country or a place, whereas pull factors attract people to a country because of beneficial influences.	Push- und Pull-faktoren
refugee	A refugee is person who flees to another place or even to another country to escape danger or persecution. The legal status and the rights and duties of a refugee are defined by the United Nations Geneva Refugee Convention from 1951 (extended 1967), signed by 149 states so far.	Geflüchtete/-r, Flüchtling
world trade	World trade refers to all the trade which takes place on the entire globe. The expansion of world trade is closely related to the process of globalization.	Welthandel

7. Young consumers

English word	Description	German translation
advertising	Advertising is a form of mass communication that companies use to promote their products or services to sell them, not only by adverts or posters, but also by product placements in films or recommendations from influencers, etc.	Werbung
competition	Competition means having a rival in another person or company. Our market economy is based on free competition between companies.	Wettbewerb
consumer	A consumer is a person or a private household who buys a product or a service. The counterpart of the consumer is the producer.	Verbraucher/-in, Konsument/-in
creditor	A creditor is a person or a firm to whom someone owes money. The opposite of the creditor is the debtor.	Gläubiger/-in
customer	A customer is basically the same as a consumer. However, the term customer includes companies that buy something from other companies, whereas the term consumer is used mostly for private persons and households.	Kundin / Kunde
debt	Debt is the amount of money that a person owes to someone else (for example, a person or a firm).	Schulden
debtor	A debtor is a person who owes money to someone else (for example, a person or a firm). The opposite of a debtor is a creditor.	Schuldner/-in
investment	The aim of an investment is to make a profit from putting money to use. There are different types of investments with different levels of risk of losing money.	Vermögensanlage
label	Many labels show you the contents of the product that is sold, for example, food labels. However, you should always look closely, as all kinds of parties (for example, the state, companies, organizations) can give labels according to different criteria.	Kennzeichnung, Label
marketing	Marketing includes all the measures which companies use to sell their products and services. Advertising, pricing, and product development are all part of marketing.	Vermarktung, Marketing
needs	Needs arise from scarcity. A need can be anything from what you must have to survive, such as food, sleep, or clothing, to luxury goods or recognition by others.	Bedürfnisse
opportunity cost	Every economic choice among several options has opportunity cost. These are the costs or the lost benefit of the option that was not chosen.	Opportunitätskosten
purchasing decision	To purchase means to buy something. In every purchasing decision we make, various factors play a role, such as advertising or recommendations from friends and family, the presentation of the product, how much money we have, and more.	Kaufentscheidung
sales	Sales are the number of products or services sold. This is very important for companies, as they calculate their profit from the sales minus the costs.	Verkauf / Absatz
scarcity	Scarcity means not having enough of a limited resource. Because our needs are in principle infinite, but almost all goods are scarce, dealing with scarcity is considered the central problem of our economy.	Knappheit
sustainability	Sustainability means not consuming more of our planet's resources than can be replaced to ensure a good life for everyone and for future generations.	Nachhaltigkeit

8. Markets and prices

English word	Description	German translation
allocation	Allocation is the economic term for the distribution of resources or production factors (labour, land, capital) in an economy.	Verteilung, Allokation
circular flow of economics	The circular flow of economics is a model showing the flow of money and resources in an economy. In English this model is also called circular flow of income, circular flow of the economy, circular flow of economic actions/activity or just circular flow model.	Wirtschaftskreislauf
demand	Demand is the desire and willingness to purchase goods or services at different prices in a market.	Nachfrage
digitalization	Digitalization refers to the integration and use of digital technologies in all areas of life.	Digitalisierung
digitization	Digitization means changing information or data into digital format.	Digitalisierung
e-commerce	E-commerce refers to buying and selling goods or services using the internet. The term is also often used in German.	elektronischer Handel
economics	Economics is a social science that deals with the production, distribution, and consumption of goods and services. One focus is the analysis of scarce resources. Various fields of specialization in economics refer either to individual companies or to entire countries.	Wirtschafts- wissenschaften
economy	The economy is the system of production, distribution, and consumption of goods and services within a society or region.	Wirtschaft, Ökonomie
equilibrium price	The equilibrium price refers to the price at which supply equals demand. At the equilibrium price, the quantities supplied and demanded are also in equilibrium (= equilibrium quantity).	Gleichgewichtspreis
market	A market is a real or virtual place where goods or services are bought and sold.	Markt
market mechanism	Market mechanism describes how supply and demand interact to determine prices.	Marktmechanismus
market structure	Market structure describes how a market is organized, including the amount of firms in it, how they compete, and what makes them different. There are four basic market structures: perfect competition (in German often called Polypol), monopolistic competition, oligopoly, and monopoly.	Marktform
monopolistic competition	Monopolistic competition is a market structure with many firms selling similar but slightly different products.	monopolistischer Wettbewerb
monopoly	A monopoly is a market structure with one seller dominating the market.	Monopol
oligopoly	An oligopoly is a market structure with a small number of large firms dominating the market.	Oligopol
online shopping	Online shopping refers to the purchase of goods or services via the internet. The English term is also often used in German.	Internetkauf
perfect market	The perfect market is a theoretical model. There is perfect competition without entry or exit barriers, the products and services are identical, there are many buyers and seller, and all buyers have complete information and no preferences.	vollkommener Markt
price	Price is the amount of money needed to buy or sell a good or service. In a market economy, the price is formed by the interplay of supply and demand in the market.	Preis
supply	Supply is the amount of goods or services on offer for sale at different prices in a market.	Angebot